PRAISE FOR

A SPIRITUA

guide to th

"*A Spiritual Renegade's Guide to the Good Life* is so good I wish I had written it myself! Seriously, you really should try to overcome your fear of bliss and start living the way Lama Marut suggests. I recommend this delightful book that should accompany your day to day from now on."

—**Robert A. F. "Tenzin" Thurman,**
Jey Tsong Khapa Professor of Buddhist Studies,
Columbia University, cofounder of Tibet House US,
and author of *Why The Dalai Lama Matters*

"While reading this book, thinking about this book, and trying [Lama Marut's] suggestions, I have begun to experience what life is like when one puts 'the horse before the cart.' I am experiencing a lot more time and a lot more love, and I am extremely grateful. It's brilliant."

—**Mary McDonnell,**
twice Academy Award-nominated actress
and star of shows *Battlestar Galactica* and *Major Crimes*

"I can think of few teachers of spirituality more capable of offering the profound and rich traditions of Buddhism and the visionary voices of yoga. When you meet Lama Marut you encounter greatness, a place where the heart and mind are one, and the company you keep presents a rare presence that can change your life."

—**Douglas R. Brooks,**
professor of religion, University of Rochester,
and founder of Rajanaka Yoga

WATCH VIDEOS WHILE YOU READ

BEYOND WORDS AUTHORS ON YOUR SMARTPHONE

Tag images like the one above are placed throughout *A Spiritual Renegade's Guide to the Good Life* to bring instant videos directly to your smartphone and enhance your spiritual renegade experience.

To watch these videos, simply download the free Microsoft Tag app at http:gettag.mobi.

Then hold your phone's camera a few inches away from the tag images, and you'll immediately be brought to the videos featuring Lama Marut teaching.

CLICK IT. READ IT.

Or you can visit *A Spiritual Renegade's Guide to the Good Life* YouTube channel at www.youtube.com/renegadesguide.

A SPIRITUAL RENEGADE'S *guide to the* GOOD LIFE

LAMA MARUT

ATRIA PAPERBACK
New York London Toronto Sydney New Delhi

Hillsboro, Oregon

A Division of Simon & Schuster, Inc.
1230 Avenue of the Americas
New York, NY 10020

20827 N.W. Cornell Road, Suite 500
Hillsboro, Oregon 97124-9808
503-531-8700 / 503-531-8773 fax
www.beyondword.com

Managing editor: Lindsay S. Brown
Editor: Henry Covey
Copyeditor: Sheila Ashdown
Proofreader: Linda M. Meyer
Design: Devon Smith
Composition: William H. Brunson Typography Services

First Atria Paperback/Beyond Words trade paperback edition June 2012

Manufactured in the United States of America

10 9 8 7 6 5

Library of Congress Cataloging-in-Publication Data

Smith, Brian K.
A spiritual renegade's guide to the good life / by Lama Marut. —
1st Atria pbk./Beyond Words trade pbk. ed.
p. cm.
Includes notes.
1. Religious life—Buddhism. 2. Happiness—Religious aspects—Buddhism.
I. Title.
BQ5395.S63 2012
294.3'444—dc23

2011053037

ISBN: 978-1-58270-373-2
ISBN: 978-1-4516-7281-7 (eBook)

The corporate mission of Beyond Words Publishing, Inc.: *Inspire to Integrity*

Contents

Preface: *A Manifesto*

This book is for desperados.

It's for those who know life is short and who are tired of wasting day after day in low-level unhappiness as they wait for the next high-level version. It's a book for those who are desperate enough to take up arms and make revolutionary inner changes in their lives before it's too late.

It's a book for people who wish to be duped no longer, who urgently want to be happy and who have figured out that the usual methods on offer in the modern world don't work. It's a guide for those tired of trying to become well-adjusted to a perverse society and who are willing—even eager—to deviate from the norm.

It's for those fed up with both the dead end of modern consumer-capitalist ideology based on selfishness and greed, and the toothless, self-absorbed navel-gazing of many contemporary spiritual self-help books. It's for those looking for a hard-core, triple-x, no-nonsense, and supremely practical guidebook to how to live the good life.

And it's for people who believe they can do it.

It's for those who are weary of feeling victimized and powerless. It's a book for heroes and heroines—people too afraid to revert back to the old, ineffectual ways or to run away from what might actually succeed.

This is a book for warriors. It's for people ready to take the bull by the horns and stop coddling their depression, anger, endless desires, jealousy, and pride. It's for those itching for the big rage-in-the-cage smack-down with their own mental afflictions, their true enemies, the demons that undermine the happiness we all seek.

It's for those who know that half-assed efforts bring half-assed results—and who are prepared to go full-assed.

If you're ready to get medieval on your suffering, this book might be for you.

The book is for those who've wised up to the callowness of being too cool to admit that we all just want to be happy—who know the way to be truly individualistic and stand apart from the crowd is to realize that we're all the same.

It's for those willing to be un-fabulous, and not for those too trendy to see that the quest for radical contentment is not just another trend.

It's for people who won't be taken in by an anti-happiness backlash, where, absurdly, being tormented and miserable is embraced as a sign of sophistication and depth.

preface

This book is for the truly compassionate—the big-hearted, not the faint-hearted—the ones who have figured out that being happy is neither superficial nor selfish but the sine qua non, the indispensable ingredient, for living a meaningful life of service to others.

It's for those who have observed that if we are to save others from drowning, we first need to learn how to swim.

It's a book for those who realize that we don't just stumble upon happiness; that happiness, like everything else, doesn't happen without reason, nor does it arise simply by positive thinking based on a magical law of attraction. It's for those who know that happiness can only be brought about through rationality, self-discipline, and persistence, and who are willing to roll up their sleeves and get to work.

This book is for those intelligent enough to discern what will really be effective and what won't, and who care about themselves and others enough to seriously commit to creating a sane, healthy way of life—and who know that in an insane world, a sane person might very well appear disordered.

It's for those desperate enough to want to make their spiritual practice into a tiger—fast and powerful—and give the beast some real teeth, so armed and dangerous that when the mental afflictions like anger, pride, and jealousy see it coming, they pee in their pants.

It's for those who are done playing footsies under the table with secularism, materialism, and consumerism, hoping such flirting might lead to something more, perhaps even a meaningful relationship someday.

It's for people who regard themselves as strangers in this strange and profane land, who are like illegal aliens in a world stripped of all values and meaning.

It's for those whose papers are definitely not in order when it comes to the status quo.

This book is for desperados, rebels, and insurrectionists willing to pit themselves against a life defined by perpetual dissatisfaction, egoism, and greed.

Is it for you?

Are you ready yet?

Are you desperate enough to really want to *incite* happiness in your life?

A Spiritual Renegade's Guide to the Good Life summarizes what I've learned from my spiritual teachers about how to live. I am especially grateful to Geshe Michael Roach for the years of training freely given. How do you thank those who have taught you the only thing that really matters? *Namo gurave.*

The book would probably never have been written without the unwavering encouragement, critical intelligence, persistent dedication, and perfect example of Cindy Lee.

David Fishman spent hours and hours of his time expertly editing the prose and helping me hone the ideas. I am so lucky to have such a good friend whose talents, obvious and undercover, perpetually amaze.

Katherine E. Fleming for many years urged me to write a book like this, and helped me envision it.

Thanks to Carmencita Penaloza and Catherine Eaton for years of work organizing volunteers to help with transcriptions of oral teachings. And I am immensely grateful to those who took the time and effort to do the tedious work of transcribing: Mitch Aase, Sarah Class, René Miranda, Irma Gomés, Lauren

Benjamin, Mira Kingsley, Margaret Remington, Grace Sullivan, Julie Upton, Morgan Adrian, Stephané Dreyfus, Carie Yonekawa, Anne Meyer, Stacey Fisher-Doyle, Mary Kay Dyer, Alvin Lee, Eric Smith, Jesse Fallon, Beverle Deerfoot, Jennifer Zipse, Douglas Smith, Jessica Perry, Rylan Perry, Zorie Barber, Denise Deniger, Karl Whiting, Cassandra Delarios, Michael Penque, Shadi Mogadime, Kate Manfredi, Patti Lounsbury, Lindsay Satchell, Ava Gerber, Terry Flowers, Eric Lucero, Christine Buchanan, Sherry Kajiwara, Krista Williams, Stephane Kirkland, Kathryn Polster, Daylin Wade, Lisa Dawes, Lora Rose, Karen Husak, Susan Lowell, Caroline Dow, Shannon Elliot, Stephanie Culen, Tamara Lovare, Elizabeth Toulan, Lindsey Dorrniro, Tam Moyer, Cole Thimsen, Jill Dunphy, Ellen Huang, Bonnie Krims, Susie Kavanagh, Angela Alaura, Ryan Dally, Mira Fairlight, Patty Fish, Jo-ann Lowney, Beth Lombardi, Anne Deneen, Jennifer Smyth, Christina Collins, and Kareen Nikiris. If you helped with the transcribing and your name inadvertently is not listed here, it doesn't mean I'm not incredibly grateful.

Thanks also to June Maker, Lauren Benjamin, Karl Whiting, Denise Deniger, Stacey Feldman, and Alicia and Tony Tolbert for their research assistance, and to David Simmons, Rick Blue, Cindy Lee, and Darin McFadyn for their professional work on the video tags, laboring under short deadlines.

For help with my somewhat shallow understanding of Christianity, I am indebted to my spiritual friends, the Reverends Anne Deneen and Brian Baker.

I am grateful to my literary agent, Molly Lyons, who never gave up on the project, and to Ava Gerber for helping me find Molly. The book was vastly improved thanks to the ministrations of my editors, Henry Covey and Emily Han.

Thank you to Douglas Paul Smith who inspired some of the visual imagery used throughout this book.

To those who have been so generous with their gifts, support, and hospitality over the past years, I remain in your debt. You know who you are, and so do I.

And I am especially thankful to all my students, who have taught me so much.

I used to live in
A cramped house with confusion
And pain.

But then I met the Friend
And started getting drunk
And singing all
Night.

Confusion and pain
Started acting nasty,
Making threats,
With talk like this,

"If you don't stop 'that'—
All that fun—

We're
Leaving."

—Hafiz
(Translation by Daniel Ladinsky)

Introduction:
Inciting Happiness

> I believe that the very purpose of our lives is to seek happiness.
> That is clear. Whether one believes in religion or not,
> whether one believes in this religion or that religion,
> we all are seeking something better in life. So, I think,
> the very motion of our lives is towards happiness.
>
> **—His Holiness the Dalai Lama**

Your Mission (Should You Choose to Accept It)

Unless you've been sleepwalking or running on automatic pilot, you've probably wondered at some point, "What, exactly, is the purpose of my life?"

The answer is simple. It's to be happy. There is no other point; there is no other reason for your existence. It is what you were put here to do. It's your mission.

Disappointed? Were you hoping for something more complicated, more onerous, more burdensome?

Does some part of you rebel against the idea that the purpose of life is to be happy?

We will never be happy unless and until we think it to be a worthwhile goal. So it's crucial to begin a book on *how* to be happy with an investigation of *why.*

I suspect that our resistance to considering happiness to be the supreme goal in life derives from one or both of two sources. We might think that happiness is a superficial aspiration in comparison to other more profound objectives. And/or we might think that the pursuit of happiness is self-centered and not befitting the higher spiritual ambitions that should take precedence when it comes to the ultimate meaning of life.

Let's start by investigating the first objection to the idea that the purpose of life is to be happy. Is happiness a shallow, superficial goal in comparison to others?

Having spent much of my life in the academic world, I know that many people in the most intelligent, talented, and artistic sectors of our society seem to embrace this notion. In such circles, there is a certain suspicion of those who come off as "too happy." In light of the deeper, more profound realities of the world—the inequities and injustices, disparities in wealth, power and its abuses, and so on—cheerfulness seems both simplistic and insensitive.

Happiness, in a word, is for airheads. Sophisticated, intelligent people should know better. Metaphorically donning berets and living in garrets like the classically tortured sensitive souls of the past, some intellectuals and artistes (and those wannabes who look up to them) spurn happiness as unworthy of their erudition and their worldliness.

There is a trickle-down effect as such an attitude filters into popular culture and mixes with the rebellious posturing of the young and disaffected. The current fashion of wearing clothes with skulls all over them and the Goth/punk style of dressing in all black, replete with tattoos and piercings of pretty much every loose flap of skin—these are the outer signifiers of the belief that it is somehow *cool to be unhappy.*

A first cousin of these cultural discontents is another group of people who have also linked their identities to suffering. The admirable solidarity with the world's oppressed among sensitive political liberals and radicals has engendered an ethos of victimhood among some. Being the (continuing) casualty of childhood trauma, of discrimination, of alcoholism and other substance abuse, and so on, provides some in our current time and place with both their sense of individuality ("I am a victim of abuse"; "I am a recovering alcoholic") and a sense of belonging to a group of similarly victimized sufferers.

For this segment of our culture, the idea of happiness is deeply suspect ("Don't ask me to forget my pain and become just another 'happy idiot'!"). For these folks too, it is not cool to be happy, for the pursuit of happiness would seem to involve denying those very realities of their past from which they derive their identities.

As we will see in chapter 4, forgiveness (one of the essential qualities of a truly happy person) does not mean forgetting. Happiness will not come from ignoring the pain and suffering in your own life, past and present, or in the lives of others. In fact, recognizing the suffering of life is a *precondition* of genuine happiness. The intellectuals and artistes; the rebels, punks, and Goths; and those who have identified themselves as victims are right to this extent: life *is* suffering, as we will investigate in detail in chapter 6.

But it is ironic that these people who are invested in unhappiness as a meaningful, deeper, and more authentic way of life are just trying to be happy too. *They are trying to be happy by being unhappy.* Adopting such a stance of unhappiness perhaps entails the unconscious belief that what we're unhappy about will change because we are unhappy about it—and then we'll be happy. But this can't work. Although it is crucial for happiness to first recognize and acknowledge suffering, suffering (need it be said) is *not* happiness and will not bring it about.

Hardwired for Happiness

The desire for happiness is actually not a choice. It is hardwired into our nature.

We all are driven, from the time we wake up in the morning to the time we go to sleep at night, by an innate urge to avoid pain and obtain things and experiences that will make us happy. There is, you might say, a kind of *will to happiness* that underlies all our efforts—our desire for food and sex, friends and family, money and things, professional fulfillment, and entertainment and amusement.

As the quote from His Holiness the Dalai Lama says at the beginning of this introduction, "the very motion of our lives is towards happiness." He has also said, "Human beings by nature want happiness and do not want suffering. With that feeling everyone tries to achieve happiness and tries to get rid of suffering, and everyone has the basic right to do this."[1]

And this is not an idea peculiar to the "Spiritual East." Many of the greatest minds in the West, past and present, have also recognized the centrality of the search for true happiness. Aristotle stated that happiness is "the human good" and that we all seek it for its own sake, and for its own sake alone.[2] Saint Augustine, one of the founders of Christian theology, in a book entitled *On the Happy Life*, writes:

> *The desire for happiness is essential to man. It is the motivator of all our acts. The most venerable, clearly understood, enlightened, and reliable constant in the world is* not only that we want to be happy, but that we want only to be so. Our very nature requires it of us.[3]

A couple of millennia later, the American philosopher William James would echo Augustine's observation, saying that "how to gain, how to keep, how to recover happiness, is in fact for most men at all times the secret motive of all they do, and of all they are willing to endure."[4] Sigmund Freud, writing in *Civilization and Its Discontents*, concurred:

> *What do they [i.e., human beings] demand of life and wish to achieve in it? The answer to this can hardly be in doubt. They strive after happiness; they want to become* happy *and remain so.*[5]

Whether East or West, the pursuit of happiness is not one of the things we're trying to do in addition to succeeding at the job, in our romantic life, or with our family. It's really the only thing that we're trying to do. We're trying to do it *through* the job, *through* the relationships, *through* the money, *through* the possessions, and so forth. We can't help but strive to happy. As Saint Augustine said, our very nature requires it of us.

But if we are, in every activity of our lives, just trying to obtain what will make us happy, why are we so bad at it?

When the Buddha achieved the perfect happiness called *nirvana*, he was, according to the scriptures, tempted to just kick back and enjoy it himself. He was (or maybe just pretended to be) reluctant to teach others how to attain it too. "It will be too hard for them," the texts have the Buddha thinking. "The others will never really get it." But the gods show up and beg him to teach, and the Buddha finally consents (thereby also starting the custom, followed in Buddhist circles to this day, of students requesting teachings before the teacher agrees to teach).

And when the Buddha "turns the wheel of the Dharma" and imparts his first sermon, the first thing he had to say is this: "Life is suffering."

We'll return later to what the Buddha meant by this seemingly pessimistic dictum. But what is relevant to notice now is that it was only from his recently attained perspective of pure, uncompromised happiness and joy that he could, for the first time, see clearly and truly the features of the state of existence that is not nirvaṇa.

Those of us who are not in nirvana cannot really know it, nor can we thoroughly and completely understand the unhappy condition we are in while we're in it. Like the water that surrounds a fish, our suffering is so ubiquitous, so all-pervasive, that we often don't even recognize it. We are, after years and years of disappointment, inured to our unhappiness, calloused to the pain, such that we usually don't acknowledge it—until and unless, of course, it is so overwhelmingly obvious that we can't help but have to confront it.

In other words, until we are enlightened, *we don't really know what happiness is*. How else can one explain surveys that show the vast majority of us in the United States, the United Kingdom, Japan, and elsewhere claiming we are "very happy" or "happy"?[6] We have, it appears, settled for very little (maybe just the temporary absence of a major disaster) and called it "happiness."

This lowballing of what will count as happiness—what Freud called, when speaking of the goal of psychotherapy, "ordinary unhappiness"—may also help to explain the resistance many of us have to the idea that happiness is a goal worth striving for.[7] Perhaps this resistance derives at least in part from our idea that happiness, conceptualized as something most of us claim to have most of the time, is a rather trivial thing. Our real goals in life should be harder to obtain than "mere happiness."

We've been conditioned by many forces—most especially by consumer capitalism—to believe that happiness lies in the material things and entertaining experiences that bring us only temporary, fleeting pleasure. When we have an abundance of consumer goods, thousands of channels on cable television, and cool vacations to Lonely Planet countries, we report to the survey givers that we are "very happy."

We have pursued happiness our whole lives and continue to do so in every activity in which we are engaged. But we've misunderstood and misdefined what happiness really is. As a result, we've been searching for happiness in all the wrong places. We have been so thoroughly misinformed about what it is and how to obtain it that, when we hear someone say that the goal in life is to be happy, we naturally assume that goal to be trivial, shallow, and superficial.

Researchers have determined that once one's annual income gets to be about $10,000, further increases do not make much of a difference in terms of the reported level of happiness. In other words, it takes only about $10,000 for us to say, "I'm pretty happy."[8] Surveys have repeatedly indicated that most people, regardless of their income level, think an increase of a mere 20 percent would be enough to make them happy.[9]

It's this kind of thinking that makes some people dubious about the claim that happiness is the ultimate goal of life. We know, or at least we should know, that a little more money will not fulfill our life's purpose! Happiness is not a consumer good and will not arise from a bump in our annual salary. At some level we must know that—although thinking that happiness is something that it isn't, we often don't act like we do.

Real happiness will not come about by just getting a few more dollars or a 20 percent spike in income. Happiness isn't just getting a promotion or better job, another fabulous girl- or boyfriend, or the latest iPod, iPhone, or other "iGadget." (In chapter 6, I'll go into more detail as to why money and things, the career, relationships, entertainment, and the health and beauty of the physical body cannot be the cause of real happiness.)

Happiness isn't just having things go right for a while in between the disasters of life.

In his book *Happiness: A Guide to Developing Life's Most Important Skill,* Matthieu Ricard wonders how such a "radical devaluation" of happiness came about. "Is it a reflection of the artificial happiness offered by the media? Is it a result of the failed efforts we use to find genuine happiness?" Happiness, Ricard notes, is not mere pleasure, or a temporary joyfulness, or a fleeting sense of well-being—let alone the attainment of an extra ten grand.

> *By* happiness *I mean here a deep sense of flourishing that arises from an exceptionally healthy mind. This is not a mere pleasurable feeling, a fleeting emotion, or a mood, but an optimal state of being.*[10]

There is a huge difference between the cheap, tinny pleasure we get from shopping and acquiring new things, on the one hand, and the deep resonance of true and genuine contentment and happiness on the other. The latter is indeed the supreme goal in life and it is this that we are really seeking. Far from being a superficial aspiration, it is a rare, difficult, and priceless achievement worthy of our greatest efforts.

The Meaning of Life
http://bit.ly/renegade1

Helpers and Helpees

But what about the second objection, that happiness is a selfish goal—that the higher spiritual purpose of our lives should entail, in one way or another, service to something or someone that transcends the egotistical desires of the individual?

It is certainly true that ultimately our mission in life is to help others live happier lives. But we cannot help others become happy if we have not figured out how to do it ourselves.

Until you're happy, forget about helping others to be happy. You don't know how. It would be akin to medical malpractice to try to help others be happy when you're not. ("I'm kind of bummed out, but I'll try to help you be happy." "Stay away from me! What do you know about happiness? You haven't finished medical school, but you want to do brain surgery on me?")

You've got to figure out how to be happy yourself before you can really help other people be happy. You can't save those who are drowning unless you know how to swim. And until then, what can you really do for others? Do you really think you're helping others by not being happy?

That's one way to think about it. Here's another way: If you are not happy, who is it that you're really thinking about? When you're not happy, you are obsessed with only one person's plight—your own. "What about me? I'm not happy. Is anyone going to help me? I'm not happy, so what are you going to do for me?"

There are two kinds of people in the world. There are the helpers and there are the "helpees."

The helpees are the unhappy people: "I'm unhappy, I'm lonely, I'm depressed, I'm dissatisfied . . . and what are you going to do about it?" That's a helpee. And then there are the helpers: "What can I do for you? Because I'm OK myself." *A helper is OK* and can start worrying about what he or she can do to help others be OK too.

And until you are OK, you don't have the mental wherewithal to think much about anybody but yourself. There's no room in your consciousness to think about anybody else's problems. That's what unhappiness is, isn't it? "I'm unhappy. What about me, what about me?"[11]

When you're unhappy you become a helpee instead of a helper. Instead of being concerned about what you can do for others, you obsess about what others can do for you. That's really why it's so important to strive to live a happy life—so that you can be a helper instead of a helpee.

Most of us have the possibility of being helpers instead of helpees. Other people might not really have that option in this life. We're not like them. We're special. We have the opportunity to be something more than just a helpee. But we have to help ourselves before we can help others. And the way to help ourselves is . . . to help others.

That's how it all works. That is the secret of life, right there, in a nutshell. Helping others in this way is in fact the recipe for obtaining our own happiness. There is, actually, no other method that will work to bring the deep, true happiness we really seek. The purpose of life is indeed to be happy—so we can help others be happy.

So that's how it goes. The way to get happy in your life is to stop worrying about your happiness all the time and to start worrying about somebody else's happiness instead. This will result in . . . your own happiness! Which will allow you to do what? To be even better at helping others to be happy.

That's all there is. The whole enchilada. That's the entire meaning of life. It doesn't really get any deeper or more esoteric than that. In order to succeed in this mission, you must have your cake and eat it too.

So we have to get over the huge resistance we all have to being happy. The principal way to do this is to use our reason, our intelligence, to overcome what is basically an unexamined force that puts up this opposition. The spiritual life is not so much about faith or belief as it is about finally using our head and figuring out what's what.

The resistance to happiness that is within all of us is one very powerful manifestation of the force of evil. There is evil in the world. And evil often looks like some kind of pseudo-rational or faux altruistic argument for unhappiness.

Where's the resistance to happiness in you? Identify it. And then give it a name: that's the force of evil. That's a demon.

When you see a depiction of demons—all red, with pitchforks and a funny tail—they're not smiling. Demons are unhappy. Demons are the very embodiment of unhappiness. So if there's some part of you that doesn't want to be happy, you have to find it, label it for what it is, and then exorcise it: "Demon, come out!"

Anything in you that's suggesting that you shouldn't be happy is a demon. It's evil. You can't be of use to other people until that demon goes. You'll be a helpee forever, which is just what the devil wants!

Learning to Be Happy—All the Time

It is, in general, a revolutionary act to think deeply and clearly about the value of happiness and its true causes. Most people never do so, and much of the ideological machinery of consumer capitalism is geared to keeping us in the dark about these, the most important questions in life. A true spiritual practitioner must necessarily, in this case as in others, be a *deviant.*

It is especially radical to take full responsibility for producing happiness in your own life—to not expect others to do it for you, and to not blame others if you don't have it. The spiritual life begins by taking such responsibility. We are the sole architects of our own suffering, and so it is that we can be our own saviors.

It is unusual to have the spiritual maturity—and, let's face it, the intelligence and courage—necessary to realize that *happiness is in our own hands.* To paraphrase the old language of the Marxists, we just need to *seize the means of production.* I have structured this book to do just that.

In chapter 1, we will further explore the contention that our true purpose in life is to learn to be happy, and we will do this by learning how to be content with our present life and with what we have. We can't become truly happy until and unless we are first content—instead of always wanting more, or longing to be somewhere (or some time) other than where we are now. Contentment is the gateway to higher forms of happiness, and we will never obtain these higher forms without it. Contentment, one might say, is entry-level happiness.

In chapter 2, we will observe that, given the many, many advantages we already have in this kind of blessed life, we are perfectly positioned to achieve the ultimate goal. We have these insanely charmed lives, complete with miraculous gadgetry like computers, cell phones, MP3 players, and televisions. But we're mostly frittering them away with our consumerism and insatiable need to entertain ourselves—to keep ourselves amused with eating, shopping, watching poisonous television shows and movies, playing computer games, and going on endless holidays.

It's hard to let go of our old and familiar habits in order to embrace the new and unknown. We're all afraid to make a radical change in our lives.

But such revolutionary transfiguration is also our only chance at true happiness. We can turn things around, and, as we will see in chapter 3, it is possible to change because everything is in the nexus of causality. If we can uncover the true causes for happiness, we can stop wasting time seeking it in what cannot deliver it, and we can start living our lives more productively. Because of causality, everything's possible.

So ends the first part, but this is where we pick up steam. In the remaining three parts of the book, we'll learn how to take control of our own lives and change the things that are keeping us from attaining happiness. To do this, we first need to overcome the obstacles to happiness—and we can categorize the main impediments into three types: We are unhappy about our past, about our future, and about our present.

First, we'll never achieve happiness if we continue to hold on to feelings of anger, bitterness, and pain about the past. In part 2, "Changing the Past," we will see how in order to be happy we must cultivate forgiveness and gratitude instead of resentment and bad feelings when it comes to our memories. The past is changeable, and because it is we can gift ourselves with a personal history that is more serviceable to our quest for happiness.

Secondly, our search for true happiness is thwarted by our anxieties about the future. We spend enormous amounts of time and mental energy worrying about what might happen in the times ahead. And unless we do our best to lead our lives according to the principles of morality and true causality, we will have good reason to be anxious about our future! In part 3, "Controlling the Future," we find that, in order to diminish and eventually eradicate our apprehension about the future, we must not overly invest ourselves in things that won't bring the happiness we seek. Putting all our eggs in such baskets merely invites the disastrous results we're trying to avoid!

If we want a nice future, we must familiarize ourselves with the karmic rules of cause and effect, for the future will be a perfect reflection of what we are doing in the present. We must always be gardening for the time ahead by being attentive to the kind of seeds we are planting now. When we have learned the laws of karma and can assiduously manipulate them by living a moral life, we can have faith, trust, and confidence in a future that is entirely within our present—and now conscious—control.

Finally, in part 4, "Relaxing into the Present," having transformed unhappiness about the past through forgiveness and gratitude, and having eradicated anxiety about the future by taking control of the real causes of subsequent effects, we are left only with our present. Being happy in the present will be a whole lot easier when we have unburdened ourselves of resentments about the past and angst about the future. But then we must master how to stay happy no matter what the present circumstances.

In this last part of the book, you'll learn about many useful tools and tips on how to lead an authentically happy life, including how to disappear an irritating person in three easy steps; how to instantly transform "problems" into "opportunities"; and how to set yourself free from the fears that can waylay even the grittiest and most rebellious of spiritual desperados.

And we'll discuss the key that unlocks every door to happiness. The real secret of happiness . . . are you ready? . . . *is to stop worrying about your own happiness all the time and worry instead about the happiness of others.* There is one person who is preventing you from achieving the contentment, happiness, joy, and bliss that is your birthright . . . and it's you! Altruism and self-sacrifice are our passport to the fulfillment of our highest dreams. We have to get ourselves out of the way if we are to be different, happy beings!

To help you make the necessary changes that will result in deep and lasting happiness, at the end of each chapter are two sections: a "Couch Potato Contemplation" and an "Action Plan" that are designed to help make what I'm talking about a reality in your own life.

Finally, at the end of the book, there is a takeaway tool for inciting the revolutionary new way of living that we've been pointing to. Just a few simple changes in the structure of your day—I call them the "Components of Living a Sane Life"—can result in a major increase in your happiness and will help you make the most of this miraculous existence of yours.

As we shall see throughout the book, there is never a time when it makes any sense at all to be anything other than happy.

Staying happy is always one's best strategy. Being unhappy about the past, the present, or the future never helps. On the contrary, being upset and disgruntled only makes matters worse.

Our goal is to be happy. And one of the primary means to that goal is . . . to be happy, always.

Easier said than done.

But if you want to learn how, read on.

Part I

Igniting the Happiness Revolution

1

Burning with Desire:
Consumerism and Its Alternative—Radical Contentment

He who knows enough is enough will always have enough.

—**Lao Tzu**

Getting Happy

I grew up in a religious household. My father and grandfather were both ordained Baptist ministers. Our meals and bedtimes were occasions for prayer, Mom led us in regular Bible study, and the family went to church all the time—three times a week, at least (Sunday morning's traditional service, Sunday evening for "youth group," and Wednesday evening for some long-forgotten reason). And nobody was that happy about it.

We kids didn't want to go. We had to take baths and put on uncomfortable clothes and were precluded from watching television or playing with our friends during the time we were in church. So we were all crying. This irritated our parents, who were not only unhappy with us kids but, soon enough, were fighting with one another.

Then we'd get to church and we'd sit for an hour and a half in those intentionally uncomfortable pews they make especially and only for churches and synagogues. Dad more or less immediately fell asleep; the kids fidgeted the whole time; and Mom stayed busy trying to contain the fidgeting kids. Everyone was looking at their watches to see if it was almost over yet. We could hardly wait until the religious part of the week was finished so that we could go back to the more enjoyable aspects of our lives.

What's wrong with this picture? Something was seriously askew. Why, if the purpose of religion is to bring contentment, happiness, and joy, can the practice of religion seem so tedious to so many of us?

Religion is not supposed to be mind-numbingly dreary. If the goal of a spiritual life is to bring its practitioners to happiness, the means to that goal cannot be to make them as bored and uncomfortable as possible until—presto chango!—suddenly somehow everyone's joyful.

I know that everyone's experience of religion was not like the one I had growing up. Once or twice a year, we got to go visit our sister congregation in the African-American community. It was eye-opening to me to see people having fun in church—singing, dancing, shouting, and waving their arms in the air. They even had an expression for it: "Get happy." As in, "We go to church to 'get happy.'" I remember thinking, "How come we can't have fun in church like they do?"

It's very important to get this straight from the start: The purpose of a spiritual practice is indeed to "get happy." And if it's an authentic tradition that has lasted for thousands of years, you should be getting happier by putting into practice what the tradition teaches. If you're not getting happier, it's almost a 100 percent certainty that it's not a problem with the time-tested religion. It's not like religion doesn't work. You're just not doing it right. You're not practicing your spirituality properly.

Among other things, this means that in order to derive the fruit of a spiritual way of life—the happiness it will bring—one has to actually practice it, on a daily basis. We can't expect to get much out of a spiritual discipline that we access in a cursory, reluctant way once a week for an hour or so, or only on two or three religious holidays per year. At various junctures in this book, we'll talk about the components of a daily practice, and in the epilogue we'll summarize what should be included every day in order to really get the juice out of your spiritual training. But unless there is a daily discipline, you can't really expect your spiritual life to do what it can do for you.

So if you are connected to an authentic spiritual tradition, a good gauge of how well you're practicing is to ask yourself: Are you getting happier? Are you getting closer, little by little, to the promise and the end of all religious traditions—the ultimate state of peace, joy, and happiness? Achieving that goal won't happen automatically. It takes regular, sustained, and substantial effort on the part of the practitioner.

In the Eastern traditions they talk about the goal as nirvana (the "blowing out" or "extinguishing" of all unhappiness) or *moksha*, "freedom" or "liberation" from suffering. When one is free of unhappiness, it is said, one is left with perfect bliss.

The Western religions have also always promised such a result at the end of the path. But at least in my experience, some of us in the West seem to have forgotten that this is the point of religion.

As I was sitting, bored, in church or Sunday school, I often heard about "heaven." I was told that if I went to church and listened to sermons (and didn't fidget so much), I'd go to heaven after I died.

"So what will it be like in heaven?" I'd ask the Sunday school teacher.

"Well, there are golden roads and pearly gates, and you'll have wings, and you'll sit on a cloud, and you'll play a harp all day."

A harp? Don't they have any electric guitars up there? Heaven didn't sound like that much fun either!

When I was a kid and heard adults describing the goal of religion, no one ever really emphasized the idea that you would *be in ecstatic bliss the whole time.* (In fact, I don't recall anyone ever even using the word "bliss" in my Baptist church, except maybe when talking about things you shouldn't do.) No one mentioned that in heaven we would never again be unhappy, or troubled, or worried. That we would have no problems, or anxieties, or disappointments. That we would enter a state w*here everything was perfect forever*.

It was only in the so-called Negro spirituals that I got even an inkling of what the real goal of spirituality was:

O Lord! Shout for Joy!
O Lord! Shout for Joy!
Early in the morning
Shout for joy
Early in the morning
Shout for joy

O Lord! Shout for Joy!
O Lord! Shout for Joy!

Feeling like shouting
Shout for joy
Feeling like shouting

O Lord! Shout for Joy!
O Lord! Shout for Joy!
Feeling like praying
Shout for joy
Feeling like praying
Shout for joy

O Lord! Shout for Joy!
O Lord! Shout for Joy!
Now I'm getting happy
Shout for joy
Now I'm getting happy
Shout for joy![1]

Perhaps it was only those who really understood the pain of life—the slaves and their ancestors, but also the poor white folks who sang similar hymns in their churches—who really understood and longed for the alternative that religion was offering.

Maybe one of the reasons so many people have stopped going to church, synagogue, or mosque in modern Western culture is that they've forgotten the goal (ultimate happiness), and, because they haven't invested time and energy in a real religious practice, they do not experience the means to the goal as happiness-producing. So they turn to other avenues as outlets for the pursuit of happiness—crazy hours on the job, consumerism, serial boyfriends or girlfriends, exotic vacations, and so on.

The serious, dedicated practice of a spiritual life should be fun. And as you progress in your practice, it should get funner. And finally one should reach the ultimate goal, which in the past has been called "salvation" or "heaven" or "nirvana," but which we might think of as . . . *the funnest*!

Fight the Power! Be Content.

So the goal of an authentic spiritual practice of any variety is to stop suffering and attain perfect happiness. And on the way to perfect happiness, one should be getting happier and happier. It is, as I've said above, a very good measure to how well you understand what one needs to do and how assiduously you are practicing your religion—"Is my life improving? Am I waking up with more optimism rather than dread? Am I getting gradually happier?"

In order to achieve ultimate happiness, we have to start with lesser versions. Did you really think that you'd just be unhappy for a long time and then suddenly become happy? Generally things don't work that way. One doesn't become a concert-level musician overnight, without years and years of lessons and rehearsing. Change occurs slowly and gradually, in small increments—and through regular practice. And that's how it works with the quest for happiness too.

In Sanskrit texts there is a helpful vocabulary for this progression toward the ultimate goal of spiritual practice. We start with *santosha* ("contentment"), about which we'll say more in a minute. *Santosha* leads to *sukha*, usually translated as "happiness," that deep-seated sense of well-being that leads you to wake up looking forward to each new day. *Sukha* eventually evolves into *mudita*, or "joy," the kind of irrepressible elation we see in people like the present Dalai Lama. Eventually and with continued efforts, *mudita* morphs into the highest form of happiness, our goal in life—*ananda* or "bliss, ecstasy."

The starting point, the "entry level" for true and deep happiness, is *santosha* or "contentment." It is impossible to achieve the higher forms of happiness until and unless we attain contentment. Many of us seem to resist this fact. We seem to think that we can somehow become happy without first learning how to just be content.

"So what more do I need to obtain in order to achieve contentment?" It is this very question that has thus far precluded us from attaining it. *We don't need to get anything more to be content. We need to be happy with what we have.* And when that happens, we are content. And until that happens we will never be content.

I think there are basically two ways to think about contentment. The first is to stay happy in the moment—to be content with the present. Everything is fine right now—here and now. And for people living charmed lives, like most of us do, that shouldn't be too hard, at least most of the time. For people like us, things actually are just fine in the here and now about 99 percent of the time.

Contentment would be a harder sell if we were speaking to any of the millions of people in our world who are living totally marginal economic lives, or to those in the middle of a war zone. But for people like most of us—people who have enough to eat; who have air-conditioning and central heating; who have security, family and friends, and a good education—for most of us, most of the time, everything is pretty much fine. Isn't it?

I used to spend a lot of time in India, where I would often rent an apartment in one of the finer neighborhoods of Pune.

In India, poverty isn't segregated the way it is in the West. The poor live on the same streets as the wealthy, and many would ask for help as the wealthy (of which I, the beneficiary of a generous US scholarship, certainly was one) walked by on the way to or from their homes.

There were just too many needy people to help. So I would ask the advice of my upper-middle-class Indian neighbors, who had developed a sort of survival technique for their consciences. They recommended that I choose *one* of the many poor as my sort of "designated beggar" and at least give a little something to him every day.

Anyway, when I feel sort of crabby and find myself kvetching about the things that go wrong in my life, I sometimes bring to mind my "designated beggar" from Pune. I picture him in front of me and then force myself to tell him—someone who is living in a cardboard box on the street, with inadequate food, rags for clothes, and so on—what's upsetting me today. My "problems" are usually so trivial compared to his that it's not long before I'm too embarrassed to feel that upset about them anymore. From a comparative perspective, the "first-world problems" we usually complain about are nothing.[2]

We're usually scab-pickers. You know how it is, when you have a little scab on your hand or arm and you just can't leave it alone? Your whole body is fine, but you obsess about the little scab. Our problems are mostly like little scabs compared to the vast majority of things that are just fine.

Of course, there are times when, even for the very luckiest of us, things aren't OK. If you've just been hit by a truck, or received bad news about your health from the doctor, or just lost a loved one, things at that moment are not fine. You are in the middle of what Buddhism calls "the suffering of suffering"—

unmistakable pain. You are *in* the disaster instead of being *between* disasters.

We'll deal more with "the suffering of suffering" in chapter 6, but for people like most of us, most of the time, we are in that in-between state where everything is pretty much just fine. Everything actually is OK, but we're just discontent and unhappy anyway. We wish we were somewhere else or sometime else. We daydream nostalgically about times gone by, or, even more often, we anticipate times that have not yet come. We're almost never content with being in the here and now.

So that's one level of *santosha*. The road to happiness begins with just staying happy in the present. Which is hard—there's no doubt about it—no matter how well things are going for us. If you don't believe me, just try it. Just try to spend a day, even an hour or ten minutes, being content in the present place and time. We'll return to the difficulty of "being here, now" and offer some tricks for cultivating happiness in the present in part 4 of this book.

The second kind of *santosha* is also difficult—maybe even more so now than ever. It is to be content with what you have. Contentment with one's things (and also with one's experiences—the Lonely Planet countries visited on holiday; the television shows, DVDs, and feature films watched; the sexual escapades enjoyed; and so on) has gotten even more difficult for those of us living now in the maw of unbridled consumer capitalism.

Staying content with what we have should be a lot easier for us than it seems to be most of the time. For people living unbelievably blessed lives like most of us, it is a little surprising (when we stop to think about it) and also more than a little shameful to always want even more than we already have—

more consumer goods, more exotic vacations, more and better relationships, more promotions at work, more entertainment experiences.

But we also have to recognize that, at every turn, our own worst tendencies are encouraged and exacerbated. In case you haven't noticed, the whole economic structure is arrayed to convince us that we don't have enough. All the time and from every angle—from the television, radio, billboards, and internet ads—we are bombarded with the same message: "Don't be satisfied. You need more."

In order to get even the starter-kit version of happiness that is *santosha*, we are going to have to swim upstream from the flow of the dominant and all-pervasive forces aligned against us. A spiritual renegade should not strive to become well adjusted in a society where the economy is powered by discontent. We're going to have to fight the power if we want to be happy. We're going to have to resist the siren song of consumer capitalism.

And it *is* the power. To fight the power, we have to recognize it as the power. Most of the time we're so immersed in and bedazzled by it that we don't even see how all-encompassing it is. We have to pay attention, especially during those critical moments when the real face of the power peeks out from behind one of its many masks.

One of those times occurred in the aftermath of the tragic events of September 11, 2001 ("9/11"). Do you remember? Thousands of innocent people killed, an entire nation traumatized, and what did we hear from some of our leaders? "Don't let the terrorists win! Don't be afraid! Return to the malls and resume shopping!"

The dominant power we live under is not democracy or some other noble ideal—it is consumerism! And we are constantly encouraged by this power to be dissatisfied with our present lives and circumstances. This is, in fact, the essence of the consumer-capitalist society we live in—to never stop wanting, acquiring, devouring; to never be happy with what we currently have. We are bombarded daily by messages ranging from television commercials to pop-ups on the internet to political propaganda, all of which exhort us to desire and to buy more . . . and more, and more, without end, without satiety.

Contentment is the antithesis of the consumerist value system at the center of our current culture. And it is sine qua non of happiness, its essential precondition. Without contentment, we can never be happy.

So what does that tell you about our shopping-mall culture? Your unhappiness is its life's blood! Rebelling against a force like this is just an expression of sanity; remaining complacent is a recipe for certain grief. Among the most revolutionary actions a person could take in a society like ours is really no action at all. *Just stop. Don't buy any more stuff. Don't even want to buy stuff. Just be content.*

Whenever we feel dissatisfied with our material lives, we might want to get back in touch with the hard facts. Go to globalrichlist.com, enter your annual income, and find out how you rank in the world. You'll be amazed by how high on the hog you are living.

Check out a few of the stats:

- The average income in the United States is the second highest in the world. (Only Luxembourg's is higher.)

- The 20 percent of the world's people living in the highest-income countries account for 86 percent of total private consumption expenditures, while the poorest 20 percent consume a minuscule 1.3 percent of the total.
- The richest fifth consume 45 percent of all meat and fish, the poorest fifth, 5 percent.
- The wealthiest 20 percent consume 58 percent of total energy, the poorest fifth, less than 4 percent.
- Two billion people in our world live on one dollar per day, and, according to some statistics, 50 percent suffer from malnutrition.

And on it goes. These statistics are not meant to make us feel guilty. They are meant to make us aware of the reality of our lives. We should call them to mind when we succumb to the temptation of thinking we somehow don't have enough.

I have invented a mantra—a set of sacred words, a prayer, or a magical spell—that I impart to my students to help them achieve *santosha*. You can call it the "Contentment Mantra." You say it over and over again—especially when tempted by ads for new products and billboards for the latest blockbuster movie. And when you believe what the mantra is saying, you will have contentment.

Like most mantras, the Contentment Mantra has some Sanskrit in it (to let you know it's a mantra). But it also has English in it so you know what it means. Here it is. Repeat it out loud:

> Om, I have enough, ah hum!

"*Om*" is the traditional way to begin a mantra; it means "here comes a mantra." "*Ah hum*" is one way to signal the end of the mantra; it means "the mantra's now finished." That's the Sanskrit part.

"I have enough" means exactly what it says: "I have enough. I have enough money. I have enough clothes. I have enough cars. I have enough room in my apartment or house. I have enough friends. I have enough success at the job. I have enough entertainment experiences." We have enough.

Say the Contentment Mantra over and over, all day long. When you believe it, you'll have *santosha* and you'll be on the road to the higher levels of happiness. But until you believe it, you'll never have contentment and won't even have begun fulfilling the very purpose of your life.

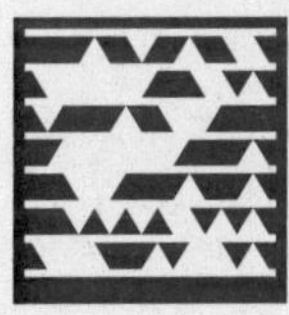

Radical Contentment
http://bit.ly/renegade02

Couch Potato Contemplation: Really Wanting to Be Happy

Hunker down in your favorite chair, get comfortable on the couch, or settle into your BarcaLounger and put it all the way back, on "full Barca." Let go of all the activities, plans, and anxieties of the day. They'll all be there when you come back in a few minutes!

Relax every part of your body from head to toe. Take a few deep breaths and bring your mind into the present moment. Spend a few minutes focusing your concentration, trying not to think of anything else but the process of your breathing. Try to get riveted on your breath, like it's the best movie you've seen all year.

Now, think about what you really want out of life. Try to identify the things you are pursuing—material prosperity, good relationships, success at the job, a nice home to live in—and then ask yourself why you want them. What do you think they'll do for you?

You think they'll make you happy, right? You're dreaming of and working for these things because you believe they will bring happiness to your life, yes? Just try to get clear on that: You are, in fact, driven by the same urge all other living beings have—to achieve happiness and avoid pain.

Next, try to identify in yourself the voices that suggest there's something wrong with being happy. Maybe they're whispering, "What a trivial goal! You should strive for greater things!" Or maybe they're trying to entice you with the idea that pursuing your own happiness is selfish, or that you somehow don't deserve to be happy.

Finally, review the points we've made in this chapter. The pursuit of happiness is not a silly or lesser goal; it is, in fact, rather difficult to achieve! If you're looking for a real challenge, try just being content! In any event, it is hardwired into our nature to want to be happy and to strive to obtain happiness—it informs everything we do, all day long. Lose the idea that the pursuit of your own true happiness is somehow at the expense of caring about others, or that it is inimical to a spiritual life conceptualized as inherently dreary and laborious. How can we truly be of benefit to others if we're not happy ourselves? How can we be helpers if we remain helpees?

End the contemplation with a resolution to try to be more aware of the parts of yourself that resist being happy, and vow to combat them with the tools of reason and true compassion for others.

Action Plan: The Consumption Fast

Go on a "consumption fast" for one day a week. Resolve not to buy anything you don't need for twenty-four hours (food, fuel for the car in order to get to work, and similar things are excluded). Note when you catch yourself wanting a new CD, another pair of shoes, a bigger house, or whatever. Try to just be content—for one day a week—with what you already have, and start habituating yourself to that satisfied state of mind.

2

Waking Up: *Recognizing the Miraculous Nature of Our Lives*

Miracles are not contrary to nature,
but only contrary to what we know about nature.
—**Saint Augustine**

Two Ways to Live

In the last chapter, we learned that the first step on the path to ultimate happiness is to be content with our present life and with what we have. We can't become truly happy until and unless we are first content. Contentment, we may recall, is "entry-level," the foundation and condition of possibility for joy, euphoria, bliss, ecstasy, or any other of the more intense forms of happiness. Instead of always wanting more, or longing to be somewhere (or some time) other than where we are now, we need to be able to just say, "I have enough. I'm satisfied with what I have here and now." When we can say and believe this, we will have obtained contentment. And not until then.

But is contentment really within our reach—right here and right now? Is our present life basically OK? Do we really have enough of everything?

As Albert Einstein said, "There are only two ways to live your life. One is as though nothing is a miracle. The other is as though everything is a miracle."[1] Which of these two ways would be a happier and more interesting way to live? Which would be more conducive to our quest for contentment with our lives? Which is more descriptive of the actual lives we are already leading?

We are living in a time and place where, for a hundred years or more, many of our intellectual and scientific leaders have been trying to drain life out of the miraculous. (Albert Einstein would not fall into this camp.) The official worldview of our culture—the one ratified by the great majority of our academic mandarins—is a secular perspective that is, by definition, the very opposite of a religious viewpoint.

When we deplete the world of the sacred, we're left with the profane—a life in which nothing is extraordinary, everything is (at least theoretically) explainable (and "explain-away-able"), and everything is just commonplace.

As Nietzsche said at the end of the nineteenth century, "God is dead." He also noted, "And it is we who have killed Him."[2]

This perception of the world as ordinary and unexceptional is, among other things, quite boring. Recent polls show that most of us are in deep revolt against this war waged by some of our intellectual leaders to uproot the esoteric and miraculous from our daily lives.[3]

But do miracles happen exceptionally and only once in a great while? One way that we can start convincing ourselves that our seemingly ordinary lives cannot be "normal" is to be a bit more observant. If we pay attention, we may notice that our daily lives are not only OK but are truly amazing and extraordinary. We don't have to make things up or squint or don rose-colored glasses in order to see that our lives are totally blessed. The possibility of contentment with our lives as they are will not require us to do much more than just pay attention to reality.

In the open, exoteric teachings of Tibetan Buddhism, it is said that the greatest "sin" (or probably the better word in this context would be "mistake") we can make is seeing things as if they were "out there," independently and objectively existing apart from our perceptions of them. The biggest error, in other words, is assuming that things are coming *at* you and not *from* you. But in the esoteric and secret teachings, the most serious of all our misperceptions is seeing our lives as just ordinary and not as astonishing marvels and full-on miracles.

Statistics indicate that the vast majority of us actually do believe in the possibility of the extraordinary occurring in our everyday lives. A large majority of us accept the idea that things such as angels and demons are active in the world. But we don't have to wait for things that go bump in the night to show up in order to find proof of the extraordinary. The real miracles are all around us, all the time. They are disguised as what appears to us most of the time as "ordinary life."

Going through life as if everything were ordinary, just "normal," is a mistake. It is contrary to the facts. One very easy way to start living a happier life is to be aware of reality. When we take a realistic look at our lives, it is hard not to believe in the second of Einstein's choices, and the option the vast majority of us say we actually believe in: the miracles are all around us.

Leisure and Fortune

In the Tibetan Buddhist tradition, we are encouraged early and often in our training to contemplate and meditate on what is called our "leisure and fortune." It is thought to be quite pertinent to the development of a serious practice to first reflect upon the facts of our present lives.

"Leisure" here means we are presently *free from* many very serious disabilities that other beings currently experience—disabilities that would prevent us from making any progress on a spiritual path. The original Sanskrit term translated as "leisure" is *kshana,* which is also a term for a unit of time—a very short unit of time, like a "moment" or a "blink of the eye."

So, built into the very term is the idea that our "leisure," our freedom from obstacles and conditions that would make it impossible to make any real improvements in our spiritual lives, *is a temporary situation.* It is a brief window of opportunity, a "blink of the eye." And the window can shut at any moment.

When I reflect on this part of the "leisure and fortune" meditation, I think about those ads you see on television or hear on the radio, where some salesperson is jumping up and down, screaming about how they're having this *craaazy* sale where the products have been *insanely* reduced in price—a "once-in-a-lifetime opportunity!" And the commercials always seem to end their pitch for this weekend sale or whatever with the phrase *for a limited time only.*

We've got this unbelievable opportunity, but it's *for a limited time only.* It's only a *kshana,* a moment, a blip on the cosmic screen. So we should learn to appreciate it and not squander it any longer with meaningless or frivolous pursuits.

The second term, "fortune," means that we are *free to* do important, meaningful things with the kind of life we're leading. The Sanskrit word translated here—*sampatti*—is derived from a verbal root *pat-*, "to fall." With the prefix *sam* ("wholly, completely, perfectly") the word means "to fall together." Things have "fallen together" for us very nicely. We have this fortunate chance—a lucky roll of the dice. Things have come together for us perfectly in this kind of life.

So that's the meaning of the terms "leisure" and "fortune." In the traditional Tibetan Buddhist presentation, the actual contemplation or meditation proceeds in three parts:

The first step is to simply *recognize* our leisure and fortune, to identify the incredible opportunity we have in this lifetime. The texts specify things like the fact that we are free from being born as an animal or in a hell realm, or as a human who is for some reason incapable of spiritual progress. And we have the good fortune to have a human life in a place where and a time when we have opportunities to learn and practice spirituality.

The point here is to get clear on the facts of the life that we're leading and to stop spacing out. We first need to be a bit more cognizant of the realities of our present circumstances. When we do a little "comparison shopping" and observe the lives other beings are living, it's not too hard to realize, pretty quickly, that we are extraordinarily fortunate in all kinds of ways.

The second step in the meditation is to contemplate the great importance, the significance, of having a life like this—to think about what it's for. What's the purpose of such a life?

The answer is not supposed to be "to live it up" or "to simply enjoy myself"—until the end comes. This pursuit of trivial and superficial pleasure—as opposed to a deep contentment and happiness—is what most of us seem to be doing with the leisure and fortune we've somehow acquired.

We were put here to do something meaningful with our lives. With the kind of lives we have, we have the possibility of doing something important and significant.

And it's relatively easy! With lives like ours, we could, without too much difficulty, cultivate the virtuous attitudes and actions which would bring about real happiness. And what a waste not to take advantage of this temporary window of opportunity! The texts say it would be like an explorer who discovers a whole island of precious gems and then leaves for home without pocketing any of them. Arya Nagarjuna, one of the great saints of Mahayana Buddhism, couched this same idea in more graphic terms in his *Letter to a Friend*: "Even more stupid than one who fills a jewel-embellished, gold vessel with excrement is he who, having been born a human, performs evil deeds."

To waste this kind of life would be truly tragic and genuinely misguided. In the great Buddhist classic by Master Shantideva, *Guide to the Bodhisattva's Way of Life*, we read:

There is nothing more deluded,
Nothing more fraudulent,
Than for me to have found such an opportunity as this one
And yet not to have used it to cultivate virtue.[4]

The third step in the traditional meditation on leisure and fortune is to consider how rare it is to have a life like the one we are currently living, and how difficult it is to put together the causes and conditions to have things "fall together perfectly" like this. To quote again from Master Shantideva's guide:

You must make use of this boat which is the human life,
To cross over the great river of suffering.
O foolish one, don't just sit there sleeping,
For this boat will be very hard to find again later.[5]

Finding a life like this one, says Master Shantideva, will be "hard to find again later," so don't just sit there like an airhead, asleep, and let it go by!

So how hard could it be to get a life like this one? Sometimes Buddhist teachers hesitate at this point to go into the details. Let's just say the chances are said to be virtually nil. If we truly understood and believed in karma, in cause and effect, we'd realize how it is almost impossible to have all the elements of our present lives come together in one package.

The teachers are perhaps reluctant to spell this out for fear that, if we believe what they say, our heads will explode! We'll go mad thinking about all the reruns of *Friends* we've watched during our lives—all the ways we've squandered years, months, weeks, days, and minutes of an unbelievably precious life, a life we're not likely to get again anytime soon.

Having things come together in such a way as to produce a life like this is rare—*extremely rare.* It is a standard trope in Tibetan Buddhist texts that the chances are as rare as a blind turtle, living on the bottom of the ocean, who surfaces once every hundred years and just happens to put its neck through a golden hoop that is floating on the vast surface of the sea—they say that's about the odds of getting a life like the one we have.

Another such story is when the Buddha was asked what the chances were of again obtaining a life like this, endowed with leisure and fortune. The Buddha put his index finger on the ground and said, "About that of the number of particles of earth on my finger tip." Those listening perhaps got their hopes up, counting the minute specks of dirt on the Buddha's finger. "But the chances of not getting such a life," the teacher then said, "are like the number of all the existing particles of earth *not* on my finger."

The audience was pretty impressed, and some commented upon what a powerful metaphor the Buddha had employed.

"No metaphor," corrected the Buddha. "Those are the actual odds. Those are the real stats. That's the rarity."

Doing the Math: Our Lives in Context

So that's an overview of the leisure and fortune contemplation as handed down in the Buddhist texts from ancient India and Tibet. And I think it's important to note that these texts were composed and studied by people *who were leading lives nothing like the ones we're enjoying here and now.* Indians and Tibetans of the past, meditating on how incredibly lucky they were to be living their pre-modern, Third World lives, could not even have begun to imagine the kinds of lifestyles we enjoy—and mostly just take for granted.

We all are subject to the "grass is greener" syndrome. We're prone to romanticize other people's lives. We tend to think, "If only I were living there and then, it would be easy to be spiritually inclined and disciplined—maybe even to achieve nirvana!" And we're especially predisposed to idealize the lives led in the traditional "spiritual East," where somehow metaphysical things were just "in the air" and everyone was sort of naturally easing into advanced mystical states of mind.

But it wasn't like that in the historical "spiritual East" any more than it is like that in today's India and Tibet. Twelve hundred years ago, Master Shantideva (who lived in a Buddhist monastery!) was pining for solitariness and peace and quiet, and those of us who have visited modern-day India and Tibet can attest to the relative absence there of those things even today.[6]

The traditional Indians and Tibetans who were extolling their unbelievably rare and valuable lives did not lead lives that had much privacy and tranquility. They did not, by and large, have grand, spacious homes with lots of rooms with wall-to-wall carpeting and thick, soundproof walls. They certainly did not have central air-conditioning for when the temperature got too high and heating for when it got a bit nippy. They mostly did not have abundant food and clothing; and virtually no one had what we would consider proper healthcare or education.

Nor did ordinary people in traditional societies, East and West, have real access to spiritual information and wisdom. (If you were a woman, forget about any such access.) Religious texts circulated in the hands of the very, very few—the literate monks and priests, the crème de la crème of the religious elite.

Imagine what a person from traditional India or Tibet who was magically transported to the twenty-first century West would think of our lives! They would see us as gods living in some kind of heavenly realm! Their minds would totally be blown!

And would they really be wrong? Until we're forced to think comparatively, all of us regard our own lives as ordinary. Traditional assessments of leisure and fortune were made with reference to beings living in hell realms or humans who were severely disabled, unfortunate, or barbaric. For us, however, the comparison will have to be with every possible kind of life.

Accordingly, in comparison to pretty much everyone else living in our present world, our lives are off-the-charts extraordinary. And in comparison to every being of the past, in every part of the world, our lives are unimaginably peerless.

When we compare ourselves to those who lived in the past, it is no exaggeration to say that almost every one of us now is living a life of material prosperity comparable historically only to those of royalty. And not only this. The average person living in the West today not only has the affluence of kings and queens but also the education of the monastic and priestly elite.

The amount of information that we are capable of putting onto our portable tablets and iPods is equivalent to what once comprised entire libraries. Our easy and nearly universal access to the internet puts us in touch with a wealth of information totally inconceivable to even the most learned scholars of the not-so-distant past.

When we start to look at them objectively and comparatively, it's not too much to contend that our lives are more than just "fortunate." "Fortunate" doesn't quite capture it. More like "miraculous."

Everyday Miracles and Our Supernatural Powers

I will suggest something radical to you. The lives we are leading are chock-full with miracles. Not only that: The appearance of such miracles in our lives is indicative of how close we are to reaching the final goal of a spiritual practice. We are getting very, very near to what has been called nirvana, liberation, heaven, or salvation.

As my teacher says, we're like bullets that have been flying through the air since beginningless time that are just now piercing their final target. We're that close.

Telltale signs that we are almost done are appearing. With a little bit of effort, we could finish it off in this life. The portents of our nearing the end are the miracles manifesting all around us—marvels and wonders that we are mostly oblivious to and taking for granted.

The miracles happen so gradually and are integrated so seamlessly into our "ordinary" lives that we don't even notice them. Until, perhaps, they're pointed out to us. When my own life begins to seem humdrum and ordinary, I like to remember one of the more obvious miracles that has occurred over the past few decades.

When I was in high school in the 1960s, one of the most valuable classes I took was typing—a skill I have used almost daily throughout my whole life. I learned to type on a manual typewriter. I venture to say that some people reading this have never even seen a manual typewriter. They have more or less disappeared from existence. But those of us old enough to remember can tell you about them and the tedious nature of their use.

And then everything changed. Suddenly. Drastically. Dramatically.

Personal computers were made widely available to the general public. Typing became instantly obsolete as "word processing" became possible. Machines had "memory." Computers could do repetitive functions like change all your footnotes to endnotes automatically at a touch of a button. Correcting, changing, and cutting and pasting text could now be done quickly and with ease. There was even spell check.

And much, much more was made possible with computers. There was all of a sudden something called email. There was the World Wide Web.

A revolution overnight. A miracle, really and truly.

If you don't believe that nearly instantaneous widespread availability of personal computers and the invention of the internet are miracles, you're "miracle-proof."

In the next chapter, we'll discuss how often such miracles occur. Suffice it to say they are not just accidental. It's not a kind of random coincidence that we are living in a place and time where such innovations in technology are rapidly and irrevocably changing our lives. We have, in a very real sense, *created* these miracles.

But first, let's see these recent changes in our "normal" lives for what they are. As I said above, lives like ours really can't be considered ordinary in any way. The features of our lives are more than just extraordinary. Again, it is useful to use comparison in order to see our own reality more clearly. Our lives are what others, looking from the outside in, would surely regard as supernatural or magical. They are what others would clearly perceive of as miracles. And they are what some spiritual traditions would see as evidence of our proximity in this lifetime to the goal we've been striving for—the perfect happiness of an enlightened being.

In the yoga texts of ancient India and Tibet, it was expected that as the advanced practitioner moved closer and closer to the end of their quest, they would acquire supernormal powers called *siddhis*. They would become what is termed *mahasiddhas*, "great accomplished ones." Wizards. Wonder-workers. Magicians.

The depiction of such powers in the ancient texts is interesting when seen through modern eyes. Signs of such advanced practice included the ability to quickly traverse great distances, to fly through the sky, and to travel speedily over water. Such a wizard would also obtain the ability to communicate to others from miles away, and to see even small things from a great distance. Or be able to become so small that they could perceive infinitesimally tiny atoms, or so large that they could see planets up close.

Sound familiar? Can we do these things? We actually do have the ability to travel great distances quickly (cars), and to fly (airplanes), and to go fast over water (speed boats and jet skis). We communicate instantaneously with others on different continents by pushing a series of buttons on our tiny, hand-held cell phones. We have telescopes and microscopes and satellites taking pictures of Saturn, which we all can view on our television sets, where events around the world are made visible to us without leaving our own homes.

Are we the very mahasiddhas the ancients described in their sacred literature? "Oh, those things don't count!" one might object. "Those aren't *really* supernatural powers. That's just *technology*."

But the technology has made it possible for us to acquire the very powers imagined in the old texts. We discount such abilities only because they seem routine and commonplace—*to us*. But do you suppose that if the ancients were transported into our world *they* would dismiss these capabilities as "just technology"? Or would they perhaps say, "Yes! That's what we meant by 'flying.' You go up in the sky and fly, like a bird." And way more comfortably than having to flap wings, scrape insects from our faces, and get our hair all messed up. Come on! What would our lives look like *to them?*

There's a hilarious riff on this topic by the comedian Louis C.K. Check it out on YouTube: "Everything's Amazing and

Nobody's Happy." He reminisces about the old days, when you had to actually dial phones in order to make a call (and thus were aggravated at people who had too many zeros in their phone numbers), versus now, when we get impatient if our cell phones don't instantly connect: "*Give it minute! It's going to space!*" We bitch and moan about the food or crappy movie they're showing on the airplane that is transporting us coast to coast in a matter of hours instead of marveling over the fact that we're actually flying: "You're sitting in a chair in the sky!" And our response? "*Yeah, but it doesn't go back far enough.*"[7]

One could argue that we have recently procured even some of the more outlandish and seemingly impossible *siddhis* listed in the yogic texts. For example, at advanced stages of spiritual development, one is said to begin to acquire the ability to know everything (*sarva-jna*, "to know all"). With the creation of and general access to the internet, we may be closer than we realize to the omniscience imagined in the ancient books.

I've got two words for you in this regard: "Google it!"

Your Miraculous Life
http://bit.ly/renegade3

Amnesiac Yogis

When my teacher had finished twenty years of study in the Tibetan Buddhist monastery and had been awarded the degree of *geshe*, his monastic preceptors informed him that he was now finally eligible to engage in the most advanced practices.

As my teacher tells the story, one of his mentors, an old and rather feeble-looking Tibetan monk, took him into a back room. Thrilled to be finally gaining entry into the reserved and carefully safeguarded secrets of this tradition, my teacher was somewhat confused when his gnarly, Yoda-like mentor instructed him to *do a downward facing dog yogic pose.* And then a spinal twist. And then a forward bend. And so on.

It soon dawned on my teacher that what had been kept so secret and saved until after the completion of twenty years of preparatory study was . . . *yoga.*

He stopped and asked of his teacher, "Are these postures the secret, advanced teachings we in the monastery are only taught after decades of study?"

"Yes," his instructor replied proudly.

"I'm sorry to have tell you this, but your 'secret' is sort of out. There are tens of millions of Westerners regularly doing these very same poses."

And my teacher was right; according to a "Yoga in America" study released in early 2008 by *Yoga Journal,* there are 15.8 million practitioners of yoga in the United States, with another 18.3 million non-practitioners saying they are very or extremely interested in yoga (triple the number since 2004), and, of these, 9.4 million say they will definitely try yoga within the next year.[8]

So my teacher thought to himself, somewhat chagrined, "Don't they have any better secrets?"

Assuming that his monastic yoga guru would be dismayed to learn that the esoteric exercises of Tibetan Buddhism were presently being performed in yoga studios throughout the Western world, my teacher was taken aback to see the monk break out in a wide grin.

"Really?" the wizened lama replied. "Imagine! Millions of advanced yogic practitioners, of *mahasiddhas* . . . all reborn at the same time in the same place!"

From the perspective of karma and rebirth that is assumed among Buddhists, to have tens of millions of people practicing yoga is wholly extraordinary. To be able to hear the word "yoga," to be interested in it, let alone to actually learn and practice the poses, assumes many, many lifetimes of previous experience with such techniques as a spiritual adept.

From the point of view of karma and rebirth, those of us in the "yoga boom" actually have to be what my teacher has called "amnesiac yogis."

Amnesiac means, of course, that we have forgotten who we really are.

We may chuckle over what seems to us to be the quaint naiveté reflected in an old Tibetan monk's explanation of the current explosion of interest in yoga in the West. That's because we persist in thinking that we're just normal. We think it's just normal to have what the yoga practitioners of the past would have undoubtedly identified as the *siddhis* or supernormal powers that accompany very advanced levels of spiritual progress. We think it's normal to live in cities or towns where yoga studios are as omnipresent as Starbucks; studios where what were once the most esoteric and rarefied techniques, designed to speed up the final stages to complete enlightenment, have been made available to us for fifteen dollars or less per class!

When enumerating the *siddhis*, the yogic texts are always careful to warn the adept about getting waylaid by their allure. These powers are said to come naturally as part of a long-term and sustained spiritual practice. But they are not the end of the journey. They are meant only to be tools—means to an end, and not the end itself.

There is a danger inherent in the privileges and powers acquired through good karma and serious spiritual effort. We might think that the point of our lives is simply to gain and enjoy all the toys and gizmos. But it's not the toys that will deliver the true, deep happiness we're really looking for. The gadgets and magical abilities are useful—maybe even necessary—for achieving our higher goals. But they should not be mistaken for the goal itself.

No One Has Had a Better Shot

We have huge advantages that humanity before us could only dream of—there can be no doubt of this. If we pause to consider the details of our lives, it becomes clear that we can't be ordinary people. Even if you can't accept the argument above—that we are somehow great yogic wizards reborn with all of our powers in order to finish it off in this very lifetime—even if all that seems too far-fetched, at the very least we can agree that when we look at our lives in a comparative manner they have to appear unusually blessed.

As we will see in the next chapter, it *is* possible to turn things around, because everything is in the nexus of causality. If we can uncover the causes for happiness, we can stop wasting time seeking it in all the wrong places, and we can start using our lives more productively. To do so, however, we have to really get clear on those three things the Buddhist texts enumerate when discussing our leisure and fortune.

- We first have to *recognize* our advantageous situation for what it really is. Most of us remain by and large oblivious to the unbelievable facts of the lives we are leading. Perhaps regularly reviewing the points made in this chapter will help to remind us that we are truly the fortunate ones of our world. And maybe, if you think even harder and deeper, you will come to the astonishing conclusion that you are far more than just "lucky"—that you are perhaps an "amnesiac yogi" equipped with the powers necessary to complete your quest in this very lifetime.
- Secondly, we have to realize what a life like this is really for. We have to recognize what we could do with this life if we just made a few adjustments. If we reorganized our priorities a bit, with advantages like ours we could achieve the happiness we really want and which a spiritual life—if pursued with diligence and vigor—could deliver. We could, in this very lifetime, reach the contentment, happiness, joy, and even bliss that would then put us in a position to truly help others do the same. We could, with a life like ours, easily move from being a helpee to a helper. *There is no one else on the planet who has a better shot at reaching the highest goals that religion has always held out.* For us, everything is perfect; all lights are green. The only thing holding us back is our own lack of belief and our addiction to diversions.
- And thirdly, the texts say we must also be aware of how very, very rare a fantastic, magical, and blessed life like ours really is. Do the math; don't forget the statistics. Acquaint yourself with the facts of your life. And then stop the obliviousness and the wastefulness with which you've been conducting it.

Choose to see that there are miracles—and that your life is proof of it!

Couch Potato Contemplation: Your Blessed Life

I like to do this contemplation in bed, first thing in the morning. Before you leap out of bed to start your busy day, take a few minutes in that delicious time between sleep and waking consciousness to do what I call the "morning loll."

Loll around in bed for a while every morning. And spend five or ten minutes at a minimum, before anything else, thinking about all the things that are going right in your life.

Think about the facts of your relative affluence. You have plenty to eat. You have shelter. You have heat when it's cold and fans or air conditioning when it's hot. You have clothes—lots of them. You probably have a car and enough money for gas to go pretty much wherever you want. You probably have enough money to take vacations, or to go to school if you wish, or to buy gifts for your friends and family. You have gadgets galore—television sets, radios, computers, iPods, iPads, phones, GPS, and so on.

Reflect on the many people who love you, who care about you and your happiness. Think about your friends and family and how great it is to have them.

Contemplate your health. If you aren't sick or disabled or in pain, think about how great that is. If you are, think about how fortunate you are to have access to medical care. If you can't think of anything else that's good about your health, be glad that you woke up today! You're alive for another day!

Then think about the education you have received. You can read and write. You know things about the world around you, thanks to your teachers and the classes you took. You have learned how to reason and how to cogently argue your point of view.

Finally, consider how fortunate you are to have at least some connection to an authentic spiritual tradition and to have the freedom to practice your religion without persecution. Be grateful that you have another opportunity today to try to put your spiritual principles into action and to live a good life.

Wake up happy! So much is going right for you!

Action Plan: Un-squandering the Miracle

Beginning today, resolve to watch one half hour less television per day. And then make a plan about how you will use that extra time. Maybe you'll use it to take that jog you've wanted to do but couldn't find the time for. Or to interact with your kids or husband or wife. Or to begin a daily meditation practice. Think about something you've been meaning to do but didn't seem to have the time for, and use the half hour you've gained in your schedule to do it!

3

Getting Stoked: *Seizing the Means of the Production of Happiness*

God does not play dice with the universe.

—**Albert Einstein**

How Things Really Work: The Karmic Worldview

If it is true that we are living blessed lives of privilege and opportunity, we also need to know how such lives came about. Figuring out how things happen not only explains how we got the lives we have, but will also help us to take advantage of our circumstances in order to move ourselves into an even higher destiny—one in which suffering is eliminated, perfection is realized, and we can begin our true mission to really help others terminate their unhappiness too.

Lazy agnosticism on the question of how the world is working does not count as a worldview, and certainly will not help us learn to become happy people. Not taking the time to think about life and its mechanisms will not further one's spiritual growth. As Socrates famously said, "The unexamined life is not worth living." And he was right. There's no virtue in being a bubblehead.

So how do things happen? How does life really work?

One possibility is that things happen randomly, arbitrarily, and haphazardly, and this is actually and somewhat surprisingly one of the mainstream viewpoints of our current cultural milieu. We see it at work "explaining" life at various levels. We call upon this worldview in our everyday experiences (interpreting unwanted events as "bad luck," for example), and it is reinforced and underwritten at the highest levels of our society (e.g., the Big Bang theory—where the entire universe is said to have come into existence "for no reason"—or "random mutation" as an "explanation" for the mechanism of evolution).

If things happen randomly, there is really no reason to try to do anything at all. For who knows if any action will pay off? It's all just the luck of the draw. If we assume that things happen arbitrarily, we have absolutely no control over our lives. We remain disempowered, feeling victimized and without hope.

A second possible explanation for why things happen the way they do is that God is micromanaging the universe. It's all just God's will. But choosing this mode of explication has the same downside as saying everything happens randomly and for no reason. Seeing everything as God's will precludes our own free will. Again, we are left completely out of control of our own lives. If everything is being determined for us, then there is nothing we can do for ourselves. And the question of why things happen remains inexplicable.

Many of us have learned not to push the inquiry too far. We've ceased to ask what I call the "Why, Daddy?" question. If you have had kids (or if you've been one), you know how this goes. When children are young, they're constantly asking Daddy or Mommy why—why do things happen the way they do?

Kids pursue this line of questioning to the bitter end; they don't stay satisfied with superficial or provisional answers. "But why, Daddy? Why?"

And you know where the conversation goes from here. We've all been through it ourselves, both as children and as grown-ups trying to answer kids' questions. Sooner or later, after we decide that the whys have gone on long enough, we lose patience and give The Real Answer: *Just because! It happened just because!*

It's just "luck" (good or bad) or "God's will." Which is to say, no reason—or at least no reason we can discern.

We adults should belabor the "Why, Daddy?" question with as much dogged persistence as we did as children. Accepting any version of the answer "no reason" is not only intellectually defeatist but also disempowering and irresponsible. Like the curious and determined child, the spiritual renegade will not give up easily on the "Why, Daddy?" question.

There actually *are* explanations and reasons behind things—*nothing* happens just by "luck," randomly and inexplicably, or by the arbitrary will of an inscrutable God. We have full responsibility over our lives and therefore everything we do matters.

Everything is an effect of a previous cause and in turn acts as a cause for a future effect. And not just sometimes. All the time! Everything is caused, always; everything is a result of an earlier action. Everything, without exception, lies within this nexus of cause and effect.

In the East, causality is called karma. But the first thing we have to recognize is that it is not some concept foreign to us in the West. Karma was not invented in India a few thousand years ago and then finally exported to the West in the 1960s as an exotic consumer good—unloaded off the boat together with sitar music, spicy cuisine, and turban-wearing gurus.

What was called "karma" in the East lies at the heart of all religious ethical systems worldwide. For how could there be a moral system that did not assume such causality and the personal accountability of one's actions? The truth of karma is found repeatedly enunciated, for example, in the Christian scriptures:

Do unto others as you would have them do unto you.
I swear to you that one day you will give an accounting of every word you have ever spoken.
Give, and you shall receive.
You cannot get grapes from thistles.
You shall reap what you sow.

"Reap? Sow? What's that mean? I'm a city boy! I haven't 'reaped' anything lately! How does that apply to my life?"

What Jesus meant, of course, using the agricultural metaphor, was that you get back what you put out. The Golden Rule (a version of which is found in all authentic spiritual traditions) encapsulates this: People will do to you what you have done to others.

So karma is not an idea that is alien to us. It is found in our own Western religious traditions as well as those of the

East. It is also integrated into some of our popular idioms for explaining why things happen: "What goes around, comes around," as we say colloquially. We get back in life what we have put out.

The laws of karma require us to take total responsibility for everything that happens to us in life—which is why at times we wish to deny them in favor of some other worldviews that allow us to abdicate culpability for our actions and their consequences. Karma holds our feet to the fire when it comes to the question of blame and liability.

But karma is also the only worldview that gives us hope, direction, and control over our future. If you want a good life, if you want a happy life, if you want good relationships, if you want wealth and material wherewithal, if you want good experiences, if you want people to be kind to you, if you want people to be honest with you—well, you've got to first create the causes for these things. It has to first go out before it can come back; a desired effect requires the appropriate cause.

Our lives are like an echo. We shout out "hello!" and it comes back: "HELLO, Hello, hello." What we send out returns to us. That's karma.

Later, in chapter 7, we'll look closely at the laws that govern karma: the rules of life we need to know in order to be conscious operators of the system and not just the ignorant victims of the principles at work in the universe. But enough has already been said here for us to be able to identify—or rather, just recognize—a worldview we are, to some extent, already familiar with.

It's the worldview that assumes causality.

Everything is caused.

But not the way we usually think.

How Things Work
http://bit.ly/renegade4

THINGS THAT MAKE YOU GO "HMM"

I think most of us, most of the time, believe in causality. We actually do mostly live our lives as if our actions function as causes that bring about the effects we desire. We go to work in the belief that working will be the cause that results in a paycheck, which, in turn, will allow us to live in our homes, drive our cars, go to the movies, and so on. In fact, everything we do in life is calculated to bring about a desired end. Everything we do is designed to bring about a happier life and to avoid pain.

Even if we haven't made some kind of conscious philosophical choice, things are caused; that's why they happen. But although we usually do subscribe to some form of cause and effect as the explanation for why things happen, *the form of causality we ordinarily believe in is fallacious.* Things cannot actually be happening the way we think. Hard work, in reality, is not the cause of money, and having money is not the cause of having a home or a car, or being able to go to the movies. Things are caused—but not the way we think.

It is a crucial part of what the spiritual traditions call "wisdom" to realize that *the way things appear is not how they really are.* If things existed in just the way they seem—if, for example, cause and effect were obvious and transparent—there would be no need for wisdom.

So if we are going to accept karma as our guide to life, we have to understand what a "cause" really is—and is not. A cause for a particular effect is not something that brings about that effect some of the time, or just for some people. And an effect is not something that could ever be brought about without its specific cause. In the eighth-century Buddhist classic *Guide to the Bodhisattva's Way of Life,* the principle of causality is laid out in clear and unequivocal terms:

> *A cause of something is that thing which when it is absent its effect cannot happen, and when it is present the effect must happen.*[1]

That's real causality. So let's check to see if the causality we ordinarily believe in holds up to this criterion.

Is hard work the cause of money? I think most of us usually assume that if we need money, we'll also need to get a job and work hard at it. But let's see, according to the principles of causality, if that's really how we get money. Does *everyone* who works hard *always* earn lots of money? There are billions of people in our world who don't have enough money even though they work harder than most of us have ever worked in our lives. And there are plenty of people who don't work hard—or don't even work at all—who get plenty of money.

So, hard work simply cannot be the real cause of money. And money, in turn, cannot be the real cause of having a nice home, or a car, or the ability to go to the movies. Again, let's check. If money were the cause of having a nice home, *nobody* would *ever* have a nice home without money, and *everyone* with money would *always* have a nice home. Without the cause, the effect is impossible; with the cause, the effect is inevitable. And the same goes for cars, the ability to go to movies, take nice holidays, buy new MP3 players, and so on.

Let's try another example. Does exercise—let's say, doing yoga poses regularly—bring about strength, good health, and longevity? It cannot. It cannot be the cause of any of these. Why? If strength, good health, and longevity came from conscientiously doing yoga poses, then *everyone* who did their yoga practice daily would *always* be strong, healthy, and live to a ripe old age. And *no one* who *didn't* do yoga would *ever* be strong, healthy, and long lived. The fact that statistics now suggest that as many as 25 percent of people who do yoga have sustained an injury that they attribute to doing that very activity indicates that yoga actually can't be working the way we may think it does.[2]

And it's not just yoga, of course. Before the yoga craze, there was running and jogging. Remember Jim Fixx? The famous runner who dropped dead of a heart attack at the age of fifty-two one day after his morning run? If running brought good health and long life, how come Jim Fixx died at such an early age . . . *after running*?

Cases like Jim Fixx's are "things that make you go 'hmm'" when it comes to our belief in the kind of causality we ordinarily believe in. "Well, that was just an anomaly," we might say—meaning an exception to causality. Or, "There were other factors at work," which in this case meant that running was, somewhat abnormally, not a cause for health but rather a cause for a heart attack.

So the so-called causality we usually and somewhat unthinkingly buy into actually only works sometimes or for some people, with all kinds of escape clauses for exceptional circumstances and other intervening factors. In other words, it's not really causality at all.

In the ancient Sanskrit texts, a distinction is made between the "cause" (*hetu*) and the "condition" (*pratyaya*). The latter are the things like hard work when it comes to money, and yoga or running when it comes to health. They are the conditions under which the real causes for things might find expression.

But the real causes of things are what we can call karma. If one has the right karma, doing yoga regularly or running will bring good health, and working hard will result in a lot of money. But if the karma is not there, it won't. It's as simple as that. It's difficult sometimes to see and believe in, but that's the way it has to be.

Yoga and running are merely two possible *delivery systems for karma*—and they can deliver health and physical well-being (if the karma of protecting life and caring for the bodies of others is there), or bodily injury and a heart attack (two ways the karma of physically harming or killing others could manifest). It all depends on the karma.

Similarly, hard work can be the means by which the real cause of money (i.e., a previous act of generosity) finds expression, or it can be a frustrating, grueling, and unrewarding experience—the way a different kind of karmic cause has found a way to realize its appropriate effect.

The karmic worldview assumes that all the things that happen to us in life are caused. That's why they happen. But it also embraces a real causality and not the fake, imposter version of cause and effect that we ordinarily subscribe to.

If we are to adopt karma, we must adhere to a causality that works all the time, the same everywhere and for everybody, and without exception. That's karma. And there are no karma-free zones.

Sticking to Your Guns, Especially When Appearances Deceive

Everything we do, say, and think matters. Everything is in the web of causality. The "good" (i.e., the selfless, the compassionate, and the kind) produces a pleasant result, and the "bad" (i.e., the selfish, the cruel, and the uncaring) brings about an unpleasant effect.

Nothing ever "just happens"—nothing good ever goes for naught, and nothing bad ever goes unpunished. As it says in the Bhagavad Gita, "No action in this world goes for naught or brings about a contrary result."[3]

Such a principle is the only one that will underwrite a coherent moral system and provide a consistent set of guidelines for controlling and improving one's life. And it is the central assumption of karmic worldview.

But we are sometimes tempted to abandon this explanatory and ethical compass because we do not see it always working in the short run. We are taken in by the mere appearances of things—and appearances do indeed deceive.

We have already witnessed how we are often fooled by a false causality, whereby things are said to be causes for other things even when they don't always bring about the result, or when the result can occur without the supposed cause. This faux causality substitutes for real causality because, at least sometimes, for some people, it appears that hard work is indeed the cause of money and exercise is the true cause of good health.

Here's another example of how we are deceived by appearances: If, for example, I do something kind and generous for someone else and receive a mean and ungrateful response, was the former the "cause" of the latter? Can an unpleasant result ever come from a good cause? And what about when I do something I know, at some level, not to be right and it seems to bring about a pleasant result? Say I tell a lie in order to get a promotion at work and I do indeed get the new, better position. Did the promotion "come from" (i.e. was it "caused by") the lie? Can an agreeable result ever come from a morally corrupt cause?

It seems like it can, doesn't it? At least sometimes. It's the old problem of theodicy all over again, with or without an omnipotent God in the picture. And it's exactly these kinds of false appearances that keep us from having any real, consistent loyalty to the laws of karma. In such cases, we take recourse in a fallacious explanatory system wherein it is possible to suspend the fundamental principles of causality and morality—that good never goes unrewarded, and bad never goes unpunished—and say, "Well, in this case, it did."

Opening such a door to irregularity completely undercuts the ethical life. There can be no real basis for morality if it only works some of the time. When one allows for exceptions to the ruling principles of karma, one is really just reverting back to the worldview where sometimes good is rewarded and bad is punished—but sometimes it isn't. And there's really no telling when it will be and when it won't. It's all just random.

Cases like those described above do indeed happen. There are times when the immediate sequel to our kind action is that the other is unkind in return; and there are occasions when we seem to "get away" with negative actions, or are even rewarded in their wake.

It's hard. But it has to be like this: There is really no cause-and-effect relationship at all between these disparate things. If a negative thing (someone is unkind to you) occurs after you have done a positive thing (you've been kind to someone), there can be no causal correlation between the two, despite the appearance of one. Conversely, if you've done something negative (lied) and something positive occurs (you get a promotion), again, there can be no cause-and-effect connection between these two things.

So how can we explain such things? Why was someone mean to me when I had just been kind to them? Because I haven't always been kind to people. The mean response was caused by a previous instance when I was angry and unpleasant to others. It had nothing to do with the kindness I had just shown. And the kind act will definitely, in the future, have a pleasant result. As for the other case, the promotion came from a past cause like selflessly helping others to advance, and was completely unrelated to the lie I just told. And the lie will definitely come back to me in the future in the form of others being deceitful toward me.

There is always a time gap between cause and effect. Karma, despite the famous John Lennon song, is not "instant." If it were, we would achieve perfect happiness in no time at all, for we would never do the things that cause our suffering and preclude our happiness.

If karma were instant and, say, your arm broke as soon as you killed an ant crawling on your kitchen counter, how many more ants would you ever kill? Maybe one more, at most, to "replicate the experiment." And then, with two broken arms, you would resolve very sincerely to never harm another living being again, right?

"Mind the gap," as it says in the London Tube. Be aware of the fact that there is always a time delay between creating the cause and experiencing the result.

If you've decided that karma is your pony, then back that horse all the way! Stick to your guns! And have faith, knowing that if things always worked the way they appeared to work, there would be no true causality at all—a causality that works all the time, for everybody.

The fact that there is a real causality at work is very good news indeed. For it means that everything happens according to rules (the "laws of karma") and that everything is therefore changeable. There are no accidents, mistakes, or anomalies, and there is nothing in our lives that lies outside of our personal control. We can have real confidence that if we learn the rules (and live by them) we can not only sustain our already miraculous existence, we can bring our lives to their ultimate culmination—perfect and everlasting happiness and bliss.

Couch Potato Contemplation: Causality—Real and Fake

Spend at least ten to fifteen minutes a day, for at least a week's time, thinking about causality and how things are really working.

Examine your own tendency to abandon causality altogether when it's not comfortable to take responsibility for having yourself caused the unwanted events in your life. Review the last time something unpleasant happened to you and see if you blamed someone else for it or just chalked it up to bad luck.

Next, think about what real causality entails: *A cause of something is that thing which when it is absent its effect cannot happen, and when it is present the effect must happen.*

Investigate whether the things you think are causes conform to these criteria:

- Do good health and longevity really come directly from exercise or diet?
- Do beauty and physical attractiveness result from losing a few pounds, getting in better shape, having your hair done, or getting a Botox shot or facelift?
- Does money come from hard work? Or from financial investments in stocks, bonds, real estate, and so on?
- Do promotions and advancements in one's profession come from doing the job well? Or from buttering up the boss?

Try to work out what might be the true causes of health and longevity, beauty and physical attractiveness, money, or professional promotions. What would they be if one were guided by the principle "you reap what you sow"?

Action Plan: Do unto Others

What is currently the biggest problem in your life? Analyze it under the assumption that everything is caused by one's moral actions in the past. Then determine to systematically put into play the true cause for its alleviation.

Say the problem is money. Resolve to be more generous. If the problem is with a person or relationship, do unto others as you would have them do unto you. If the problem is physical health, take care of the body or bodies of others.

Do something at least once a day that will plant these new seeds. And keep a journal where you note each day what you did. Continue for at least a month (or until the problem evaporates).

Part II
Changing the Past

4

Preemptive and Unilateral Forgiveness: *Ending the Repeated Resurrection of Frankenstein's Monster*

The stupid neither forgive nor forget; the naïve forgive and forget; the wise forgive but do not forget.

—**Thomas Szasz**

Stop Running with Scissors!

In his *Guide to the Bodhisattva's Way of Life*, Master Shantideva reveals the depressing fact that our suffering is basically self-induced. We continually make ourselves unhappy. We do so in part by vigorously pursuing the very things that will hurt us:

> *People who want to be rid of suffering instead madly dash toward it. Even though they want to be happy, because of their delusion they destroy their own happiness as if it were an enemy.*[1]

We should cherish our happiness enough to stop doing the very things that would undermine it. But instead, we're like masochists in denial. We say we want to be happy while simultaneously doing things that preclude the very happiness that we seek. To shift the metaphor (or is it a metaphor?), spiritually, we're like children:

> *Children want no suffering but at the same time they thirst for the things that bring them pain.*[2]

When it comes to acting wisely and in our enlightened self-interest, we're like little kids stuck in cosmic kindergarten. We're children recklessly running with scissors. Didn't your mom tell you not to do this? But we don't seem to know any better, and so we trip and inflict injury after injury on ourselves.

"Ow, ow, I hurt! I hurt! What should I do? Ow, ow, ow, I'm cutting myself!" But when the cosmic kindergarten teacher comes and says, "Just give me the scissors," we resist. "No, don't take my scissors! Ow, ow, ow! It hurts! But don't take my scissors!"

That's about where we're at, unfortunately. We won't loosen our grip on the things that are hurting us. But if we are going to be happy, we're going to have to relinquish the scissors.

So what are these scissors? What are we holding on to (and wielding self-destructively) that is inflicting so much pain? As we shall see, there are several versions of the scissors. Ultimately, however, all of them entail some form of the two-fold mistaken idea that *happiness comes from any other place than within ourselves and that other people and events have the power to make us unhappy.*

In the first place, we're fundamentally ignorant and deluded about where happiness is to be found and how we will obtain it. Although we seek happiness, we're looking for it in all the wrong places (i.e., outside of ourselves): in money or possessions, in our job or profession, in our vacations and entertainment, and, perhaps most often, in other people.

We believe that other people—our partners, friends, or children—somehow have the ability, as well as the obligation, to make us happy. And they don't have either one. We set them up to fail, over and over again. And then we become unhappy because we thought they should do something they didn't do . . . *because they couldn't do it.*

On and on and on we go, like caged gerbils running on a wheel. That's what was meant in the ancient Indian texts by the term "samsara"—the cycle of continuous and repeated suffering. Samsara is the gerbil wheel we can't seem to get off of. We're trying to be happy but we're making the same mistakes over and over and over again—thinking, for example, that happiness is in something "out there" somewhere, or that other people can bestow it upon us.

Other people cannot make us happy. Thinking that they can, and then being repeatedly disappointed when they don't, is one version of the scissors we're running with, and one of the ways we keep ourselves on the samsaric gerbil wheel of suffering. *No one can make you happy but you.* We'll return to this theme in part 3, where we discuss how to be more realistic and savvy about where the happiness we hope for in the future will actually come from. In the meantime, because we have put our eggs in the wrong baskets, we remain needlessly anxious and apprehensive about what will happen to us in the future.

But if other people cannot make us happy, by the same token *other people cannot make us unhappy either.* They don't have that in their power any more than they have the capability to induce happiness in us. While it may be convenient to blame others for our distress ("You made me so unhappy!") if we are to live according to the laws of karma, we must take total responsibility for *both* our happiness *and* our unhappiness.

The Alchemical Magic of Forgiveness

In this chapter and the next, we'll concentrate on how we can begin to ease our pain and start living happier lives simply by undertaking something we have in our power to do any time we choose. It is to reconceptualize our past, to think differently about what we think has happened to us. When we supply ourselves with a new, more positive vision of our personal history, our present is immediately and beneficially affected. We'll feel happier in the here and now when we have a more favorable and constructive view of our past.

This chapter is about the first step in rehabilitating the past: learning to let go of the pain, resentment, and anger we're carrying about what has happened to us in our lives. And there's only one way to do this. It is to forgive—preemptively and unilaterally. When we take this initial step, we will have created the possibility of moving on to an even higher level of overhauling the past. We'll be able to generate gratitude for the events and people of our lives, which will be the subject of the next chapter.

Perhaps resistance to forgiveness is already rising up in you. We all have it, and some of us have it big time. I've had people walk out of talks I've given on this subject, their body language distinctly declaring, "No way am I going to forgive him! He hurt me and he hurt me badly! I'm not staying to have this crazy monk tell me I have to forgive . . ."

Forgiveness is hard and we really don't want to do it. So we need to be as clear and forceful as possible with our reluctant selves. *Holding on to grudges simply perpetuates our own suffering.* Instead of letting go and moving on, we repeatedly aggravate these past hurts by dredging them up and reliving them, over and over again. It's like running electrodes through Frankenstein's monster so it can rise and live once more! We're *re-membering* instead of *dis-membering* the horrific demon that is terrorizing us and undermining any hope of our attaining happiness.

We don't need to continue running and stabbing ourselves with these particular scissors. We can just drop them anytime we decide to. And when we do, we'll immediately feel better.

But doing what is good for us often seems difficult. We resist change. We've become quite accustomed to carrying our scissors, and we are habituated to cutting ourselves with them. To free ourselves of bitterness and to end the repeated cycle of pain, we'll need once again to assume the role of a spiritual renegade and do what our conservative nature very much resists—practice radical forgiveness!

If we want to incite happiness in our present lives, we must let go of our resentment about the past. We'll have to forgive those who hurt us. And we'll have to overcome the huge resistance to doing so. We'll need to use our heads to overcome our gut instinct to hold on to the resentment, the anger, and the pain.

If we are going to finally surrender our scissors of acrimony and ill will—the self-inflicted pain that comes from holding on to resentment about the past—it will be important to get clear about three things:

First, we must think it's possible to change the past.

If we are going to set out to do something—especially something difficult—we have to believe it can be done. We have to believe we can succeed if we try.

Radical forgiveness goes beyond merely forgetting and moving on. We're not advocating a coping mechanism, just trying to "get over" the past. We're interested here in a more thoroughgoing and subversive solution to the problem of retrospective angst.

So we'll start below by investigating the crucial question: Can we do more than just try to overlook or forget about the past? Can we, in fact, actually change the past through the alchemical magic of forgiveness? Some of the memories we have now are tormenting us and ruining our chances for true happiness. Can we think differently—more positively and beneficially—about what has happened to us in a way that will then provide us with a different sense not only of our past but also of our present?

Second, we need to persuade ourselves that we can truly benefit by forgiving others.

We'll need to be very clear about the fact that we cannot be happy in the here and now if we continue to harbor these grudges and remain full of bitterness, sadness, and anger about what others have done to us in the past. We must recognize, first and foremost, that it is not in our enlightened self-interest to repeatedly poison ourselves with this kind of rancor.

Practicing forgiveness is like taking medicine for an illness: at first it may be hard to choke down, but it is the only thing that will cure us. Our present happiness is being spoiled by our anger and sadness about the past.

Third, we need to know precisely what forgiveness is, and what it isn't.

We are, perhaps, reluctant to forgive, or maybe we excuse ourselves from doing so because we have fostered a mistaken idea about it. We may think that forgiveness entails something that it doesn't, or that it will require us to do something that we suspect is undesirable or even impossible.

At the end of this chapter is something of a laundry list of what forgiveness really involves. Being realistic about what forgiveness is, and what it isn't, will be the final step to actually doing it!

The Greatest Enemy

"It is a simple but sometimes forgotten truth," remarked former Australian Prime Minister Robert G. Menzies, "that the greatest enemy to present joy and high hopes is the cultivation of retrospective bitterness."[3]

Not forgiving those who hurt or disappoint us is one of the biggest reasons we are not happy in the here and now. But make no mistake about it: Letting go of our "retrospective bitterness" will not be an easy task. For it forces us to contemplate doing something we don't really want to do, taking medicine we truly abhor.

So, to counteract our strong resistance to this, we must first believe it is possible to change. And we'll need to be clear about what forgiveness really is and what it entails. Most of all, we'll have to jimmy up some strong desire—a powerful enough wish to be happy in the present that we'll be willing to do the very thing we least want to do with those who have hurt, betrayed, or abandoned us in the past.

Cultivating this deep desire to be happy, to diminish our suffering, will result in our willingness—even eagerness—to finally do what we've resisted for so long: to forgive.

The Past Is Never Like It Used to Be

We'll never even try to do something that we're already reluctant to do if we don't think that it's possible to do it. We won't even try to forgive others if we don't believe that one can really do something about what has happened. Such an attitude can result in a defeatist appeal to just "let bygones be bygones" or "let sleeping dogs lie."

But these sleeping dogs don't just lie there. Left untreated, the resentments we have about the past just fester and throb. Our personal happiness in the present requires a more proactive and subversive approach to our "retrospective bitterness" about what has happened in the past.

So we'll begin by reposing the question above: *Can we change the past?*

On the one hand, the answer is "of course not." What happened, happened; what's done is done. You can't just up and decide that you weren't born where and when and into the family you were, as a person of a certain race, nationality, socioeconomic class, and so forth.

These are the hard facts, the data, of our individual lives. And this holds true for the shocks, injuries, and traumas that have happened along the way. These too are among the facts of life. We can't just wish them away.

But on the other hand, we can learn to see them in a new light, and we can stop privileging one kind of narrative over others. The belief that the past is more powerful than the present is part of a victim's mentality, and not that of the spiritual renegade. When we take up the power we have over the past in the present, the very nature of the facts of our lives will transform. The past will change when we look at it differently. To comprehend why this is so requires us to think carefully about what the past actually is.

In what way does the past really exist? If the past is truly past, if it refers to a time that is "done and gone," then one cannot say that it exists anymore. And if the past does not exist, then how can it function to affect our present state of mind?

Of course, the past in another sense does exist. *It exists as a part of the present.* In this sense, William Faulkner was right when he said, "The past is not dead. In fact, it's not even past."[4] What we mean by "the past" is, upon analysis, nothing other than an idea of what has already occurred, which we then carry around in our present minds. "What happened" is really just (and always) an interpretation—it's what we *think* happened, or more accurately, it's what we *presently think* happened.

This being so, we can certainly learn to interpret and understand the past differently, in a healthier, more positive way, such that we are no longer resurrecting Frankenstein's monster every time we remember. We can transform our past because although the basic facts of what happened may be immutable, what they signify to us in the present is a matter of interpretation.

We can change our *understanding* of the past. And adjusting one's current understanding of the past *is to change the only past that actually exists.*

So, can we change the past? Of course we can. Not only can we change the past, we do so every time we revisit it.

The past, one could say, *is never like it used to be.*

The official keepers of our group history have understood this for decades now. If we went to the history department at Harvard or Stanford and asked one of the professors there, "Do the accounts we give of the past change over time and among different historians?" what do you suppose they would say?

Come on! It's obvious: History has a history—that is, the stories we tell about the past are modified over time. Every historian has a point of view. The teller of the story puts a distinctive stamp on the story being told.

So at the cultural or social level, the official narratives of the collective past are constantly being revamped and are inevitably colored by the perspective of the narrator. The history of a nation like the United States, for example, is perpetually being revised every time it is retold. The triumphant narrative of "How the West Was Won," to take one illustration, is not recounted anymore by anyone other than retrograde extremists, and certainly would not be the storyline of any Native American historian.

History—the account we give of the past, as a people and as individuals—is *presentist* and *perspectival.* What that means is that the accounts given of the past are coming from and are in the service of the present circumstances of the storyteller. As they say in Hollywood, things depend on one's POV (point of view).

And as they also say in "The Business," every character needs a "backstory." The past is not only coming from the present, it is in service of the present. History gives a group or a nation a backstory, a past context for their present situation. And it is the history we think we have that helps us to construct our communal sense of present identity.

The stories we tell ourselves and others about our individual and personal past operate in exactly the same manner as our collective histories: they too are told from the POV of our present (from what other temporal standpoint could we be narrating?), and they function to give a backstory to our current situation and sense of self.

There is no past apart from the backstory we give our present. The past is used to help explain why and how we got to be who we are, here and now. Put otherwise, our sense of the past is both coming from and creating our present, and it changes as the present changes (just as the present changes when we shift our story about the past).

History, both personal and collective, is *always* "revisionist." It's not only that we *can* and *do* change the past; it's that we *can't help* but do so.

Mark Twain once quipped, "I'm an old man and have known a great many troubles, but most of them never happened."[5] We need not go that far in order to recognize the truth being communicated: the past is never what it used to be. If the past is presentist and perspectival, then of course we can change it. So why not take control of this process? Why not take advantage of the presentist and revisionist nature of recollection—*and start telling ourselves a better story about what happened?*

When we do, we'll simultaneously be thinking better thoughts about our present lives. We'll live happier in the here and now when we project happier times then and there.

It's neither useful nor inevitable to prolong our well-worn personal narratives of victimization. We can drop those scissors. And since we can, why don't we?

The past is just a story *about* the past, and we are who we think we once were. So who do you want to be? The embittered, unhappy self who is holding on to stories of the traumas and tragedies of the past? Or a healthy and happy self who has changed his or her backstory through the application of the healing balm of forgiveness?

Why Forgiving Is Good for You (and Not Forgiving Isn't)

To revise history—to tell ourselves a different and more beneficial story of our past—we must clean the slate of our current dysfunctional narrative. To reconstruct a past more in accord with our present interest in leading a happy life, we must first deconstruct less helpful accounts of what happened.

When we think about our past, we usually do so using one of two filters. Sometimes (and it happens more often the older we get) we get all nostalgic about "the good old days." We fondly reminisce about our youth and how everything was so much better back then: the music was superior (especially compared to the "noise" produced by the present day groups), people were friendlier and more trustworthy, goods and services were of a higher quality, and so on.

In light of what we discussed in the last section, we need to ask ourselves: Is this "good old days syndrome" conducive to our present happiness? Actually, it's not. It serves only to cast the present in a negative light in relation to an idealized, rose-colored version of the past. The present is measured against an impossibly romanticized edition of the past and, inevitably, it comes up short.

Contentment with the present is precluded when we glorify the past. And make no mistake: the nostalgic vision of the past is indeed a glamorized version. If you have some version of the "good old days syndrome," it generally can be corrected by just being more realistic and honest. The good old days were never really that good, and, even more importantly, nostalgia for an irrecoverable past is not a useful game plan for a happy life in the here and now. "We seem to be going through a period of nostalgia, and everyone seems to think yesterday was better than today," humorist Art Buchwald once wrote. "I don't think it was, and I would advise you not to wait ten years before admitting today was great. If you're hung up on nostalgia, pretend today is yesterday and just go out and have one hell of a time."[6]

For most of us, however, it is another, quite different mode that dominates when we review our past. This is the lens that skews the narrative in the opposite direction. Instead of denigrating the present by means of comparison with an idealized past, we subvert happiness in the present by obsessing about bygone sorrows, regrets, and catastrophes. We become like those ghosts in the cartoons, hobbling our way through life while burdened with the chains and weights of our disappointing past.

Let's be clear: everyone has had difficulties in the past. It's not just you. Terrible things have happened to everyone. This is not to minimize the truly horrific traumas some people have suffered and have to cope with for the rest of their lives. But it is to acknowledge that even those who have seemingly been gifted with charmed lives have had their ordeals too: they too have been betrayed or abandoned; they too have had their hopes and dreams dashed.

There's a story in the Buddhist texts about a mother who loses her only child. Distraught, she goes to the Buddha and begs him to restore her son to life. The Buddha agrees, but conditionally: "Just bring me a mustard seed from the kitchen of a home in the village that hasn't had a tragedy like yours." And, of course, as the woman goes from household to household, she learns that every family in the village has suffered some tragedy or another.

We're all unhappy, every one of us, in part because of our past. We're all nursing our grievances, harboring our ill will, and bearing with our bitterness and pain. There are different degrees of injury, but we're all the walking wounded.

And let's be clear about another thing. Re-envisioning the past doesn't mean you can just make stuff up or pretend that things didn't really occur. It's neither helpful nor intelligent to disingenuously make believe that what happened didn't. It did happen. The sh*t did happen—maybe not exactly as you are remembering it, but something did occur and that something hurts.

As we shall see below, when it comes to letting go of pain from the past, the point is not to try to just "forgive and forget." The work is not to repress or ignore the pain; the task at hand is to transform—to transform suffering into happiness. What we're talking about here is a kind of alchemy, turning something base into something precious. Or you can think about it as a metamorphosis, converting the Frankenstein monster—the unhappiness you feel about the past—into a loveable teddy bear you will willingly embrace.

Let's begin with what life will look like if we don't forgive, if we don't transform the poison of rancor and resentment. Let's look at what's behind our reluctance to forgive and why this is just perpetuating our own suffering. If you check, you'll probably uncover in yourself some version of this twisted logic: "By refusing to forgive her, I am exacting my revenge. I'll show her! I'll just hold on to this grudge forever, and then she'll be sorry!"

Ridiculous, right? Refusing to forgive does not bring about what we intend it to. As someone once observed, *not forgiving is like eating poison and hoping the offending party will die.*

Not forgiving someone who hurt you doesn't hurt them. It hurts you! It destroys your peace of mind, and it undercuts any hope you might have of finding happiness. You cannot enjoy the pleasant things about your present life when you are fixated on painful memories about the past. The resentment begins to affect every aspect of your life—you lose your appetite and your sleep is disrupted.

In his *Guide*, Master Shantideva nicely summarizes the disadvantages of not forgiving and of staying angry:

When one has the thorn of anger lodged in the heart,
There can be no peace of mind or happiness.
One can't sleep and nothing satisfies.[7]

So if we're now clear on the disadvantages of not forgiving, we can move on to the advantages of doing this difficult act. Will there be a payoff for me if I forgive the ones who have injured me?

Of course there will!

This is the real reason why forgiveness is universally recognized by the great spiritual teachers as one of the principal virtues. Spiritual traditions, being in the business of producing happy people, tend to speak in one voice when it comes to the importance of forgiving those who have offended us.

- "You have heard that it was said, 'Eye for eye, and tooth for tooth.' But I tell you, do not resist an evil person. If someone strikes you on the right cheek, turn to him the other also. And if someone wants to sue you and take your tunic, let him have your cloak as well. If someone forces you to go one mile, go with him two miles. Give to the one who asks you, and do not turn away from the one who wants to borrow from you. You have heard that it was said, 'Love your neighbor and hate your enemy.' But I tell you: Love your enemies and pray for those that persecute you, that you may be sons of your Father in heaven." (Jesus, Matthew 5:38–44)[†]
- "If anyone should give you a blow with his hand, with a stick, or with a knife, you should abandon any desire [to retaliate] and utter no evil words." (The Buddha, Majjhima Nikaya 21.6)[‡]
- "Let [us] pardon and forbear. Do you not wish that God should forgive you? God is All-Forgiving, All-Compassionate." (Qur'an 24.22)[§]
- "You shall not take vengeance or bear a grudge against any of your people, but you shall love your neighbour as yourself." (Leviticus 19:18)[†]
- "Hatreds do not ever cease in this world by hating, but by love; this is an eternal truth. . . . Overcome anger by love, overcome evil by good. Overcome the miser by giving, overcome the liar by truth." (The Buddha, Dhammapada 1.5; 17.3)[*]
- "Love your enemies, do good to those who hate you, bless those who curse you, pray for those who abuse you." (Luke 6:27–28)[†]
- "The recompense of an evil deed can only be evil equal to it; but whoever pardons and makes reconciliation, his reward is due from God." (Qur'an 42:40)[§]

- "He, indeed, is a wise and excellent person who has conquered his wrath and shows forgiveness even when insulted, oppressed, and angered by a strong person. The man of power who controls his wrath enjoys numerous everlasting regions; while he that is angry is called foolish and meets with destruction both in this and the other world." (Mahabharata, Vana Parva, Section XXVIII)[||]

Forgiveness, extolled by all the great religious traditions, is a quality of the saintly. It is good, morally, to forgive—we all know this. In a Gallup poll conducted back in 1988, 94 percent of the respondents admitted it was important to forgive. But, interestingly enough, 85 percent also said that they were going to need some outside help in order to do so in their own lives.[8]

It seems so hard to do the right thing. We know that we should forgive, but we feel unable to actually do it. We're like Saint Paul, who in the book of Romans sadly observed, "I do not understand my own actions. For I do not do what I want, but I do the very thing I hate."[9]

But forgiveness is not only morally good; it is also good for us. It is conducive to our well-being and will help us motivate ourselves to actually do it. We have to be clear about the advantages (and, as we noted above, clear also about the disadvantages of not doing it).

So it is important to review over and over again the following: *We cannot be happy people without letting go of the unhappiness we feel as a result of not forgiving.*

Increasingly this is being recognized by modern psychology, once again ratifying what the religious traditions have been propounding for millennia. Studies have shown that people who forgive are happier, more optimistic, more compassionate, and more self-confident than those who cling to their grudges.[10] Organizations such as the International Forgiveness Institute have sprung up to help individuals and groups to forgive others in the interest of emotional healing.[11]

Think about it.

Wouldn't it be nice—wouldn't it make for a more pleasant life—to not have to carry enmity and injuries any longer? Wouldn't it be better to just drop the resentment, anger, and pain that are like poison in our hearts? Wouldn't it be a better way to live to be free of all this "retrospective bitterness"?

So if we believe that it is both *possible* to give ourselves a different feeling about our past and *desirable* to do so, we are in a position to think seriously about embarking upon the difficult work of forgiveness. The last thing we need to know is what we will actually be doing when we practice forgiveness. We'll have to understand what forgiveness really entails—what it means to forgive, and what it doesn't.

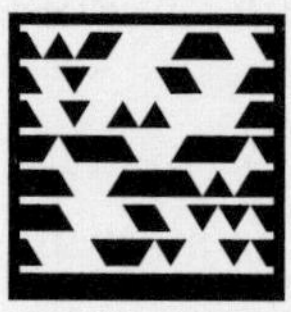

Forgiveness
http://bit.ly/renegade5

What Forgiveness Is—and Isn't

It is important to be clear about what forgiveness is, and not just so we know what we're doing when we finally get around to doing it. We also want to expose and explode any false rationale we might be using as an excuse not to forgive. As we've repeatedly underscored in this chapter, it feels very difficult to pardon people who have hurt, betrayed, and disappointed us in the past. We don't really want to do it, and we may be consciously or unconsciously relying on mistaken ideas about what forgiveness involves in order to justify our reluctance.

So here we go: a checklist of what forgiveness is, and what it isn't.

Forgiveness ISN'T about forgetting or denying what happened.

We should feel a little better already about proceeding further along this path of forgiveness knowing that we won't have to go all amnesiac to do it. "Yeah, that's right! Damned if I'm going to just pretend it didn't happen!"

Don't worry, you don't have to. Forget about forgetting. You probably can't do it anyway. If you do attempt to suppress or push down what you know really happened, it will just ooze out around the sides and work on you in misdirected and inappropriate ways. It's not the point to try to repress, deny, or otherwise somehow put out of your mind those painful memories. As Freud rightly said, mental health can only come about if we put the ego where the id was. We must make conscious what is unconscious in order to defuse the latter's surreptitious power and influence.

Chances are that many of us do need to be a bit more conscious of the bad feelings we have about others. If we are going to work on these sentiments, we have to admit that we possess them. Sometimes we try to repress what we are feeling, not only because it hurts to remember but also because we're embarrassed that we feel the way we do. We're ashamed of our own negative feelings. Especially if we are trying to be a good, kind, spiritual person, we may be reluctant to admit that we harbor such ugliness within ourselves, such anger and hatred toward others.

But denial won't help here. *You have to feel in order to heal!* So don't try to deny that you are upset about the past, and don't think that you'll achieve the purpose by some simplistic version of "forgive and forget."

Forgive, yes. But true forgiveness arises from first admitting both the pain and the feelings one has in response to that pain. Don't forget what Thomas Szasz said (we used it above as the epigraph for this chapter): "The stupid neither forgive nor forget; the naïve forgive and forget; the wise forgive but do not forget."

Forgiveness ISN'T about condoning or excusing.

One of the most common errors—and an excuse we rely on to avoid forgiving—is the contention that to forgive the ones who hurt us would imply somehow also excusing, accepting, or disregarding the cruel and harmful behavior that brought the pain to us.

In order to practice forgiveness, there is, presumably, some wrongful action that one is pardoning. Someone hurt, betrayed, or abused you—and it's not right or good to hurt others. Forgiveness depends upon there being something to forgive. If forgiveness went hand in hand with condoning the action you were forgiving, what, exactly, would you be forgiving?

Forgiveness entails the recognition that a harmful act has occurred. And it's as wrong for others to hurt us as it is for us to hurt them. Isn't this, in fact, one of the reasons to practice forgiveness in the first place? As we have seen above, we don't forgive others in part out of the delusional idea that our withholding will somehow hurt them. Such a truculent attitude in and of itself is destructive to our peace of mind; the wish to harm others is a cause for harm to come to ourselves. Forgiveness is the antidote to this wish for retaliation, for returning harm for harm. It was Gandhi who reputedly said, "An eye for an eye makes the whole world blind."[12]

Forgiveness ISN'T about whether or not the offending person "deserves" forgiveness.

Just as forgiveness is not about condoning an action that was truly harmful, it also isn't contingent upon whether the person who hurt us is deserving of our forgiveness. The spiritual renegade realizes that it doesn't matter (as we shall see below) whether the person has asked for our forgiveness, or apologized, or in some other way shown us the deference we think we deserve. It doesn't matter if the offending party has changed and is now a kinder, gentler version of him- or herself in comparison to how they once were.

It doesn't matter. It's not about the offending person. Forgiveness is about you.

At the Forgiveness Institute, they have a nice definition of what's really at the heart of the virtue we're speaking about here: "It is the foregoing of resentment or revenge when the wrongdoer's actions deserve it and giving the gifts of mercy, generosity, and love when the wrongdoer does not deserve them."[13]

Forgiveness ISN'T dependent on the other person apologizing or reconciling with you, but any such reconciliation IS dependent on first forgiving.

Here is another of our favorite excuses as to why we do not forgive another: they haven't apologized yet! They are not worthy of forgiveness because they have not admitted their guilt and said they were sorry!

Chances are you are entertaining a forgiveness fantasy that looks something like this: Someday your offenders will finally come to you on bended knee, groveling and supplicant, and admit that they haven't slept a wink for lo these many years, racked with guilt about what they did to you and how much they regret it. They then plead with you to please, please exonerate them from this terrible burden so they can get on with their lives. And then you look down upon them and sternly give them the scolding they so richly deserve (and that you have been rehearsing for quite some time):

> *That's right. You hurt me; you were very, very wrong. It's good that you know how much you hurt me and how mistaken you were to do it. It's good that you've felt so bad about it!*

And then, having made sure they really and truly feel super bad and guilty, you will, with great magnanimity, *deign to forgive them.*

This scenario almost certainly is not going to occur. Out of the thousands of people I've talked to about forgiveness, only one has come up to me and reported that something like the above chain of events actually happened to him. That's about the odds: about one in several thousand. You can wait a long, long time—maybe your whole life—before your offender comes groveling to you to apologize. If your act of forgiveness is tied to the other person asking for it, forgiveness, for you, will probably not be happening any time soon.

Maybe the offender is too embarrassed or lacks the moral fiber to apologize. In that case, we'll need to be strong enough to preemptively forgive those who are not strong enough to say they're sorry. Remember, forgiveness isn't about them; it's about you.

Conversely, it's possible that the person you are so angry with doesn't even remember the incident you have been replaying in your mind over and over again. Has this ever happened to you? You tell someone that you want to talk to them about this hugely traumatic event in your life that you're holding them responsible for—and they don't even know what you're talking about! It's only you who has regarded it as so significant; it's only you who has kept it alive by running the electrodes through Frankenstein's monster, over and over and over again.

But if, on the one hand, forgiveness is not dependent upon the other person admitting culpability, saying they are sorry, and pleading for reconciliation, then, on the other hand, there is no reconciliation possible without forgiveness. You cannot expect a rift between you and a person from whom you are estranged to heal on its own. And since, as we've seen, it is unlikely that the other person is going to make the first move, it's up to you to do the right thing—for yourself, first and foremost, but also for all those concerned.

Forgiveness ISN'T an act of weakness; it IS an act of great strength.

Perhaps it's a sort of macho thing (regardless of gender) to think that it is "wimpy" or "wussy" to forgive. Forgiveness might seem like weakness; a strong person holds his or her ground, refusing to relent.

In the Hindu epic, the Mahabharata, it is admitted that "There is only one defect in forgiving persons, and that defect is that people take a forgiving person to be weak." The text goes on to say, "That defect, however, should not be taken into consideration, for forgiveness is a great power. Forgiveness is a virtue of the weak, and an ornament of the strong."[14]

Mahatma Gandhi, surely one of the world's greatest practitioners of forgiveness, puts it even more starkly: "The weak can never forgive. Forgiveness is the attribute of the strong."[15] And if you don't think the Mahatma was right, try it. Forgiving is really, really hard! It seems much easier not to do it, never mind the negative consequences.

Real strength is required to overcome our own habitual negative feelings—feelings like bitterness, resentment, anger, and vengefulness. The power of these mental afflictions should not be underestimated. It is because we have such compelling feelings that we so easily and "naturally" strike back and retaliate. If someone hurts us—or runs planes into our buildings—well, then, someone is going to have to pay! Our knee-jerk response to offense is to be offensive back.

Jesus said that when someone strikes you on one cheek, to turn the other one. In Buddhism too we vow to try not to respond with the same when someone yells at us, is angry with us, criticizes us, or does us physical harm. But it's really hard to forego retribution. It takes a lot of strength and inner discipline to not just follow our instinctual response. We have to overcome some of our strongest inclinations, knowing, however, that we are badly wired. So in such cases, as always, we try to use our heads and do what we know to be the right thing, instead of what we just feel like doing.

We have to once again step up and be the spiritual warrior who is determined to achieve the goal of radical contentment. We remember that when we try to get even with those who harmed us, we indeed become even with them. Those who hurt others are not happy themselves, and neither are those who return harm with harm.

To incite happiness, the spiritual renegade has to restrain the urge for revenge.

Forgiveness ISN'T an act of capitulation; it ISN'T "losing." It IS an act of triumph over your negative tendencies that prevent your happiness.

Just as forgiveness isn't an act of weakness but rather of strength, it also isn't a defeat but rather a great victory. If you believe that forgiving another somehow entails knuckling under in some great showdown or war of wills, consider this: Who's really the loser if you don't forgive? Who are you really hurting by refusing to drop these particular scissors you're so stubbornly running with?

As Barry Lubetkin, psychologist and director of the Institute for Behavior Therapy, observes, "Holding a grudge takes mental, emotional, and physical energy. It makes you obsessive, angry, and depressed. There's a strong connection between anger and a wide spectrum of health miseries—chronic stomach upset, heart problems, and skin conditions among them. Without question, the more anger we experience within, the more stress we're under."[16]

Who's the loser when refusing to give up the anger and resentment is physically killing you, never mind the consequences on your mental state? If you think that withholding your forgiveness is somehow winning, you should look up what it means when we say a victory is "pyrrhic."

If you want to pick on somebody, pick on someone your own size—and you're exactly your own size! The greatest battles are internal, and succeeding in forgiving others will be among the most monumental of your inner victories.

Forgiveness ISN'T primarily an act you do for the other. It IS the best thing you could do for yourself.

If you've followed along so far, you probably have already come to the conclusion that the one who really benefits from forgiveness is not the perpetrator of the harmful deed; forgiveness is for the redemption of the victim. Forgiveness, in fact, emancipates and transforms the victim into an empowered master—someone who is resolved to get on with his or her life and overcome the paralysis of past pain.

Forgiveness is for you, not for them. As Booker T. Washington put it, "I shall allow no man to belittle my soul by making me hate him."[17] Hatred, resentment, and ill will toward others make us less than the person we want to be. We forgive, then, in order to recover our humanity, as well as our happiness.

Forgiveness IS a unilateral and preemptive act on the part of the offended party.

We have seen how forgiveness is not dependent on the perpetrator first admitting guilt and apologizing. While that might be a good thing for him or her to do, it's really not within your power to make that happen. Your own actions, however, are within your control. Forgiveness is something you can do—on your own, without the necessary participation of anyone else—that will make your life better. It's up to you to do it, and you have the power to do so.

"Unilateral" means regardless of what the other party does. You forgive without any expectation of the other. And "pre-emptive" means to prevent the continued suffering you will experience by not forgiving.

So let's say you have finally decided to take control of the situation and do what you know to be not only the right thing but that which is most advantageous to yourself, what's most conducive to your happiness. You have enough compassion for yourself to want to stop the needless pain of holding on to anger and resentment.

And so you begin practicing forgiveness by exercising it on yourself—you forgive yourself for all of those weeks, months, or years of not having forgiven! You forgive yourself for being so stubborn and willfully ignorant about what was in your true self-interest all along.

You review what you've learned about what and where "the past" really is and how it is changeable. You reconsider all the benefits of forgiveness and rehearse the many downsides of not forgiving. You go over the list of what forgiveness is and isn't, and work to overcome any remnants of reluctance.

And then you just do it. It may be that you want to meet face to face with the one you are forgiving. But be careful here! Be careful about even subconsciously using forgiveness to punish the other person with your supposed superiority: "Yes, I'm the better person here. I forgive you. Now don't you feel bad?"

Probably better, if you want to have a personal encounter, to forgive implicitly through an explicit apology:

I just wanted to meet with you to say that I'm really sorry for anything I may have done to bring about the conflict between us, and to ask you what I could do to help heal it.

And then just shut up and listen. No recriminations; no repeated revivals of the incident in question; no expectations of an apology from their side; no further argumentation.

It is, however, both necessary (*before* any such personal meeting) and sufficient in and of itself (if such a meeting seems inappropriate or too fraught) to do the forgiving in your own mind. The Action Plan for this chapter provides guidelines for doing so. Even if you wish to do the personal encounter thing, this forgiveness exercise must be done first. You must be sure that there is no rancor left in your heart before any actual meeting with the person you're forgiving.

Forgiveness ISN'T an act you do once in a while; it ultimately IS an ongoing state of mind. Forgiveness should become a lifestyle.

It is important to exercise forgiveness on the big resentments, the greatest traumas, of one's past. But it will be easier to do the major work if you are training these muscles all day long. "Forgiveness is not an occasional act," said Martin Luther King, Jr. "It is a permanent attitude."[18] For true happiness, forgiveness should become second nature, a permanent part of your spiritual warrior's lifestyle.

There will be plenty of opportunities to enter the forgiveness gym for a little workout as you go through your day. Someone cuts you off in traffic on the way to work. "Big deal. I forgive you." Someone lies about you to the boss in order to save face. "I'm sorry you are so fearful and insecure. I forgive you." A salesperson tries to cheat you by giving you back the wrong change. "How sad to be so concerned with such trifling sums of money. I forgive you." Another person insults you. "Just words, coming from an obviously unhappy person. I forgive you."

The big ones will be hard—we've been repeating this over and over throughout this chapter. But as Master Shantideva notes, through practice everything gets easier—even forgiveness:

> *There is nothing that remains difficult if one practices.*
> *Because one has practiced with small difficulties*
> *One will succeed with the large ones.*[19]

Couch Potato Contemplation: Why to Forgive and What It Is and Isn't

Dedicate a few minutes a day to think about the disadvantages of not forgiving those who have disappointed, hurt, or betrayed you in the past. Contemplate how important forgiveness is for you—how you cannot be happy and hold a grudge at the same time.

Review over and over what forgiveness IS (*it is a unilateral act done in the interest of your own happiness; in fact, it's among the best things you can do for yourself*) and what it ISN'T (*it isn't forgetting, condoning, or excusing; it isn't about whether the offending party "deserves" your forgiveness or not; it isn't dependent on the other person asking you to forgive them; it isn't an act of weakness, but rather an act of strength; and it isn't a capitulation—you are not "losing" by forgiving, but rather by not forgiving*).

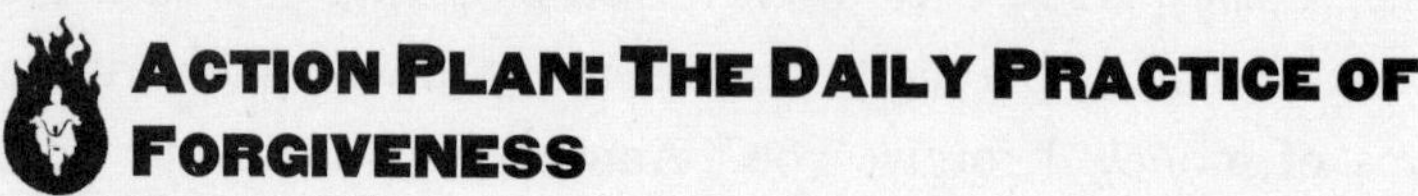

Action Plan: The Daily Practice of Forgiveness

Think about the wrongs committed against you. Be specific about who, what, when, and so on. *Feel* the resentment, anger, and hurt that you are carrying in regard to these people and incidents, and resolve to be rid of such crippling, negative feelings.

Make a list of who you are upset with and why. Then, one by one, unilaterally and preemptively forgive them. Say to yourself, for each one, "I forgive you, so and so, for what you did that hurt me. I let go now of any and all resentment, anger, and hurt I feel about it. I forgive you, unconditionally and totally."

Resolve to make forgiveness a daily part of your spiritual practice until you have truly forgiven each and every one of the people who have hurt you.

5

Revisionist History: *Being Grateful for Everything*

In our daily lives, we must see that it is not happiness that makes us grateful, but the gratefulness that makes us happy.
—**Albert Clarke**

Completing the Job: From Forgiveness to Gratitude

In the last chapter we learned something very encouraging. Every day truly does offer an opportunity to begin again. Every day is like New Year's. It is possible to cast off the ball and chain we are lugging around, our dysfunctional and unnecessary bitterness about the past, and start again, fresh and clean.

We don't need to undergo some special religious ritual to be "born again." Each day is another chance to renew and redeem ourselves. The option is always there, should we decide to avail ourselves of it. We can at any time upgrade our present by doing what's necessary to alter our memories of the past.

The past is mutable; we can change it. We do it all the time. Remember, the past is never like it used to be. History, both collective and personal, is just an ever-changing part of our ever-changing present, and when one of them—either our idea of the past or experience of the present—undergoes a shift, the other is symbiotically modified. When we begin to take control of this process and forgive those who have hurt us, we take a giant stride toward rehabilitating the past, pacifying what was once a source of pain and bitterness and reworking it into something more useful to our project of achieving happiness and contentment in the present.

But to complete the job of auto-redemption, to thoroughly effectuate the metamorphosis brought about through revisionist history, there is a further step. Having dropped our crippling narrative of the past by forgiving, we are now in a position to compose the story in a more advantageous key. Once we let go of our negative depiction of the past, we can go further and replace it with a positive account of what happened.

We move from forgiveness to gratitude.

While there are many deep-seated emotions and feelings that are counterproductive to our happiness—greed, jealousy, anger, pride, and so on—there are others that we should cherish and foster. Gratitude is certainly among them. Most of us fortunately have within our personalities at least a modicum of this noble quality. We are appreciative of and grateful to our friends, family, and loved ones—for the special kindnesses they show us, the gifts they give us, and the assistance they provide us. If you're not grateful, at least sometimes and to some degree, there is something profoundly missing in your psychic makeup.

But no beneficial quality such as this endures without cultivation. We must exercise gratitude if we wish to continue to feel it, let alone expand and increase it. So in this chapter we will be speaking about gratitude as a practice. Just as we must work at and train for forgiveness if we are to eliminate the animosity and resentment we feel toward those who have hurt us in the past, so too will we need to make strong and regular efforts if we are to go further and begin to cultivate gratitude. Gratitude toward those who have hurt or angered us in the past will not come easy, any more than forgiveness did. But if we are to complete the process of gifting ourselves with a new and improved past in order to increase our happiness level in the present, this is the next step.

In order to develop our ability to do anything, one way to start is to consider the advantages of acquiring that skill. So we'll begin there: with a look at how advantageous it would be to be more grateful in general. And then we can move on to generate thankfulness for the many things others have done for us in the past. Here, it's really just a matter of remembering those kindnesses instead of spacing out. We can begin by recalling the many people who have loved and cared for us; all those who have taught us all manner of things, ranging from how to tie our shoes and go to the bathroom, to the skills for making a living and learning how to live the good life; the friends and family who supported us in hard times and rejoiced with us when times were good; and so on.

Having strengthened our gratitude muscles in this relatively easy way, we can then move on to a more difficult job: Can we feel grateful even, and especially, for those who have brought us what would otherwise be regarded as nothing but suffering, hurt, and betrayal? Can we learn not only to forgive them but to feel gratitude for them?

In this chapter, we'll review some radical techniques that will enable us to achieve this ability to feel grateful even when it's hard to. We'll see that there are actually advantages to suffering and that one can always learn from things that bring pain. In fact, there is a wisdom that we never could have realized were it not for those special experiences with the difficult people in our lives. When we can begin to think of them as teachers and these painful events as teachings, they will cease to be either meaningless or purely negative, and will become instead the focus of our gratitude.

Comprehensive appreciation and thankfulness for everything that has occurred in the past has an equally far-reaching beneficial effect on our understanding of the here and now. Among other things, this new and radically different interpretation of our past incites happiness by engendering a deeper appreciation for the people and events in our present life.

We no longer go through life with blinders on when it comes to the many people who are constantly helping us and generally making our world a better place to live. Instead, having cultivated the practice of gratitude, we pay better attention, and as a result we see more and more for which to be grateful. Our happiness increases, because (as the epigraph to this chapter points out) it's not happiness that makes us grateful, but the gratitude that makes us happy.

The Advantages of Gratitude

Before we begin a review of the advantages of being grateful, we might first want to consider the disadvantages of the opposite, just as we did for forgiveness. The very terms we use for the antithesis of gratitude point to our disapproval when we notice it in ourselves or observe it in others. To be ungrateful is to be unappreciative of what others have done for us, to be ungracious in our insolent refusal to acknowledge the graciousness of others.

We become acutely aware of how awful ingratitude is when we are the recipients of it. Parents especially will have had experience of this. You spend three hours cooking a nice, healthy meal for your kids, and when you ask them how they like it, they say something like, "Whatever. Could we have McDonald's next time?" If you don't like it when others are ungrateful for your efforts, imagine how they feel when you are the same.

Those who are ungrateful are self-absorbed, spaced out, and narcissistic. The Latin poet Ausonius summed it up: "Nothing more detestable does the earth produce than an ungrateful man."[1] Most of us, I would think, would rather not appear to ourselves or to others as this kind of person.

So we want to cultivate the virtue of gratitude in part to avoid the opposite vice. And there are, of course, lots of advantages to developing the positive quality of thankfulness. We'll later go into what we should be grateful for; here we're still concerned with the question of why we should be interested in the practice of nurturing and expanding our sense of gratitude.

The reason to be grateful is quite simple. Cultivating gratitude is one of the easiest and most effective ways to incite more happiness in your life. And this happiness derives not from dreams or hallucinations about "if only," but from seeing things as they really are, here and now. Gratitude brings happiness by putting us in touch with reality, with what is actually happening. Psychotherapist Richard Carlson explains:

Throughout history, wise men and women have encouraged us to feel grateful for what we have. Why? Very simply because gratitude makes us feel good. When you're feeling grateful, your mind is clear, and therefore you have access to your greatest wisdom and common sense. You see the big picture.[2]

In other words, you see reality as it is. There's so much to be grateful for if we simply pay attention! People are actually helping us and showing kindness to us all the time. If we just observe what is really happening, we immediately feel happier about life.

Gratitude is the opposite of taking things for granted. And the more thankful and appreciative we are, the more things we will observe in life for which to be grateful. Gratitude in this way snowballs into more gratitude.

It is impossible to be sad and grateful at the same time, and so gratitude also serves as a natural cure for depression. Depression and gratitude can't exist concurrently in the same mind. The mind isn't capable of holding those two thoughts simultaneously. It's showdown at OK Corral. "This town ain't big enough for the both of us." When it comes to depression and gratitude, one or the other has to go. So if depression walks into your town, send gratitude out for the face-off!

In order to feel thankful, you have to first notice how much is going right for you, how many people care about you and your welfare. Once your mind has turned in that direction, you no longer feel sorry for yourself. Presto chango—gratitude has turned depression into appreciation and thankfulness.

Being grateful also fosters other beneficial qualities. The Roman philosopher Cicero long ago observed, "Gratitude is not only the greatest of virtues, but the parent of all the others."[3] From a sense of gratefulness spring forth all kinds of beneficial qualities: generosity, compassion, loving-kindness, friendliness, and so on. Gratitude, like forgiveness, is good for you. It makes you both happier in yourself and a better person to others.

Should you need further convincing, modern studies are proving this. Psychologists Dr. Michael McCullough, of Southern Methodist University in Dallas, Texas, and Dr. Robert Emmons, of the University of California at Davis, recently conducted what they dubbed the "Research Project on Gratitude and Thanksgiving."[4]

Members of one group were asked to engage in daily or weekly gratitude exercises such as keeping a list or a journal (see below for this chapter's Action Plan). In comparison to a control group where no such exercises were required, those keeping a weekly gratitude journal were found to exercise more regularly, reported fewer physical symptoms, felt better about their lives as a whole, and were more optimistic about the upcoming week. Participants who kept gratitude lists were more likely to have made progress toward important personal goals. Those engaged in daily gratefulness exercises reported higher levels of the positive states of alertness, enthusiasm, determination, attentiveness, and energy. In a sample of adults with neuromuscular disease, a twenty-one-day "gratitude regimen" resulted in greater amounts of energy, positive moods, a greater sense of feeling connected to others, more optimistic ratings of one's life, and better sleep duration and sleep quality, relative to a control group.

What's more, the researchers found that thankfulness also resulted in people being kinder to others. Not only were they likely to feel more loved, but participants also reported that they were more inclined to help someone with a personal problem or offer emotional support to another. McCullough and Emmons noted that gratitude instigated "a positive cycle of reciprocal kindness" among people; one act of gratitude encourages another.

We can make a difference in the world around us. One easy way to do so is to start practicing more gratitude. Gratitude both increases our own happiness and makes us nicer people to be with. The more gratitude we have, the more we have to be grateful for, and as gratitude mushrooms in our lives, it also has a beneficial ripple effect on the people around us. The more grateful we are, the more likely it is that we will perform acts of kindness for which others, in turn, can be grateful.

Gratitude proliferates, and with it, happiness.

Re-cognizing: Gratitude for Past Kindnesses

Now that we know *why* it would be good to practice gratitude, we can next think about whether there's anything in our lives for which to be thankful. If you even have to ask the question, "What do I have to be grateful for?" you are clearly not in touch with the realities of your own life. No matter what—no matter how bad things are going, no matter how depressed, worn down, or discouraged you may feel—there's *always* something to be grateful for.

It's said that the Buddha recommended the following daily affirmation:

> *Let us rise up and be thankful, for if we didn't learn a lot today, at least we learned a little, and if we didn't learn a*

little, at least we didn't get sick, and if we got sick, at least we didn't die; so, let us all be thankful.[5]

So that's the bare minimum, the foundation upon which more things to be grateful for can rest. We can be grateful that we're still alive, and this will help us stop taking our short and precious lives for granted. It is because we haven't cultivated sufficient gratitude that we are so complacent and blasé. One wise person remarked, "When I was asked if my cup is half-full or half-empty, my only response was that I am thankful I have a cup."

With gratitude for life itself as the base, we can then go further. In order to become a master in the practice of gratitude, two skills are necessary. One is to *pay attention* and observe what is actually happening in your life: many, many people are helping you, being kind to you, showing you all kinds of courtesy, all day long, every day. This is one application of what the Buddhists call *mindfulness*. Just noticing what's going on in our lives on a day-to-day basis will keep our practice of gratitude active on an ongoing basis. We'll return at the end of this chapter to this topic of how to stay grateful every day, all day.

For now, let's focus on the second skill we'll need in order to practice gratitude well. It relates to our task of revisionist history: *remember* what others have done for you in the past. When we actually sit down and spend a few moments in reflection, we will discover lots to be grateful for. Our past is replete with kindnesses others have shown us, but if gratitude for them is going to arise, we must recall them.

According to one dictionary definition, gratitude is "the recognition of what others have done for you." This is a good word, "recognition." When we remember, we re-cognize—think about something again. Recognizing assumes that we did, at one time, cognize; that we paid attention and were mindful enough to realize that somebody did a nice thing for us. So it's not like you have to make up something that didn't happen. To practice gratitude when it comes to the past is simply to acknowledge and re-cognize all that has happened that we can be thankful for.

We can begin with our parents (either our biological parents or those who played equivalent caregiver roles in our lives). Our parents—and especially our mother—were, you could say, the first and most obvious of the appearances of Divine Beings in our lives. They served us and sacrificed for us for years and years. They gave up major chunks of their lives and their resources in order to care for us. If we can't be grateful to our parents, who have done so much for us, how can we expect to appreciate the lesser acts of kindness shown to us by others?

There's a classical meditation in the Tibetan Buddhist tradition, designed to engender more compassion and responsibility for others. It begins with the radical assumption that, given countless previous lifetimes, all beings have served (repeatedly) as your mother. The meditator first reviews all that the mother in this life has done for him or her, and then extrapolates that to all other living beings. The objective is to generate such intense feelings of indebtedness that one then strongly wishes to repay others by seeing to it that they are happy and free of suffering.

When the Tibetan teachers brought this meditation to the West, they were greeted with a totally unexpected response. The lamas were aghast when their Western students objected, complaining that they were unable to engender feelings of love and compassion for all beings by thinking about their mothers because their mothers had been so mean to them. "How can I be grateful to my mother? It's because of her that I've been in therapy for the past twenty years!"

While it is unfortunately the case that, in a few rare and extreme cases, people have had truly catastrophic relationships with their mothers, for the vast majority of us it is embarrassing to complain about what is really just trivial in comparison to our mothers' self-sacrifices and service. For nine months your mother carried you in her womb, forfeiting her physical comfort as her body became distended and bloated. She spent hours, sometimes days, in unimaginable agony while delivering you, not to mention year after year of feeding on demand, changing diapers, and going without a good night's sleep, her entire life dedicated to keeping you alive. Our mothers taught us how to eat, to speak, to survive. And that's just infancy. It goes on from there . . . for decades.

To focus on relatively small failings while ignoring many years of selfless service to us seems petty, small-minded, and . . . ungrateful. So remember and recognize what your mother and father did for you. And then spend some time expanding your re-cognition to include your brothers and sisters and other family members, your teachers, your friends, and even strangers who have helped you in the past. Think of how much you have received and learned from them, how much they have freely given to you out of kindness and love. If we just stop long enough to think, to remember, it shouldn't be hard to find a whole lot in our past to feel grateful for.

Albert Schweitzer once said, "To educate yourself for the feeling of gratitude means taking nothing for granted, but to always seek out and value the kindness that stands behind the action."[6] When we're practicing gratitude, we not only recognize what others have done for us, but we also remember the motivation behind such considerate and generous acts—acts inspired by kindness, impelled by goodness.

When you're grateful, you're not only recognizing how kind others have been to you. You're also rejoicing about other people's virtue. It's ironic that while we never fail to notice when others are nasty to us, we don't always pay attention to the many times people have been helpful and caring.

It's amazing that there have been so many kindhearted people in our lives. Remember. Recognize. And rejoice!

When It's Hard to Be Grateful: The Advantages of Difficulties

It's relatively easy to build up some gratitude muscles by exercising them in relation to the people in our past who have cared for and helped us. And it's an important component of the larger project of rehabilitating the past. If we just spent more time remembering the many unselfish, compassionate things others have done for us, and less time obsessing over our complaints and resentments about past wrongs, we'd be happier campers. We'd be more inclined to have a healthier view of our lives because we'd be accentuating the positive rather than repeatedly dwelling on the negative.

But if we are to truly and thoroughly refurbish and revamp the past, the practice of gratitude has to expand to include not just the easy cases, but also the difficult people in our lives. Having spent time in the last chapter discussing how and why to forgive those who have injured us in the past, we now need to take the next step and see if we can't actually practice gratitude toward them as well.

We often hear from our spiritual traditions that we should be compassionate and kind to those who have harmed us—turn the other cheek, and all that—and maybe by now we have an idea as to why it's a good idea to do so. We may also understand that we can't be happy without letting go of our grudges and the poisonous urge for revenge.

Forgiveness is one thing. But why (and how) should we be grateful to those who have hurt, betrayed, or abused us in the past?

The answer lies in a relatively simple fact: There are things we can learn through pain and adversity that we could never learn otherwise. Had it not been for the difficult people in our lives, and the grief we experienced through our interaction with them, it would be impossible to really grasp certain important truths and acquire valuable personal qualities.

Part of revisionary history is to go back and see if we have, in fact, learned anything from the difficult times. To paraphrase George Santayana's famous dictum, if we don't learn from the past, we are doomed to relive it.

If we haven't already learned from the past, it is possible to do so retroactively. The past is never like it used to be; we have power to change it. We can transform it from a series of more or less meaningless traumas into a book of precious lessons. We can look back at the past as a string of invaluable (if difficult) teachings—and be grateful for them and for those who educated us.

The transformative magic lies right here: *if we can see a problem as a teaching, it is no longer a problem.* If we can learn from them, the difficult times we've had in the past cease to be either meaningless or irredeemable. We can then be grateful for everything that has happened to us and for everyone with whom we have ever interacted.

The Two Un-confirmable Assumptions

The process goes like this: When we review painful encounters with those special, difficult people of our past, we engage in a form of revisionist history. (Remember, we can and do change the past by continually reinterpreting it.) We intentionally try to take a different (equally possible, but much healthier) view of what happened.

Rather than regard the past as a series of problems, traumas, and disappointments, we can reenvision those very experiences as a set of educational opportunities. We may, retrospectively, realize that we did indeed learn crucial lessons from those important, if trying, episodes in our lives; lessons that made us into better people. "What doesn't kill me makes me stronger," as Nietzsche famously said. And even if we didn't learn anything in the immediate wake of those painful incidents, we can derive meaning from those experiences retroactively and with the perspective of time.

In either case, recognizing ("re-cognizing") challenging past events as *lessons* for which we can be grateful, rather than *lesions* that continue to spoil our happiness, is the only way to truly heal past wounds.

Just as the experiences themselves can be rehabilitated into something beneficial, so too can we reinterpret all those seemingly mean and hurtful people who brought us the painful experiences. When we encounter another person, we have two *un-confirmable* possible assumptions. Either one is equally plausible since neither is confirmable.

We can assume that the other person is in fact what they might at first seem to us to be—uncaring, harmful, cruel, or otherwise disreputable. But we actually don't know *who* they are. We only know how they *seem*. Our other choice is to assume that the way they appear to us on first sight is *not* who they are. If we go with that second assumption, then who they are could be different from the hurtful, mean person they seem to be. They could, in fact, be someone trying to help me learn something I need to learn.

We can reenvision them as teachers or guardian angels, only trying to help. Instead of thinking of others with paranoia—"Everyone's just out to get me"—we can practice the opposite, or "pronoia": "Everyone's just out to get me—enlightened!"

It's understandable, if simpleminded, to assume that teachers should always be nice to us, supporting us and propping up our egos at every turn. But actually, if we think about it, it is often the case that our most memorable and effective teachers have actually been sort of the opposite. I really don't remember the names and faces of most of the teachers I had in high school, many of whom I'm sure were encouraging and affirming. But I do remember my eleventh-grade English teacher named Mr. Mao, who had an interesting name for a white, Occidental dude in the 1960s. Sort of suspicious, looking back. In any case, Mr. Mao was not nurturing. Mr. Mao kicked my ass. Mr. Mao didn't let me get away with anything. The lessons he taught me about English literature I recall to this day, as well as his name and face.

And it's not just our high-school educators who can be our teachers. If we can learn something from anyone—including someone who reproaches us, insults us, or otherwise hurts our feelings—then we have transformed them too into teachers. They become, by virtue of our own ability to see the encounter with them as positive rather than negative, people for whom we can be thankful.

So what can we learn from those tough encounters with challenging people? "I have learned silence from the talkative," said Kahlil Gibran, "toleration from the intolerant, and kindness from the unkind; yet, strangely, I am ungrateful to those teachers."[7] If nothing else, these difficult people and painful experiences can be used as negative images that, by contrast, highlight their positive opposites. We can, as Gibran observes, learn the value of silence from those who intrude on it; the virtue of tolerance by paying attention to what intolerance looks like; and the importance of kindness, made vividly apparent when we are subject to the unkindness of others.

Master Shantideva takes a somewhat different tack as he sums up what he labels the "good things about suffering":[8]

> *And besides, there are good things about suffering: because of it, I lose my pride; it brings compassion for those in the cycle of suffering, fear of doing bad things, and a longing to be a Conqueror (a Buddha).*[9]

Let's dissect each of Shantideva's points about how to transform suffering into something positive.

"I lose my pride."

When things are going too well for us, we tend to get complacent and, truth be told, somewhat arrogant. We think at some level that it is our God-given right to have things go well for us. We feel that we richly deserve our privilege—and that somehow those for whom life isn't so easy and pleasant do not.

But when unwanted events occur, when we meet up with someone who pops our little balloon of smugness, we have the opportunity to wake up to our pride and to our inflated self-regard. We are taken down a notch or two; we join the rest of humanity with our newfound realization that we are really no different than others. Our fantasies of being somehow naturally or inevitably immune from the problems others face dissipate as we are presented with the chance to gain a healthy detachment from the sources of our pride—our status, reputation, privilege, beauty, or whatever.

We are humbled by encounters that humiliate us. And such events can truly be transformative. One thing we know about the great saints, from the Buddha, Lao Tse, and Jesus to Gandhi, Mother Teresa, Bishop Tutu, and the present Dalai Lama is that *they are humble.* As Rabindranath Tagore observed, "We come nearest to the great when we are great in humility."[10]

It is especially those who defame, slander, and humiliate us who can be our best and perhaps only teachers of the importance of identifying and overcoming our pride. Again, from Master Shantideva:

> *Obtaining honor is a bond which is not conducive for my longing for liberation. How could I be angry with those who are liberating me from my chains?... I want to enter a house of suffering [the consequence of holding on to pride] and, like blessings from the Buddhas, there are those who are barring the door. How could I be angry with them?*[11]

So if you have had someone in your past who has in this way tried to "liberate you" from the chains of egoism and vanity, give thanks for them! This special person can be perceived as your teacher—the bestower of the "blessings from the Buddhas"—for such a person was just trying to help you by pointing out something within you that is preventing real happiness.

"It brings compassion for those in the cycle of suffering."

It is not really until unwanted things happen to us that we know how others who are in the same situation really feel. Our compassion for the suffering of others is theoretical and relatively superficial until we feel the pain ourselves. "Oh, *this* is how it feels to have someone I love leave me." "So *this* is how it feels to have another person betray (cheat, falsely accuse, disparage, and so on) me. Now I *really* know how others in this same position feel, and have always felt, while I remained oblivious."

The pain we feel can be the prerequisite, and the *only* truly effective prerequisite, for genuine sensitivity to the suffering of others. And if we agree that being more compassionate—and less callous about others' problems and pain—would be a good thing, then again we are in a position to be grateful for those who help us develop this deeper empathy.

Those who have hurt us provide us with an opportunity to know what it is to hurt. True suffering comes not from pain but from the self-absorption pain can foster in us. In order to *heal* from our real malady—our selfishness itself—we have to first *feel* the suffering of others.

We can only know what others must be experiencing when we experience it ourselves. So be grateful to those who have helped you experience pain, and thereby given you the opportunity to develop true compassion for the suffering of others who have been and are in exactly the same situation.

"It brings fear of doing bad things."

Most people are big fans of causality when things are going well, but then they tend to abandon it when things don't go their way. "How could this have happened to me?" "There's no rhyme or reason to this!" "This is so random!"

When we look back on past difficulties, we can either see them as random, haphazard, and therefore meaningless events, or we can choose to scrutinize them for what they can teach us about karma. What goes around, comes around. "What must I have done to others in the past to have brought me this person, this challenging experience?" If someone has cheated you, you must have cheated others; if someone has been unfaithful to you, it points to a similar cause in your past actions.

Reviewing in this way the difficulties we've experienced in the past leads us to a determination not to replicate the causes for such occurrences in the future. We think about the Golden Rule in both its positive and negative forms, as we resolve *to do unto others as we would have them do unto us, and* ***not*** *do unto others as we would* ***not*** *have them do unto us*. In this way, painful past experiences become useful object lessons in causality. They bring us "fear of doing bad things" to others because we don't want to repeatedly suffer from the consequences of such actions.

If we look at our past as a set of karmic lessons, we can also view the people in our past differently. From this vantage point, they appear as the agents of our own karma, the delivery system for bringing to us only what we have previously visited upon others. As such, they deserve our thanks, not our hatred.

"It brings a longing to be a Conqueror (a Buddha)."

Finally, the difficult people in our lives and the tough experiences they have brought to us can instill in us a longing to be a person who is immune from suffering altogether—a perfected human being, a Buddha.

Ultimately, the only reason others can hurt us is because we are vulnerable. The only reason others can push our buttons is because *we have buttons to push*.

What's more, it is only those who push our buttons who have the ability to show us that we indeed have those buttons. We can go through long periods of time convinced that we are a thoroughly kind, caring, and patient person, until one day, along comes that special person who irritates and angers us, thereby revealing that which we have kept hidden from ourselves.

These are our greatest teachers—those who have provoked in us what we need to look at, admit, and fix. To paraphrase what Jesus taught, if you love and are grateful for your enemies, you won't have enemies. You'll just have friends and teachers, essential assistants in your quest for radical contentment and perfect happiness.

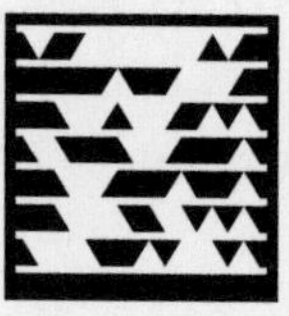

Gratitude
http://bit.ly/renegade6

How to Stay Grateful—All Day, Every Day

The past is transformable. And if we are to lead a happy life in the present, there is no alternative: we *must* redeem ourselves from the bitterness and resentment and instead cultivate gratitude and thankfulness for everything that has occurred in our lives and everyone we have encountered.

Having convinced ourselves that the past is indeed mutable, we launch our own personal historical revisionism by first forgiving those who have hurt, angered, or betrayed us. But then we must move to the next stage of our own redemption. We build up gratitude muscles by *re-cognizing* all that others have done for us over the course of our lives. We truly *re-vise*, literally "look again," at our past with eyes of thankfulness and appreciation. And then we complete the process by moving beyond forgiveness and generating gratitude for those special teachers in our lives who have, if we look at it properly, helped us so much and in ways that only they could.

The past and the present exist interdependently. When we change one, we change both. When we gift ourselves with a different past—one in which people and events have been constantly conspiring to aid us in all kinds of ways—we automatically start to see the same changes in our present. We start to notice the kindnesses that are shown to us every day and by so many. Conversely, when we pay attention in the present, appreciating those continuous acts of helpfulness and magnanimity, we are much better able to remember that our past too has been chock-full of similar incidents.

We observed at the end of the last chapter that forgiveness should become a "lifestyle," an ongoing process we can exercise all day, every day. It's the same with gratitude. Gratitude too should become a *practice*. And, as we have noted above, the more gratitude we have, the more we will see to be grateful for. Here are some tips on how we can stay grateful, all day, every day:

- *Keep a "gratitude journal."* See below for this chapter's Action Plan. If you're not keeping track of the things to be thankful for each and every day, you're almost certainly not fully aware of them. And if you don't even take notice of the things there are in life to be grateful for, how can you practice gratitude?
- *Make use of sticky notes.* You know, those little pads of paper with adhesive on the top edge? Write a question to remind you to pause during your day to *pay attention*: "What do I have to be thankful for?" or "What's going right in my life?" Slap notes like this on your bathroom mirror, your refrigerator, the rearview mirror in your car, and anywhere else you might encounter them during the day. When you come into contact with the question, just stop for a moment and take stock of your life and all the things and people there are to be grateful for.
- *Chant the gratitude mantra.* The great Christian mystic Meister Eckhart once said, "If the only prayer you ever say in your life is 'thank you,' it will be enough."[12] Try substituting "thank you" for the usual soundtrack that plays inside our heads all day ("It's too hot" / "It's too cold"; "I'm so hungry" / "I'm too full"; "This person isn't paying attention to me" / "This person won't leave me alone"). As we noted above with the "Contentment Mantra," in Eastern religions, mantras usually begin with the Sanskrit syllable *om* and often end with *ah hum*. So here's your official "Gratitude Mantra": *Om thank you ah hum; om thank you ah hum; om thank you ah hum.* Chant it all day long, and you'll be reminding yourself to remember all the things there are to be thankful for.
- *Go on a "complaining fast" once a week.* You can do this by yourself or, if you live with your family, this is a great group

activity. Declare a moratorium on complaining for one day every week. No one's allowed to bellyache about anything for one day a week. You'll probably find this to be a very difficult practice (since, if we pay attention, it's alarming to notice how much we grumble!), which is why it would be good to have a spouse, children, or a friend help you. They can point out (preferably with kindness and uncomplainingly!) when your kvetching starts. Stop the whining for one day a week! And you'll then be cultivating a habit that will carry over into the other six days!

- *Say a prayer of gratitude before eating.* If you had a religious upbringing, chances are good that you already know some kind of prayer to say before meals. It's a great practice. And if you don't know a meal prayer, here's one from the Buddhist repertoire. Just stop before eating (which for some of us will be eight or ten times a day!) and bring gratitude to mind:

The joys and pains of all beings
are present in the gift of this food.
Let us receive it in love
and gratitude.

And in mindfulness of our sisters and brothers
among living beings of every kind
who are hungry or homeless,
sick or injured,
or suffering in any way.

Remember, the more often we can remind ourselves to be grateful, the more we will be aware of how much there is to be grateful for. Gratitude begets more gratitude—being thankful for everything and everyone in our past helps us be more grateful for what's happening to us here and now. And vice versa.

Gratitude begets more gratitude, and more gratitude begets more happiness. Thanks to gratitude, we can obtain a better, healthier, and saner view of our past. And thanks to gratitude, we can stay happy and healthy-minded continuously, each and every day.

All History Is Revisionist History

In this section on "Changing the Past," we discussed how to take control of our own happiness in relation to our personal history. Since some part of our present dissatisfaction with life derives from the burdens of resentment and bitterness we are carrying regarding our past, happiness in the here and now requires changing what we think happened there and then.

We begin the process of rehabilitating our stories about what happened by abandoning the myth of the un-alterability of history. Of course the past is changeable! We do it all the time! There is *no history that isn't revisionist history*. The question is not can we change the past, but *can we take responsibility* for the stories we tell ourselves about our past. What's really important to know is *how* to change the past *in a way that is beneficial* to ourselves and those around us. The "facts" need not change, only the interpretation of those facts. How can we understand the past in a way that will be more advantageous to our present desire for a happy life, free of all bad feelings we have about what previously happened to us?

In this and in the previous chapter, we've revealed the answer to that question. Nothing really astoundingly new; just the old, time-tested advice you can find in countless authentic religious scriptures and philosophical texts (and now ratified by modern psychology). It is through forgiveness and gratitude that we will redeem the past in the service of present happiness. While neither will be easy, there is really no other way to achieve liberation from the animosity and rancor that is despoiling our chances for true and meaningful happiness in the present.

The past is never like it used to be, and thank God for that! So change it! Begin today to bestow upon yourself a better past, and your experience of the present will immediately improve.

Couch Potato Contemplation: Learning from Difficult People

Review the list, which you compiled as part of last chapter's Action Plan, of people who have upset or hurt you. You know, the list of all those people you have now forgiven, right? Now consider each person on the list, remembering what he or she did or said, and see if there is something you can feel grateful for about the person and incident.

Did you learn something as a result? Have you been able to generate more compassion toward others who were and are in your same position? Has your wisdom about why things really happen increased because you were forced to think about why such a person was in your life and why they did what they did to you?

Reflect on what you have learned from each and every person on your list. Think about the fact that you could not be the person you are now had not everything happened in just the way it did.

Practice being grateful for every aspect of your past, and for everyone whom you've encountered. It is crucial for your full embrace of the present.

Action Plan: Keeping Track, Keeping Grateful

Keep a gratitude journal. At the beginning of each day, write "Today I am grateful for" and make a note of the people and situations in your life you are most grateful for, and why. At the end of the day, make an entry under the heading "Today I was grateful for," and review the important events of the day and why you are grateful for them.

Concentrate on the difficult people and events in your life. See if you can find reasons to really feel grateful even—no, *especially*—for them.

Part III
Controlling the Future

6

Letting Go of the Burning Coal: *Detaching from the Sources of Suffering*

> The future influences the present just as much as the past.
>
> —**Friedrich Nietzsche**

The Future Is Now

Past, present, and future—change one, you change them all. Why? Because the past, present, and future exist only interdependently. It is impossible even to imagine any one without the other two; there literally can be no meaningful concept of a present without the necessary contrastive ideas of past and future. And the same goes for past (no such thing without a present and a future) and future (totally dependent on a present and a past).

One startling implication of this is that since each of the three times exists only dependently on the others, *past, present, and future must all be present at that same time.* No one of them can be there without the other two. And so, surprisingly enough, the past and the future are as accessible to us as the present.

Another way of making the same point is to observe that the past and future exist only as ideas within our present mind. Neither past nor future truly exists outside of the present. The past as we usually think of it is, well, past—and so it no longer exists. And the future hasn't come yet, so it doesn't really exist either. Neither the past nor the future exists truly, or, to put it another way, *independently*. But they do exist *dependently* on the present mind that is thinking about them.

Albert Einstein wrote, "The distinction between the past, present and future is only a stubbornly persistent illusion."[1] That's true; the distinction between the three parts of time is not "real" in the sense of being "out there" or "objectively existing"—but that's only half the story. Illusions, as purely conceptual entities, nevertheless function just fine. Illusions in this sense work, and so they do have a kind of reality.

Alan Watts preferred to call the past and future "real illusions." They're real in that they do exist (conceptually and dependently), but they're illusions in that they don't exist in the way we usually think of them (objectively and independently): "I have realized that the past and future are real illusions, that they exist in the present, which is what there is and all there is."[2]

Illusions, like the past and future, *exist* only in the present, but one of their main tasks is also to help *define* the present. Our current sense of self is a function of the past we think we had and the future we are anticipating.

On the one hand, *we are who we think we once were.* This is the essence of what the Eastern traditions call karma, and it is also the central assumption of modern theories of the influence of childhood events on personality. What "really" happened is not nearly as important as what we *think* happened. As we have seen in the last two chapters, our current understanding of our self changes when our conception of our past is reconfigured. We become happier people when we change our ideas of what happened through, for example, the exercise of forgiveness and gratitude.

But if "we are who we think we once were," it is also the case that *we are who we think we will become.* As Nietzsche notes in the epigraph for this chapter, the future affects the present as much as the past does. It's been said that the future is the shadow that the past and present throw in front of us, but it is equally true that the present (as well as our sense of the past) is affected by our expectations of the future. What we anticipate will happen in times to come obviously colors the present mind that is doing the foretelling; the seer is impacted by what one thinks one is seeing.

While we are often either nostalgically reminiscing or masochistically regurgitating the past, an even larger percentage of the present is consumed with projecting into the future. And while both recalling what has been and envisaging what will come can and do distract us from what's happening right now, there are better and worse ways of thinking about past and future.

It does not engender happiness to obsess about the painful experiences we've been through, repeatedly resurrecting the Frankenstein monster of the past and having it live again just so it can hurt us. On the other hand, recalling the many acts of kindness others have shown us, remembering the teachings we've received at the hands of those special tutors, and fostering gratitude for everything that has happened and everyone we have come across—this is the way to think back on the past such that we are promoting rather than undermining our present happiness.

And it's the same with thinking about the future—there are disadvantageous and beneficial ways of doing so. Much of our lives is spent thinking about what's ahead: *What's going to happen tonight, tomorrow, next week, next year?* But how many of these reveries are either realistic or pleasant visions of a future we can eagerly anticipate? Chances are that when we think about the future we're either quixotically fantasizing about it or going off on some bad trip, with hallucinations more nightmarish than dreamlike.

Just as sometimes when we think about the past we do so with a kind of nostalgic wistfulness (almost always a romanticized distortion and in every case denigrating the present by comparison), when we visualize the future we can do so in a totally unrealistic manner. We muse about perfect tropical paradises, grandiose fame and absolute power, striking it rich, titillating trysts with adoring partners, and so forth. While these fanciful and fantastical dream states may be temporarily enjoyable, they are really not that different in function from a drug- or alcohol-induced stupor. They take us out of reality and into pure fantasy—and coming back into reality is both inevitable and, in comparison with the dream, depressing.

Such fantasies of an outrageously unrealizable future, like the nostalgic portraits of an impossibly glossed-over past, are not conducive to inciting contentment and happiness in the present.

All scenarios of the future are imaginary; they are projections from the present into a time that does not yet exist. But it is a sign of our perversity that more often than not the scenarios we envision are not the agreeable, if unrealistic, daydreams we've just spoken about. Rather, they are nightmarish visions that elicit anxiety, worry, and dread. It's like we're all living in a science-fiction novel of our own composing, but almost always the future we're envisioning is dystopian, filled with potential tragedies.

Everything that possibly *could* go wrong, we imagine *will* go wrong. And then we worry. We conjure up hallucinations in our minds, and then we stress out about them. That's what worry is, right? Apprehension about what *might* happen in the future.

My mom used to say, "Don't get your bowels in an uproar!" When we worry about the future, we're getting our bowels in an uproar. And then there's another expression for the same thing: "getting your knickers in a twist." And if you put those two expressions together, well, it's not a pretty sight.

One way to begin to alleviate such anxiety is simply to recognize that our fearful visions about what could happen generally turn out to be unfounded. What we imagine might happen in the future very rarely, if ever, actually comes to pass in the way we pictured it. Minimally, the details are different. And in many, many cases the entire scenario we conjured up in our minds fails to materialize at all.

Despite our attraction to astrology and other forms of preternatural prognostication, we all know that the future is basically unpredictable. And, really, why would we want it any other way? If we could somehow know exactly what was going to happen in advance, life would actually be quite boring. In any event, most of what we anticipate with apprehension also doesn't eventuate. Even in those rare cases where what we were so anxious about actually does come to pass, we almost always find that we are able to cope with the situation in ways we were unable to foretell—and so even here the future turns out to be not what we had envisioned!

There's really no point in worrying too much about what *could* or *might* happen in the future. We have seen in previous chapters how *the past is never like it used to be.* Now we might also note that *the future never turns out to be as we predicted.* Fretting about what *might happen* is thus both illogical and counterproductive for the spiritual renegade trying to live a happy life in the present.

Worrying about what just might or possibly could happen is like rocking in a rocking chair—it gives you something to do, but it doesn't get you anywhere. Worrying doesn't help solve future problems; it only drains attention away from what's happening in the here and now. As writer Andrew Solomon observes, in extreme cases, being anxious about the future is the very essence of depression, a wretched state of mind where "all that is happening in the present is the anticipation of pain in the future, and the present qua present no longer exists at all."[3] The stress and anxiety that inevitably arises when we send ourselves on bad trips about hypothetical tragic future events not only destroys our happiness in the present, but also eliminates awareness of life in the present altogether!

Worrying about tomorrow doesn't change tomorrow. But it does change today—and not for the better.

It is important to try to live more in reality, more in the present, and we will discuss how to do so in part 4. But at the same time, we must admit that it is unrealistic to just stop thinking about or planning for the future altogether. Planning for the future—wisely, from the vantage point of the present—

is both necessary and important. But we can and need to learn *how to think about the future in ways that are conducive to rather than destructive of our present peace of mind.*

To incite more happiness in our lives, we'll want not only to *change the past* but also to *alter our expectations of the future.* Although our present conjectures about the details of the future may not be wholly realized when the future becomes the present, the expectations of *the future that we have in the present* can be modified. We need not be sending ourselves on bad LSD trips about what might happen later any more than we need to be perpetually revivifying the Frankenstein monster of past traumas.

Since what we call "the future" exists only as a part of our present, we can change it—just like we can (and do) change the past. *The future,* like the past, *is in our hands.* We don't have to feel like we are either victims of an unalterable history or slaves to an uncontrollable future. It is our responsibility to take control of time and redesign it to our advantage—and it is in our power to do so.

The future, no less than the past, is now, and it is therefore totally within our jurisdiction. All we need to do is abandon our sense of fatalism and seize the power we have over the only future that actually exists—a conceptualization of a time to come that is present, here and now.

Steer Clear of the Fire and You Won't Get Burned

The question we will be exploring in this chapter and the next is this: How can we learn to think about the future with joyful anticipation rather than with anxiety and worry? What do we need to give up or renounce, and what should we take up or adopt, such that our expectations of the future—and therefore our experience of the present—will be happier and less stressful?

In the next chapter, we'll talk turkey about what to take up—how to seize control of the causal process such that worry and anxiety about what is to come are replaced by trust and confidence. We are in charge of our future in the present, and in more ways than one. Given the infallible laws of cause and effect (remember the karmic worldview from chapter 3?), what we do, say, and think now will determine our experience in the future. The karma we're creating in the present affects our perception of what kind of future we will have—we are, in fact, actively constructing that future by planting seeds that will later come to fruition. If we are leading a morally pure life, our conscience will be clean and we can relax and not worry about things. But to do so, we need to learn the rules of how to live a good life, which are also the effective methods of how to control the future in the present.

While we may sometimes feel powerless and fatalistic about what will come, this doesn't always stop us from attempting to gain a modicum of control over it. We all do believe in causality; we take actions in our lives that we think will bring about a better future for ourselves. In order to allay our insecurities, we invest enormous time and effort in our attempts to ward off future suffering. And here's how we do it: We try to make more money, accumulate new possessions, advance our careers, improve our relationships, keep ourselves preoccupied with the latest entertainment offerings, and work to keep our bodies young, beautiful, and healthy—all in the interest of present and future happiness.

There's nothing wrong with these things in and of themselves, and it is certainly not just by giving them up that the happiness we seek will be attained. Although, as we shall see, happiness actually isn't *in* the money, things, relationships, career, entertainment, or beautiful and healthy body, it also doesn't come about just by being poor, possessionless, unemployed, lonely, bored, and ugly and out of shape! That would be too easy!

What's called for is a bit of mental detachment. We need to understand that our future well-being and security will not derive from the externals. For our own good, it's crucial that we stop ignorantly putting our faith in things outside ourselves. Linking our happiness to such external things is designed to bring us pain *when* (not *if*) they let us down.

This is why all authentic spiritual traditions have urged us to turn away from an overemphasis on worldly pursuits. Again, it's not because temporal things and activities are somehow intrinsically bad. But our naïve expectations and foolish attachments to them guarantee that they will not bring us the happiness we seek in them.

We need some *renunciation*—not of the worldly objects and pursuits themselves, but of our way of thinking about them. It is crucial to realize that happiness cannot be found outside of ourselves. Believing that more money (or a nicer car, another promotion at the job, a new and improved mate, a better vacation, or finally losing those extra pounds and getting our bodies in shape) will, at long last, make us happy will result instead in the contrary effect. We're just setting ourselves up for yet more disappointment and frustration.

In this chapter, we will offer concrete suggestions about how to think and act differently when it comes to what most of us regard as the fundamental building blocks of life, what we will hereafter refer to as The Big Five:

1. Accumulating more and more money and material goods
2. Seeking personal fulfillment in a career
3. Looking for happiness in our relationships with others
4. Endlessly pursuing more and better recreation, "infotainment," and communication with others
5. Obsessing over our physical bodies

We'll learn instead to approach these topics with more wisdom—to see them stripped of any essential happiness-producing nature, impermanent and fleeting, and not at all integral to one's self-identity or self-worth.

When it comes to money and things, we need to become consumer-capitalist dropouts! Let's finally stop thinking that just buying more stuff will make us happy and instead learn to live happily with less! Furthermore, let's de-identify with our jobs and professions, and instead work less and become more "un-busy!" Our radical inner makeover will also lead us to reduce or eliminate the meaningless and detrimental relationships we spend so much time perpetuating. We can be content on our own, without desperately looking to others to "make us happy!" We'll next review what we regard as "entertainment" and the increasingly pervasive addiction to perpetually staying "plugged in." And finally, we'll explore ways to refrain from hitching so much of our self-worth to the appearance, health, and vitality of our physical bodies.

"If you don't steer clear of the fire, you can't avoid getting burned," says Master Shantideva.[4] Our ill-advised dependency on The Big Five for our present and future happiness is one of the main causes of our suffering. Without abandoning an outmoded and ineffectual mind-set—without letting go of the coal that is burning us—we will remain enchained by our ignorance and imprisoned by our habits. Renunciation of suffering is the *sine qua non*, the necessary precondition, for happiness, but we must understand what that really means in order to practice it. When we learn to drop what hurts us, we can, in the present, look forward to a better future.

Suffering and Its Causes: Looking for Happiness in All the Wrong Places

Before separately investigating each of The Big Five, let's begin in a more general way to scrutinize why the very things we count on for our present and future happiness end up disappointing us.

It's fairly well known that the Buddha declared that life is suffering. Here's the long-playing dance version of what he said:

> *Birth is suffering, aging is suffering, illness is suffering, death is suffering; sorrow, lamentation, pain, grief, and despair are suffering; union with what is displeasing is suffering; separation from what is pleasing is suffering; not getting what one wants is suffering.*[5]

It sounds pretty pessimistic, doesn't it? But there's really no disputing that birth is suffering (oh, come on, let's not be in denial here: everyone's crying, there's blood everywhere—the whole experience is a train wreck!), let alone aging, sickness, and death. And what about "sorrow, lamentation, pain, grief, and despair?" All just synonyms for suffering, no? Or the triad of "union with what is displeasing, separation from what is pleasing, and not getting what one wants"—isn't this the very definition of what counts as unhappiness? We get what we don't want, and we don't get what we do want, and even if we do, we can't keep it!

When we've just lost a loved one, or our job, or our health—when we are in the middle of a disaster—we don't need to be convinced that "life is suffering." We know it, firsthand. It's obvious. This is what the later Buddhist tradition classified as "overt" or "explicit" suffering or, as the texts put it, "the suffering of suffering."

We're all very well acquainted with "the suffering of suffering," but its self-evident nature was really brought home to me when I lost one of my best friends. One day John ran his car 90 miles an hour into a telephone pole. His suicide was totally unforeseen by his family and friends; we were all shocked and stunned. I remember a dinner I had with John's widow a week or two after the event. I told her that his death had at least gotten me more serious about my own spiritual path. She asked me what that path was, and I told her it was Buddhism. "Well, what does Buddhism teach?" she asked. And I told her what the Buddha had said immediately upon achieving his Awakening: that *life is suffering.* Without a radical transformation like the one the Buddha accomplished, life was definitely going to entail unhappiness.

I'll never forget the way she looked across the table at me, like, "Is that controversial in some way?" She knew that life is suffering. She was in the middle of the disaster. *Of course* life is suffering when the suffering is so unmistakably manifest. When the eggs we've placed in such fragile baskets break, when the sh*t hits the fan, it's then (don't mind the mixed metaphor) that the scales fall from our eyes . . . at least temporarily.

But then life goes on, doesn't it? We pick ourselves up, shake ourselves off, and soldier on. And then, after some time, a sort of morphine haze sets back in. We say, "Yeah, that was a bad time for me, back then. But I'm feeling a bit better now, getting back on my feet and all." And then, perhaps unspoken and maybe not even consciously: "*And maybe that sort of thing won't happen to me again . . .*"

This is naïve, and will not help us prepare for the next challenge . . . which is sure to come. In our present kind of life, there are two and only two options: *You're either in a disaster or you're between them.* We don't need a Buddha to point out that when we're in a catastrophe it hurts and life sucks. But what about those times in between? Why would "life be suffering" then when, well, it just isn't—or at least it doesn't seem to be?

In addition to the "suffering of suffering," Buddhism also recognizes another kind of suffering: the "suffering of change." It's not that change is somehow intrinsically problematic and painful. But what is guaranteed to produce unhappiness is our *resistance to change.* Things do, indeed, change. This is a fact of life. But when we try to arrest change, we lose; we suffer. You can resist it, but *change isn't going to change.*

And it's the suffering of change that is most relevant to our discussion in this chapter. For our problem is due precisely to our expectation that there is some kind of *security* (i.e., changelessness) in the external things that we're attached to. We're setting ourselves up for future suffering by placing our trust in things and people outside of ourselves—all of which are changing, none of which remains stable and dependable.

To repeat: The "suffering of change" doesn't come from the fact that things change. It arises when we mistake changing things for unchanging things. It is because of our ignorance and denial of reality itself that we suffer. The thing that really needs to change is our perspective on change.

So do we ever mistake a changing thing for an unchanging thing—and suffer as a result? Let's check, shall we?

As an example, let's say we just bought a shiny, glitzy, state-of-the-art iPad. We take our new iPad home and boot it up. "Oooh, nice graphics! User friendly!" And every day we boot up our iPad. Every day we enjoy its features and convenience. Every day we boot it up, boot it up, boot it up. . . .

And then . . . one day, *the iPad doesn't boot up*. And we suffer. "My iPad isn't booting up! I'm having such a bad day! I'm so bummed!"

Well, what did you think? Did you think the iPad was *always* going to boot up? And, yes, as a matter of fact, that's exactly what we do think. We mistake impermanent, changing things for things that will always boot up. But the iPad will inevitably show you its true nature someday (and probably sooner than you think!): "I was never always going to boot up. I'm an impermanent, changing thing!"

Over and over again we suffer because we make this same mistake, because we have unrealistic expectations of changing things. And what about people? Are they changing things or unchanging things? One day your loved one won't boot up either, just like the iPad. And then so many of us go to pieces: "How could this have happened?" we wonder. Well, just like the iPad was *never always going to boot up,* so too our loved ones will not always be with us. They're as impermanent and changing as the iPad.

And what about your own life? Changing or unchanging? How about your job? Your "secure" investments? What about the 54-inch, state-of-the-art, flat-screened plasma television? Or the beautiful new dream house? The fabulous holiday in the Bahamas? How about your youth and health? Changing or unchanging? Permanent or impermanent?

We're continually grasping outside of ourselves to constantly changing things and beings, naively believing that if we could somehow get everything right and then just stabilize all the elements and freeze-frame it, then we'd finally be happy. "Things are going well at the job just now, and my health is pretty good, but I'm having a bit of trouble with the boyfriend, and I'm really bored living here in L.A., so if I just had a little more money . . ."—and so it goes. We're constantly juggling the components of life, futilely trying to get all the balls in the air at the same time and have them all just stay up there, steady and dependable.

But it's not working.

It will never work.

Everything is changing. And trying to stop change is like tilting at windmills.

If we want to be truly happy, we need to detach from our ignorant, unrealistic expectations of changing, external things. We do have some sense that the objects we are so invested in are unstable and unreliable. That's why we worry about them and *what might happen* to them in the future. We know, at some level, that we've entrusted our happiness and sense of security to what can't really be counted on, and we're anxious about it.

So what can we do?

The first step in constructing a more trustworthy future for ourselves is to stop making the same old mistakes. *Stop looking for happiness in all the wrong places!* And by the "wrong places,"

I primarily mean The Big Five. We're now ready to review them, one by one, and think about what renunciation might mean in terms of each of them.

First and foremost, we need to learn how to *think differently* about these things. We will then be able to take the necessary steps to *act differently* toward them—to live more simply, and to think more realistically about what will and will not pay off for us. Only then will we be able to live a life designed to bring us more happiness and less pain.

Money and Things

Let's begin our individual analysis of the "wrong places" in which we seek our happiness with wrong place *numero uno*: money and possessions.

We all are familiar with the truism that "money can't buy happiness." But we don't act like we believe this at all. In fact, our nonstop pursuit of money and the things money can buy indicates that we do think we'll be happier if we have more.

It's commonsensical that a certain level of material comfort and affluence is essential for a happy life. Recent studies seem to show that, up to a point, money does buy you a certain degree of comfort and security.[6] It's obviously better to have enough money than not when it comes to dealing with difficulties in life. Put in a different way, more money may or may not buy you more happiness, but it certainly can buy you a little less misery.

Jane Austen once had one of her characters declare, "A large income is the best recipe for happiness I ever heard of."[7] And the vast majority of us, regardless of our circumstances, believe this. *But we're wrong. And we sort of know it.* Study after study has repeatedly demonstrated that after a certain income is reached, happiness is no longer linked at all to money. The truth is, there is no one-to-one correlation when it comes to one's income and one's level of happiness.[8]

One doesn't really need to conduct a well-funded academic study to know that *money cannot be the cause of happiness*. The logic that proves this is very simple: If there were a causal relationship between money and happiness, the more money we had, the happier we would be. If there were a correlation between wealth and happiness—if each dollar created a smiley-faced unit of bliss—then the richest people would also be the most ecstatic. When you saw Bill Gates or Donald Trump on television, they'd practically be breaking the camera they'd be so joyous.

But this is patently not the case. There are plenty of unhappy rich people (and lots of happy poor people as well). "Yeah, but money is wasted on the rich! If only I had Bill Gates's money, then I'd be happy."

Well no, actually. Not automatically anyway. As producer and philanthropist David Geffen rightly observes, "Anybody who thinks money will make you happy, hasn't got money."[9] And, if we're honest with ourselves, we know from experience that more money isn't going to deliver the contentment and deep satisfaction we're really seeking. The inchoate, or immature, view (or is it rather the *incoherent* view!) that money will bring us happiness just keeps us on a treadmill of, at best, perpetual dissatisfaction, and, at worst, greed. We laugh at Henny Youngman's joke because we know deep down that we've inverted things: "What's the use of happiness? It can't buy you money!"[10]

And if happiness isn't in the money, neither is it in the things that money can buy. But, again, we're all a bit unclear on this—and we're kept as fuzzy-minded as possible by the forces of consumer capitalism. Really the only people for whom there ought to be a question of whether real happiness is located in material possessions should be those without such things. So what's our excuse?

We've got the goods—the houses, cars, refrigerators, washers and dryers, boats, motorcycles, televisions, stereos, computers, PDAs, CDs, DVDs, MP3s, and so on. The median household income in America (adjusted for inflation) has nearly doubled since the 1950s, and with it the capability to buy pretty much whatever our hearts desire (if not with cash, then at least on credit!).[11] But we're not happier. Our malaise and dissatisfaction is not on account of a lack of consumer goods. We're choking on our stuff! The size of the homes we look to buy or rent is often determined by the amount of possessions that we need to fit into the place. It often seems that it is not we who own things; it's the things that own us!

This is not to say that there isn't pleasure associated with buying a new car or computer or whiz-bang gadget. There is. It's nice to acquire new things, just like it's nice to have enough money to not have to worry about the many things people without money do have to worry about. As Edith Wharton observed, "The only way not to think about money is to have a great deal of it."[12] And the same goes for possessions.

Ay, but there's the rub. When is enough enough? When it comes to money and things, it often seems that there is *never* enough. "A woman can't be too thin or too rich," according to one modern axiom. Or like the old bumper sticker proclaimed (in what could be the nihilistic motto of the whole consumerist mentality that so many of us have adopted): "The one with the most toys at the end wins." In cultures like ours, the so-called hoarding phenomenon, where people literally cannot throw out their material possessions until the stuff has taken up every square inch of their home, is just a caricature of the norm.

The problem is that everything we own takes up some mental space, occupies some part of our mind: Where am I going to keep it? How can I protect it? Is it scratched? Is it still working? Will it work tomorrow? And, finally, how can I get rid of it?

Ironically, rather than producing happiness, the insatiable quest for more money, and newer and "better" things, turns out to just increase our discontent and our suffering. We know that we're not satisfied now, in the present, but we repeatedly and foolishly hope that, *if we just had a little more* then we'd find happiness in the future.

Arya Nagarjuna, sometimes referred to as the "second Buddha," wrote in his *Letter to a Friend* nearly two thousand years ago:

The more one possesses the more one will suffer,
Unlike those of modest desires.
Just as the more heads a great serpent has
The more suffering must be endured as a result.[13]

And, over on the Western side of things, Jesus put it even more strongly: "It's easier for a camel to go through the eye of a needle than for a rich man to enter the kingdom of God."[14]

But that's not because of any intrinsic problem with money, and the solution isn't to just empty our bank account and get rid of everything we own. We've argued that money can't buy happiness. But, of course, neither can poverty. If "renunciation"—which, let's remember, the spiritual traditions regard as a prerequisite to true happiness—were to be achieved through simple abandonment, the solution would be relatively easy: Just give away all your money and things and then—*Voilà!* Congratulations!—you now have renunciation!

To repeat: the problem is not in the money and things. If there's nothing inherently happiness-making in them, there's nothing unhappiness-making in them either.

The problem is in the mind, in the way we think about money and things. What perpetuates our suffering is a *belief* that money and things have the capability to convey happiness to their possessor. Or to be precise, it's not even this misguided belief that is the culprit, but rather the fact that this *belief is not born out by reality.* A bump in one's income or another material possession turns out not to bring us the contentment we believed that they would. In fact, there's only one thing worse than *not* getting what you want . . . and that's getting it.

So the solution is, first of all, to think differently—more logically and realistically—about money and possessions. Whenever you are tempted to think, "If only I had more money" or "If only I had that new house (or boat or dress or CD), *then* I'd be happy," just stop a minute and recall the last time you got more money, the last time you obtained the consumer good you once desired. This increase in income and this acquisition of a new item will likely have exactly the same half-life as before. It will be accompanied by a shot of pleasure, and then that high will wear off and you'll eventually be right back where you started: "If only I had . . ."

Remember what, at some level, you already know: *Happiness is not in the money or the things.* The spiritual renegade must break with the false consciousness that repeatedly tries to reassert itself, and that the commercial media are constantly reinforcing. Become a consumer-capitalist dropout! Cultivate a sense of fulfillment and satisfaction with what you have, materially, by chanting over and over again the Contentment Mantra that we learned in chapter 1:

> Om, I have enough, ah hum.

And specifically:

> Om, I have enough money, ah hum.
> Om, I have enough possessions, ah hum.
> Om, I have enough . . .

And once you've altered the way you *think* about money and things, you'll be in a position to change your *actions* regarding them. Remember the Action Plan entailing a "consumption fast" that I recommended at the end of chapter 1. Occasionally put yourself on a spending freeze, where you purchase only the real necessities (shelter, food, fuel) for a day, a week, or more. Train yourself in the heretical notion that *happiness does not come from buying or consuming.*

Once you've staunched the incessant incoming flow of new things, take a look at all the material possessions you already have. Do you really need all this stuff? Exercise the six-month (or one-year, or three-year) rule: If you haven't used it for that long, you don't need it. Clear out your garage, your closets, and empty out the storage locker! Just give away what you're not using. You won't miss the stuff at all; in a week or two, you won't even remember that you ever owned these things. And you'll feel cleaner, lighter, and more aware of reality.

Contentment—entry-level happiness—can never be obtained through "getting more," and that very much includes more money and more consumer goods. Rather, it comes from being satisfied with what you have. Here's Nagarjuna again:

Of all types of wealth it is contentment
Which was said by the teacher of gods and men to be the most supreme.
Strive for complete contentment, and should you achieve it,
Even without material wealth,
You will truly have found your fortune.[15]

There are two ways to get rich: make lots of money or be satisfied with what you have. Having sufficient money and the possessions that accompany a comfortable life are important. But they are only the means to an end—they provide a platform from which you can achieve higher things; they are not ends in themselves. Thinking and acting as though obtaining more money and things in the future will bring happiness is guaranteed to backfire.

The Career

Unless you are retired, rich, or have a trust fund or something, it's also important to hold down a job. Most of us need the income that working generates in order to house, feed, and clothe ourselves. Our mission in life is to learn how to be helpers, not helpees—and in all arenas. If we are wholly dependent on others for the basics of our very survival, we're stuck in the second category. And it is usually going to be through working for a living that we are able to achieve economic self-sufficiency.

So, for most of us, having a paying job of some sort is not optional, at least not at present. But it's another thing altogether to identify with and invest a huge degree of one's self-esteem in one's career. Just as believing that more cash and more stuff will bring you more happiness is setting yourself up for a fall, so too is the mistaken idea that your fulfillment and success as a human being derives from what you do for a living.

If you believe your future happiness will come from a great new job or more promotions within your present profession, think again. First off, just as there's no end to the pursuit of "enough" money or things, there's never going to be an end to the hoops one needs to jump through to reach the "pinnacle" of any given career. There's always going to be someone above you; there's always going to be a higher level. If you think happiness lies in "better" or "more" when it comes to your job, well, it'll be like Mick Jagger sang: *I can't get no . . . satisfaction.*

Everyone's career experience will be comparable to mine. I was an academic. I started out in graduate school, hoping that when I finished my PhD, I'd get a job. And I did! So happy! But my first job was as an instructor, making $18,000 a year, and I wanted more prestige and more money. So I worked hard and was promoted to assistant professor. Then I was told that with hard work (and Lady Luck on my side) I'd receive tenure and become an associate professor. Which I did. Ah, tenure! I've achieved the goal!

But there was yet another carrot to dangle in front of my nose. Next it was, "Work even harder and you might get promoted to full professor." And so I did that, too. But by this time I was beginning to wise up. I realized that there were going to be plenty more hoops left to jump through. After becoming a full professor, you then need to think about wrangling an endowed chair. And if you get an endowed chair, well, it's probably not at Harvard. And if it's an endowed chair at Harvard, it's not at Oxford. And it's likely that professors with endowed chairs at Oxford think they haven't succeeded until they are offered a chair at Harvard.

You get the point. There's no end to this. There's always "more" and "better" looming just ahead.

If you've pinned your hopes for happiness to your career, I have a homework assignment for you. Rent the movie *About Schmidt,* starring Jack Nicholson. The story depicted in this film is the best-case scenario for anyone who gives twenty, thirty, forty, fifty years of their life to the job. In the end, they'll say to you what they say in the movie to Jack's character, an insurance salesman: "Thank you very much *for your life.* Here's a dinner in your honor! Here are speeches and toasts! Here's a watch! We're so grateful. . . . Now, please go, and don't come back."

And that'll be it. They'll forget about you in about six months. Like you were never there. And that's best case. They could fire you long before you reach retirement age, or the company (or the whole economy) could go bust, or the profession you once thought was so important, interesting, and challenging could turn out to be *just a job.*

Which it is, actually. *It's just a job!* And every job is a dead-end job in that every career has the same termination. *Your job is not your life!* You are much more than what you do to make a living. Think differently. And if you need some help, here's another mantra for those of you who think your work (and you yourself, for doing this job) are so vitally important:

Om, it's just a job, ah hum.

The working classes generally get this, so chances are if you're unclear on the concept it's because you identify yourself as a "professional" something or other. *It's just a job!* Punch in, do what you are paid to do, and then punch out and leave it behind. Don't invest more of yourself than that. If you want to reduce your own suffering, think about the career, the profession, the job differently—as just what it is, a way to make a living, and no more—and this is how you'll begin the process of letting go of this particular burning coal.

The dream of technology bringing us more, and not less, freedom from work and time for leisure has transformed into a nightmare of busyness for its own sake. In testimony before a US Senate subcommittee in 1967, one expert predicted that due to time- and labor-saving advances in technology, "By 1985 people could be working just 22 hours a week or 27 weeks a year or could retire at 38."[16] But as we know, the reality turned out to be different; things actually went in the opposite direction. According to a Harris Poll, leisure time enjoyed by the average American shrunk from twenty-six hours a week in 1973 to an all-time low in 2008 of just sixteen hours a week.[17] It hasn't gotten any better over the past few years either, given the economy and the increasing prevalence of a mind-set that extols busyness for its own sake.

Instead of enjoying more free time, we're kept occupied working more. A 2006 study discovered that 80 percent of those employed in the United States work between forty and seventy-nine hours a week, with only 14 percent reporting a work week of forty hours or less.[18] One survey found that the average work week increased from forty-one hours in 1973 to nearly forty-seven hours;[19] another source gives the average now as fifty-four hours per week.[20] Lunches during the work day are rushed or choked down on the run, while 70 percent of employees say that they work beyond their scheduled time and on weekends. And more than half cite "self-imposed pressure" as the reason for putting in this additional time on the job.[21]

Does this sound familiar? So many of us have got caught up in this rat race—and willingly, thinking that somehow our busyness is proof of our value.

We're not only working more (often voluntarily) each day, but we're cheated (and cheating ourselves) when it comes to vacation time. American jobs usually give between seven and twenty-one paid vacation days a year, with the average being around ten. Compare that to what is mandated by law in France: *seven weeks of paid vacation every year*. In other European countries, it's similar—Denmark, six weeks; Finland, 35 days; Sweden, 25–32 days; Spain, 30 days; Italy, 20–30 days; Norway, 25 days. Australia gives its workers 28 paid days off. Even places like Brazil (30 days paid) and the Ukraine (24 days) are well ahead of the US average.[22]

But American workers, already comparatively shortchanged in terms of paid holidays, also *voluntarily* give back some 465,000,000 vacation days a year.[23] In the United States, at least 30 percent of all employed adults don't take all the (already relatively minimal) vacation days they are allotted.[24] And even when we do actually take our holidays, many of us continue to work away. An estimated 71 percent of baby boomers admitted to working *during* their vacations.[25]

The increase in the time we work—per day, per week, per year—may be correlated to economic reasons, which generally means an increase in "need" for a bigger home, better car, more electronic gadgets, better trips to more exotic locales, and so on. Thinking differently about work will obviously, at least to some extent, correspond to thinking and acting differently when it comes to money and things. We are, to some degree, working for a higher income and the goodies we can buy with it—or to pay off credit cards used to purchase things we couldn't really afford in the first place.[26]

But also at play here is a new version of the old Protestant work ethic, which links one's spiritual and psychological self-worth to hard work, worldly success, and general busyness. As one observer writes, "As the pace of our lives has increased, overcommitment and busyness have been elevated to socially desirable standards. Being busy is chic and trendy."[27]

Stress and busyness are not somehow proof of the importance of what you're doing with your life. And just staying busy all the time does not result in more happiness. Happiness isn't in the career ... because remember, *it's just a job* and nothing more. This doesn't mean we shouldn't try to do our best at the job we have. But it does mean that we should stop pinning all our hopes for happiness to it. With a different mind-set—one that has realized that working more or getting another advancement or finding that "perfect job" will not deliver the goods—we can begin to act differently vis-à-vis the career.

We can, for example, start thinking about ways to work less. Most of us are working way more than we need to. We're keeping very busy indeed—not, generally, because we have to but because we have convinced ourselves that our self-worth and future security are tied to our work. What if instead we were to pay off our debts, reduce our consumption, and learn to live happily with less? If you need some helpful hints for how to construct a life without so much materialistic clutter—which will free you up to work less—go to the web and Google "voluntary simplicity." You'll pull up countless websites dedicated to people just like you, people who have decided that *time is more important than money* and have changed their lives accordingly.

Renunciation and detachment when it comes to the career aren't obtained by simply quitting the job. The job won't bring you happiness, but neither will unemployment. This is important to realize before doing anything rash and irresponsible. Furthermore, if we have the right attitude toward our profession, it can be an excellent arena to practice all kinds of virtues, eight hours a day: patience, generosity, forgiveness, self-sacrifice—you name it.

What working less can bring is the freedom to do something perhaps more meaningful with the limited time we have in this life. And it's not entirely impossible that eventually we'll figure out how not to work for a paycheck at all (without, of course, being a leech on others). It's not as hard as it may sound. Lots of people just like you have done it, one way or another. But before you can even start to think about how you'll pull this off, you'll have to really want it and you'll need to have found something more important to do with your time.

You'll have to let go of the coal that is the belief that your present value and your future happiness reside in what you do for a living, for this too is an ember that will continue to burn you until you drop it.

Relationships

In chapter 4, we briefly referred to a fact of life that could save us from scorching ourselves with yet another burning coal: *Other people cannot make us happy*. Here is another arena in which we look to what is outside of ourselves for what can only come from within. We stubbornly hold on to the conviction that we would be satisfied and happy with our lives if only we could find the right partner—someone who could *make us happy*.

And so we repeatedly make the same mistake: "If only I could find Mr. Right, then, finally, I'd be happy. Those other losers didn't make me happy—in fact, they actually *made me unhappy*—but surely there's someone out there who can fulfill and complete me. Someone who can . . . *make me happy*."

We go looking for that special person, expecting that our future happiness will be delivered to us on a silver platter, and we remain unsatisfied and discontent with our lives until we think we have found him or her.

And, chances are, you know from experience what happens next: "Oh, I've finally found Ms. Right. She is so perfect! She's like an angel, sent from above! We're soul mates! Everything she says is like poetry, like music! Finally I found the right one for me. This relationship *makes me so happy!*"

For a while anyway. The half-life of this initial phase is usually no more than a few weeks or months at best. And then the next stage begins. We start to feel that the relationship isn't going so smoothly any more. It seems like it needs some tweaking here and there. "Honey, you know I love you and think you're great and all. But sometimes you kind of *make me unhappy*." Overall the relationship may still seem to be good enough to stick with, but there is definitely some "work" that needs to be done. "We've had some rocky times, but we're *working on our relationship*."

Relationships, of course, do take work. But if we have invested another with the power to *make us happy* (or to *make us unhappy*), we can also convince ourselves that it is he or she who needs to do the work! It's the other who is not doing their job and needs to work harder at *making me happy*!

If you are or have been in a relationship, you may recognize these ominous words: "Honey, we need to talk about our relationship." Decoded, what this means is that we need to sit down and listen for the next hour as our partner tells us how we have failed to *make him or her happy*—and how we need to change; how we need to work at being better, different; how we need to transform into someone who can *make them happy.*

We probably know what it feels like to be on the receiving end of such a talk, and it's also likely that we've put our partner in that very same position when we've felt the need to "talk about our relationship." But this kind of conversation puts the cart before the horse. It's not the other person who needs to change in order to "make you happy." It's *you* who needs to change. And you can begin by changing the way you think about relationships in general.

Thinking differently in regard to your partner (or friend, or family member) starts with turning what has been inverted right-side out. It's not someone else's responsibility to make you happy, nor is it even in their power. And so we can also stop blaming them when the relationship doesn't fulfill our expectations. It's not their fault. Things change. You, the other, and the relationship between you two—all three components are constantly in flux. Wishing that people and relationships didn't change won't stop them from changing. And unless you know how to control the direction of change (more about this in the next chapter), you remain the victim rather than the director of karma.

Here's another aspect of how to start thinking differently about relationships. Realize that *you don't* ***own*** *other people.*

While we may deny that we think we do, our language betrays us: *She's **my** girlfriend; he's **my** husband.* We may have even convinced ourselves that this proprietary, possessive attitude is a sign of the depth of our love, or some such nonsense. When we get jealous, we mistake a mental affliction for a display of true love: "I love you! Don't talk to him! I love you! You're *mine*."

Like the Sting song says, "If you love somebody, set them free." Real love isn't about ownership any more than it is about what the other person can or should do for you. It's about what you can do for them. If you really love someone, you want them to be happy. Real love isn't about you and what you can get out of the deal. It's about the other and the happiness you wish for them.

Thinking differently leads to acting differently. If you are taking responsibility for your relationships and if you really love someone and wish only for their happiness, you'll be having different sorts of talks with your partner.

You can start the same way—"Honey, we need to talk about our relationship"—and watch your partner start to squirm uneasily, assuming the talk will go as usual.

But then change it up on them! "Yeah, we really need to talk. What *more* can I do for you? Did you like the red roses I got last week, or would you prefer white ones? I'd like to help you take that class you were interested in, and would you like me to dry the dishes as well as wash them? Let's talk about our relationship . . ."

This kind of new and improved attitude and behavior presupposes an understanding of how things work karmically as well as a kind of renunciation of the old expectations and suppositions. If you want others to appear to be trying to make you happy, then you must *first* make efforts to do what you think will bring happiness to their lives. What goes around, comes around—but it's gotta go around first! Whether or not what you do seems to bring happiness to them is not actually in your control, any more than it is in their power to make you happy or unhappy. But that doesn't mean it's not important to *try to make your partner happy* if you want to create the causes for it to appear as though your partner were *trying to make you happy.*

Your willingness to be other-oriented rather than self-centered, and your own well-intentioned efforts that derive from such a change of attitude, will produce the happiness you're looking for. It's the self-sacrificial attitude and the concern for the others' happiness that creates the karma that will ensure that your relationships succeed.

When it comes to relationships, this relinquishing of the burning coal of selfishness both stems from and enhances true independence and a sense of responsibility for oneself. Renunciation in this arena does not mean that we should abandon all relationships. But it does entail a sense of healthy self-sufficiency and the ability to be happy alone, without being lonely. Instead of relying on others to "make us happy," we foster a mature ability to be OK on our own. We become helpers rather than helpees. We live in service to others rather than in dependence on them.

It's often the case that if we think that our happiness lies in relationships, we try to increase the sheer quantity of them. We fill our rolodexes (remember those? I mean our "computerized address book programs") with names, phone numbers, and email addresses. Instead of collecting other people like baseball cards, minimize your relationships to a few good, strong, meaningful ones.

Here's a test: Ask yourself, "Can I learn something from this person, or can I help them?" If the relationship fails to meet these criteria, it's almost certainly either trivial or toxic and you should probably drop it.

Your relationships will improve if you learn to be happy within yourself, alone and quiet. If the thought of being alone for hours, or even days or weeks, gives you the heebie-jeebies, think to yourself: Who is it, exactly, that I don't want to be alone with? It's like Mark Twain said: "The worst loneliness is not to be comfortable with yourself."[28] If you take a weekend a month and just spend it by yourself—without seeing or talking to others, and without the distractions of television and the internet—well, you might just find out you're not that bad to be around!

And you'll be far less likely to be constantly casting around for someone who could *make you happy.*

Talking about Relationships
http://bit.ly/renegade7

Entertainment and Communication

Back in 1985, Neil Postman, a professor at New York University, wrote what has become a modern classic entitled *Amusing Ourselves to Death: Public Discourse in the Age of Show Business.*[29] In this overview of our zeitgeist, Postman observes that nowadays every form of public discourse—politics, news, economics, education, religion, and so on—is packaged as entertainment. Every aspect of society and culture is regarded as just another program on television, another "reality show," another website to visit on the internet. Everything must be reducible to a sound bite or a brief video segment if we are to pay attention. The value of things is gauged to their relative ability to engage us—at least for a moment or two before the next attraction. Insatiable gluttons for entertainment, we are "amusing ourselves to death."

In the age of ceaseless diversions, communication also becomes just another way to keep ourselves occupied—and entertained. It too has been co-opted by our relentless will to be amused. Information has become infotainment. Staying in touch with one another constantly and the endless stream of breaking news serves to preoccupy us, just as the hours of daily television-watching and web-surfing do. Keeping ourselves perpetually distracted and in nonstop communication has become for many of us the highest good, the *summum bonum*, of existence.

There's certainly nothing new in the idea that happiness is found in leisure activities and entertainment. And the need to communicate with one another is as old as language itself. Nor, once again, is there anything intrinsically wrong with diversionary pastimes or the desire to stay in contact. It is indeed important to take occasional breaks and to kick back, relax, and do something fun. And it is also good to stay in touch with friends and family and to keep up with the events of the world around us.

But entertainment and constant communication have engulfed and enslaved many of us—and they have done so because at some level we are convinced that our happiness and self-worth depend on them. Many of us even seem to regard perpetual amusement and a nonstop intravenous media feed as the very purpose of life; boredom has become life's greatest evil and must be avoided at all costs.

Old-school versions of the notion that our future happiness lies in novel and amusing experiences are, of course, also still very much with us. They include traveling to Lonely Planet destinations ("If only I could holiday in Jamaica, I'd be happy"); dining out at yet another exotic restaurant ("If I could eat at that new Thai place, then I'd be happy"); going to the theater or the movies ("I've really got to see that new Brad Pitt movie"); reading the latest novel ("I'm just not going to be a complete person until I'm edified by reading that literary masterpiece by the Egyptian Nobel Prize–winning author"); not to mention the obsession many of us have with sports ("Is the game on yet?").

None of these diversions will produce the result we're looking for in them. None can fulfill our quest for real happiness. In fact, as we all know, when it comes to these kinds of experience, it's just the opposite. As soon as we succeed in getting to the Lonely Planet vacation spot of our dreams, we start thinking about the next one. The satisfaction we derive from the gourmet meal, latest Broadway show, or bestselling novel is short and fleeting and, inevitably, just morphs into a new itch we then need to scratch.

We will be saved from a lot of unnecessary disappointment by just realizing that they all bring the same half-life of temporary pleasure before they wear out and transform into another new desire. Go ahead and indulge occasionally, but mindfully and realistically. And at some point, it is important to recognize that, here too, *we have all had enough:*

> Om, I've traveled to enough places, ah hum.
>
> Om, I've tasted enough cuisines, ah hum.
>
> Om, I've seen enough blockbuster movies and avant-garde plays, ah hum.

Om, I've read enough bestselling novels, ah hum.

Om, I've seen enough football games, ah hum.

These more traditional entertainment options can amuse us only occasionally and for relatively short periods of time. Because of their ability to keep us diverted for large chunks of our waking hours, the new possibilities technology has delivered to us over the past few decades are far more addictive and all-consuming than were their predecessors. Many of us are now plugged in all the time, via our televisions, our Xboxes and our Wii players, computers, cell phones, Blackberrys, iPhones, and iPads. We have become communication and entertainment junkies who can't go hours or even minutes without another hit.

Let's run the numbers. On average, we are now watching television for nearly six hours a day, surfing the web for another two and a half hours, and listening to the radio for yet another ninety minutes.[30] And our fixation with staying plugged in is growing stronger and more compelling all the time. Even with competition from DVDs, the internet, video and computer games, and other recreational alternatives, television watching is now at an all-time high.[31] The use of the internet worldwide increased 200 percent between the years 2000 and 2006,[32] and the amount of time that we are spending online is steadily rising.[33]

Communication for its own sake also consumes large parts of our lives. It's estimated that a staggering 294 *billion* emails are now sent every day (that's 2.8 million *every second*).[34] It's reported that 43 percent of us check our email first thing every morning, and the same number sleep near their "email unit" in order not to miss every new incoming message.[35] But email is already becoming old-fashioned; text messaging is more and more popular, especially with younger people. Of the fourteen billion text messages floating through the air daily, a disproportionate number are sent and received by teenagers. According to a Nielsen poll, the average American teen sent and received 2,272 text messages per month in 2008, *almost eighty text messages a day* (more than double the average of the year earlier).[36] As many as 15 percent of teens aged twelve to seventeen, and 18 percent of young adults between the ages of eighteen and twenty-four, send and receive *more than 200 messages a day.*[37]

And then there are the online so-called social networks like Facebook (with its over *800 million* users), where we can become "friends" with people we've never met. Australian internet users lead the world in the time spent (wasted?) on these social networks, fixated for nearly seven hours a day on such sites. Americans, Italians, and the British follow close behind.[38]

Once again, renunciation when it comes to these new forms of entertainment and communication does *not* mean simply abandoning them. But it does begin with thinking differently about such distractions. This, in turn, will lead us to kick our addiction to such stimuli and to make healthy-minded changes in our behavior.

We need, first and foremost, to remember that amusement, no matter what form it takes, is just that—fun and diverting, but not the "be all and end all" of life. Taking too seriously what is ultimately rather trivial and unimportant—sports, video games, and hobbies; but also most emailing and texting, internet surfing, social networking, and so on—trivializes your life. The need to rest and rejuvenate has been recognized in many spiritual traditions, such as the concept of the Sabbath in the Western religions. Taking a day off every week (and a couple weeks of holiday every year) to relax and recharge yourself is important. But keep entertainment in its proper place—as something you do to revitalize yourself in order to return with vigor to the truly important activities of your life.

Second, pay attention to what you are consuming for your diversion. Much of what passes for entertainment in today's movies, television shows, video games, magazines, and books is just toxic—the display of other people's suffering for our amusement—and is essentially just an updated form of the barbaric cruelties of the Roman Colosseum. We watch, riveted amidst the munching of popcorn, as award-winning filmmakers realistically depict people's heads being blown off. This voyeuristic fascination with violence is a habit many of us need to break, and substituting more wholesome forms of entertainment is a beginning. Eventually you might find that your best form of "re-creation" lies in reading spiritual books or listening to podcasts on how to live a truly happy life.

Finally, when it comes to the modern obsession with communication, reflect upon whether there is something intrinsically important about being informed about everything all the time. Do we really need to be emailing and texting each other all day long, or reading each others' banal postings on Facebook? Do you think it might possibly make for a happier life to be actually *less* in touch with others and less obsessed with constantly sharing insignificant information? Could it be that such an obsession is just another burning coal we'd be better off dropping?

Even more radically, do we really need to be constantly apprised of the latest news? I've noticed that even just suggesting that it might be better to be *less* rather than more informed about current affairs evokes gasps of outrage among those of us immersed in the "information age." Staying constantly abreast of the news seems to be obviously desirable—or even a moral obligation—in and of itself.

If you are unclear that suffering in our world is ubiquitous and ongoing, then it would indeed be important to tune into CNN for a few hours or days to dispel your ignorance. But once you get the general principle, what, exactly, is the point of continually ingesting more and more of the details? *Why* do we need to know so much about the specifics of other people's suffering?

In an age where the orthodox position assumes that being informed about everything is the greatest good, maybe it's better to become an *info-heretic*!

There is no intrinsic value in information for its own sake. Before checking into CNN or spending hours surfing the web or reading newspapers and magazines for updates on current affairs, consider: *Do I plan to do anything with the information I'm gathering here? Do I plan to help those who are suffering?* If so, then by all means inform yourself thoroughly about the particulars. If you are planning to help starving people in Somalia or earthquake victims in Japan, it is certainly important to have as much detailed information about those situations as possible. But if you're really not planning to do anything about such ongoing catastrophes, then chances are that the news has just become "infotainment," another outlet for an unhealthy—perhaps even perverse—attraction to other people's problems.

As if we didn't have enough of our own!

The Body

And then there's perhaps the strongest of our attachments. Just as true happiness does not come from the pursuit of more money, more things, a better job, more fulfilling relationships, or more leisure-time recreation and infotainment, it will also not come from futile attempts at keeping the physical body forever healthy, young, and beautiful.

This is surely one of the most virulent of our delusions: if only I eat right, take vitamins, stop smoking and drinking so much, exercise regularly, do yoga, get plenty of rest, and stay focused on my grooming habits . . . well, then what? And here's the unspoken hope: *Maybe I'll never get sick, old, and die.* We, all of us, spend hours a day and countless dollars trying to forestall the inevitable—or even trying to avoid it altogether.

Once again, let's be clear: it's important to try to keep the body healthy and fit, and it's not wrong to attend to one's personal appearance. Renunciation does not mean that you simply neglect the regular care and maintenance of the body. But if we are invested in thinking that our future happiness will depend upon the well-being and attractiveness of the body, we're setting ourselves up for a fall.

Letting go of this particular coal starts by just being more realistic. While it's good to do our best to live healthy lives, let's face it: the body is fundamentally a losing proposition. Doctors lose every one of their patients, eventually. Overly investing in one's physicality is a sucker's bet.

Our health is extremely fragile; it can be taken from us at any time, no matter how many sit-ups or downward-facing dogs we do. Some readers will be old enough to remember the story of Jim Fixx, America's fitness poster-boy in the 1970s and '80s—a story we alluded to in chapter 3 when discussing the fake and real causality. Author of bestsellers like *The Complete Book of Running* and a regular on popular television talk shows, Fixx dropped dead after his daily run. He was fifty-two years old. The cause of death? A heart attack caused by blocked arteries—probably a hereditary condition, according to the experts.

Some of us are so attached to how we look that we even go to the trouble of undergoing surgery to change it or try to reverse the aging process. Over ten million such procedures are performed annually in the United States—breast augmentations (or reductions), eyelid surgery, liposuction, rhinoplasty, and nearly 2.5 million administrations of botox.[39]

These are sad signs of desperation. The attachment to the body is very, very powerful in all of us, but buying into the idea that our future happiness depends on staying youthful, attractive, and always healthy is guaranteed to bring us a big letdown.

The problem here is that we're overly identified with our physicality. At some level, we think *we are nothing but our bodies.* This is concomitant with the materialistic age we live in. If the only things that we can admit exist are those that can be measured and quantified, then when we think about who we truly are, we are left with just this body.

But you are more than your body. Renunciation in this area is a matter of detaching from this simpleminded identification with flesh and bone. The body is a vehicle, and like other conveyances should be kept in good running order. The spiritual renegade knows that placing one's faith in perpetual youth, vitality, and physical health is not a wise investment in one's future happiness.

At a deeper level, identification with the body perpetuates a sense of separation from others. Our feelings of isolation and alienation from our fellow human beings are in part due to thinking we are nothing other than the body. Delinking the sense of self from one's corporality is an important step in re-identifying oneself as part of a larger whole, a nexus of being that joins us together.

Wising Up about What to Give Up and What to Take Up

We all wish for a happy, secure future. And although it's not advisable to space out about what's going on in the present by incessantly planning for what might happen next, it's OK to think about the future in a wise and healthy-minded manner. The future we imagine influences our present; *we are who we think we will become.* So if we are to be happy in the present, we must also be able to anticipate, in the present, a happy future.

But we will not attain this goal if we don't wise up a bit. We need to be more attentive to what to give up—that is, what to renounce and detach from so we can reduce our suffering. Only then we will be in a better position to know what to take up—what we should be doing in the present in order to feel truly secure about our future.

As we have seen in this chapter, renunciation and detachment fundamentally entail a change of attitude about the things we have imbued with such critical importance. And they are helped along by a sort of world-weariness that comes from noticing that the objects we have repeatedly entrusted to bring us happiness, The Big Five, have disappointed us time after time. Given this track record, we need to get our heads around the fact that things won't be different in the future: obtaining a higher salary or a new car will turn out just like the last raise and the previous new car purchase. We will end up in the future, just as we have in the past, dissatisfied and either wanting more or something different.

With this new, more realistic perspective, we can begin to cultivate a different state of mind in the present, taking up new, more realistic actions that will actually pay off in the future. The dawning of a different mind-set provides a kind of relief, a diminishing of the anxiety that came from thinking in the old way: My future happiness depends on money and things, a good job, nice relationships, plenty of entertainment, and a strong, healthy, youthful body. Since we've wised up a bit and now know that happiness doesn't lie in these things anyway, we can drop the coal of worrying about acquiring, keeping, or increasing these things in the future.

This new attitude results in a new kind of lifestyle, one in which our actions are no longer compelled by anxiety and fear. We begin to relax a bit more about the future, knowing that our happiness isn't entirely bound up with keeping or obtaining these transient things. Only then can we really enjoy the good things of life. We will appreciate our money and things, careers, relationships, entertainment, and our physicality more, not less, if we aren't overburdening them with expectations they cannot possibly fulfill. We can chill out about the future, knowing that, as the old Who song says, *we won't get fooled again.*

And we begin to recognize that our suffering actually doesn't come either from getting or not getting the things we have instilled with such paramount importance. The suffering comes from the worry itself, from imagining a future where unwanted events occur completely out of our control, where changing things change, and do so in a way we can't seem to predict.

The Buddha was right: life is suffering, and we are clutching the very coals that are burning us. But the Buddha didn't stop there, fortunately. He didn't announce that life is suffering and then say, "So, good luck. Sorry, but I gotta go." He went on to note that suffering is caused, and that, if we stop producing the causes for future suffering and instead create the causes for future happiness, we can finally take control of the system and manipulate it to our own advantage.

Once we've wised up about what to give up, we're then ready to learn what to take up.

Couch Potato Contemplation: Where Does Happiness Come From?

Spend some time contemplating whether the sources of happiness can really be in external things. Can money, for example, bring happiness? What's the proof that it can't? What about relationships? Can another person make you happy (or unhappy, for that matter)? Review especially the spheres of life you value the most (your family, house, profession, travel, physical health, keeping in constant communication with your friends, or whatever) and check: is there something *intrinsic* in this object, person, or activity that "makes me happy"?

Action Plan: Letting Go of the Coal That's Burning You

Identify your main attachment when it comes to the external things of life that you think will, in and of themselves, bring you happiness. Maybe it's money, or maybe for you it's physical beauty or a good physique. Perhaps it's having an attractive and compatible partner, or the latest electronic gadget or entertainment experience.

Having pinpointed your principal attachment, spend a month weaning yourself from it. If your big attachment is possessions, put yourself on a spending freeze and make special efforts to rid yourselves of possessions you don't need or use. If you have invested your job with too much importance, intentionally increase the time you spend not working (and thinking about work). If your problem is worrying about whether you are popular with others, carve out some time each day to be alone, happy in solitary pursuits. If your attachment is to constant stimuli and entertainment, spend some time daily where you rediscover the peace of silence, with everything turned off and your mind quiet and at ease. And if you're overly concerned about your physicality, try a little asceticism: wear less attractive and more functional clothes, go without a haircut a little longer than usual, or (gasp) skip your habitual yoga practice or daily run!

7

Transforming the Future: *From Worry and Anxiety to Trust and Control*

Trust is good, but control is much better.

—**Vladimir Ilyich Lenin**

FUTURE SUFFERING CAN BE AVOIDED

There is a famous Sanskrit phrase found in the Yoga Sutra, an ancient text of the yoga tradition: *heyam duhkham anagatam*, or "future suffering can be avoided."[1] Just because we haven't succeeded in controlling the future in the past doesn't mean we can't do it at all. Suffering, as the Buddha pointed out, is caused, which is also why future suffering is not inevitable. If we remove the causes, we eliminate the results that are connected to those causes. Conversely, happiness also is produced and does not occur randomly; if its causes are in place, the result must come.

Gaining some detachment from the sources of pain and anxiety will contribute to a sense of optimism about the future, thereby also helping to produce a peaceful, contented state of mind in the present. Just letting go of the burning coal (which usually comes in the form of an unwise overinvestment in one or more of The Big Five we reviewed in the last chapter) automatically reduces our level of stress about what's coming. Having wised up, we then give up on strategies that cannot ensure a happy future. And with that detachment, we're able to maintain a more realistic and sensible view about life in general and the future in particular.

When we've renounced our unrealistic hopes and foolish expectations, we can take the next step. We've divested ourselves of attachments that will only result in disappointment; now it's time to invest in what will really pay off in the future. Having given up on what cannot be relied upon for future security and happiness, we can take up attitudes and activities that will deliver the goods. And by doing so, we can create a positive outlook about the future that will add yet another beneficial component to our present mind-set.

We are who we think we will become—our ideas of the future affect our present as much as our conceptions about what has already occurred. Apprehensiveness about what will come obviously engenders a fearful, agitated perspective that taints our present frame of mind. A sense of security about our future, on the other hand, will be imbued with peacefulness and calm.

But gaining an optimistic feeling about our destiny involves much more than just wishing or hoping that everything will turn out well. We need to be convinced that we are truly and actively creating the causes in the present for a future we can look forward to. We must have faith in and rely upon the karmic worldview—*everything is caused*—which is the only perspective on why things happen that gives us power over (as well as responsibility for) our lives.

We noted at the beginning of the last chapter that the future in its details never turns out the way we envisioned it. And, truth be told, why would we want to be able to drain the future of unexpected surprises? Wouldn't it be boring to be able to *completely* predict the future? But that doesn't mean that we can't do anything at all about what's coming. We have the ability to shape the basic parameters of our destiny such that we can rest assured that, no matter what specifically might occur, in general, everything will be all right.

Taking Control

Can we really control the future? Of course we can, just like we can change the past. We've asserted before that the *future is in our hands*, and we mean this in more ways than one. It's in our hands in the first place because the future, like the past, exists only as an aspect of our present mind. What has happened is gone and lives only in our present and ever-changing (and *changeable*) reconstructions of it. And what will be has not yet come, and so it too does not exist except as a concept or set of conjectures. In this sense, the future (i.e., our present conceptualization of the future) changes every time we change our idea of it, and thus it is very much in our present control.

Secondly, the time that will come later is presently being shaped by the kind of karmic seeds we're planting now. We're always in the process of creating our destiny. What we will experience in a time not yet come will be precisely determined by what we do now. There's no need for a special activity called "planning for the future." We're always already doing it—consciously or not—by acting in the present, by creating the causes for future effects. And so in this sense too the future is in our hands. But for most of us most of the time, we are not deliberately and with awareness utilizing our present actions of body, speech, and mind to construct a desirable future.

The spiritual rebel gains control over what will come by understanding the process of cause and effect. We learn how things are really working and realize that *the future is the consequence of actions in the present*, a perfect mirroring of the causes we put into place in the here and now. It's all within the nexus of causality. Just as the present is a faithful expression of the past—of who we once were and what we once did, said, or even thought—the future will reflect the kind of person we are now and what kind of karma we're presently creating.

In this chapter, we address the question of what to "take up"—that is, actions in the present that will bring about the kind of future we can look forward to. Confidence in the future will arise only when we overcome our doubts, abandon mere wishful thinking, and get motivated to put the real causes into play for the results we desire. We are then inspired to learn the time-tested principles for how to live the good life, in two senses of the phrase. We can be assured of a good life in the future—one where we need not worry about having enough money or a rewarding job or good relationships, and so on—only if we are leading a morally good life in the here and now.

As we've seen, because the present and future exist only interdependently, it's not only the case that *we are who we think we will become*; it's equally true that *we will become who we are now*. Effect follows cause; we are in every moment planting the seeds for future results. Future suffering can be avoided, but if we are to have confidence and security about what is coming, we have to know how things are really working.

To get there we will need to break through certain blockages that preclude a reasoned embrace of the laws of karma. Before proceeding further, there are two types of such impediments that we will pause to examine.

The first sort of stumbling block is doubt, and it comes in a variety of different flavors. Some forms of skepticism are extremely beneficial for the spiritual life and should be cultivated. But other sorts—what we can call "lazy doubt" or "hip cynicism"—function only to paralyze us into hopelessness and nihilistic fatalism.

The second hindrance to gaining conviction about how to really change the future is the opposite of the first. Instead of pessimistic resignation and defeatism, this obstacle entails a kind of naïve and really quite self-centered belief that we get what we want simply by wanting it. This notion of how things happen is in some ways worse than the inertia and pessimism of the Doubting Thomases. For it not only precludes our acceptance of the real laws for creating a happy future, but actually aids and abets our ingrained tendencies to re-create the causes for yet more suffering for ourselves.

When we overcome these obstacles of debilitating doubt ("lazy" or "hip") and selfish wishful thinking, we will be ready to really buckle down and learn the rules of the game. And when we do, both the anxiety and fear about what *might happen* and also our simplistic hopes for what we *desire to happen* will be put to rest. Only then will we acquire true faith and confidence about what *will happen* if we live by the real laws that govern the system.

Doubt and Faith

We will never work hard to create the good life if we don't believe we can do it. Accordingly, the motivation to take control of our future by creating the appropriate causes in the present will not come until we overcome the hesitation and doubt that immobilize us.

When we speak of "faith," we need not automatically affix the adjective "blind" in front of it. The Sanskrit term is *shraddha*, which really means the "confidence" or "trust" that comes from arriving at a conclusion. "Faith," wrote C. S. Lewis, "is the art of holding on to things your reason has once accepted in spite of your changing moods."[2]

Faith, confidence, and trust are all the antithesis of one kind of doubt. It's important to differentiate between different types of indecision and skepticism—good and bad, healthy and unhealthy. Good doubt is the sort that impels us to consider things carefully before accepting them and to remain continually alert to the dangers of complacency and closed-mindedness. This kind of healthy skepticism should be encouraged. The Buddha advised his followers to scrutinize the authenticity of his teachings like one would examine gold: "As the wise test gold by burning, cutting and rubbing it (on a touchstone), so are you to accept my words only after examining them and not merely because you revere me."[3]

Faith, therefore, is not the opposite of reason. It is the opposite of what we might call "lazy doubt," the unwillingness to wrestle intellectually, emotionally, and spiritually with the thorny questions of life. Lazy doubt can itself be subdivided into two forms: one for those who haven't started a spiritual path because they can't be bothered to think about the big questions; and another for those who are on a path but become complacent and use their faith to disguise their intellectual somnolence and/or closed-minded fanaticism.

In either case, lazy doubt is a big problem. In Buddhism it is regarded as one of the major *kleshas* or mental afflictions (it made the "top six" list), for it (a) underlies and enables inertia, thus bankrupting our hopes for self-improvement, and (b) lulls us into a kind of self-congratulatory smugness that blocks our further development.

Unfortunately, this kind of doubt has become sort of chic in certain corners of contemporary society. Being jaded and without convictions of any sort is sometimes seen as a mark of sophistication. One contemporary Buddhist teacher, Sogyal Rinpoche, writes about what he calls "mean-spirited" or "destructive" doubt, or what we've termed "hip cynicism":

> *If we were to put our minds to one powerful wisdom method and work with it directly, there is a real possibility we would become enlightened. Our minds, however, are riddled with confusion and doubt. I sometimes think that doubt is an even greater block to human evolution than is desire or attachment. Our society promotes cleverness instead of wisdom, and celebrates the most superficial, harsh, and least useful aspects of our intelligence. We have become so falsely "sophisticated" and neurotic that we take doubt itself for truth, and the doubt that is nothing more than ego's desperate attempt to defend itself from wisdom is deified as the goal and fruit of true knowledge. This form of mean-spirited doubt is the shabby emperor of samsara, served by a flock of "experts" who teach us not the open-souled and generous*

> *doubt that Buddha assured us was necessary for testing and proving the worth of the teachings, but a destructive form of doubt that leaves us nothing to believe in, nothing to hope for, and nothing to live by.*[4]

This kind of fashionable but dangerous doubt paralyzes and depresses. In contrast to it, faith serves as the precondition of a vital spiritual life aimed at true happiness. In the Buddhist as well as the yoga texts, faith (or confidence or trust) is listed as the first of the "five powers" (*panca bala*) that comprise a spiritual life. The power of faith (*shraddha*) counteracts the inaction that accompanies doubt and thus enables joyful effort (*virya*) to arise. Effort overcomes laziness and leads to mindfulness (*smirti*) that in turn empowers the concentration (*samadhi*) necessary for the cultivation of wisdom (*prajna*).

Faith is here and elsewhere regarded as the prerequisite for wisdom, as Arya Nagarjuna also notes in his *Precious Garland*: "Because of the faith one has in it, one relies on a spiritual practice. And because of the wisdom one acquires through that practice, one really knows what's what. Of these two, wisdom is the main thing and faith is its prerequisite."[5] Without faith to inspire us, we never exert any effort and therefore never learn "what's what." Immobilized by lazy doubt and trendy cynicism, we remain inert and ignorant.

It is faith that leads us to begin a rational inquiry into the purpose of life, the causes of happiness and unhappiness, and the true methods for achieving our spiritual goals. As such, faith certainly does not entail abandoning all reasoning and questioning. While overcoming one kind of doubt is necessary to even begin a spiritual life, the cultivation of another kind of doubt is the condition of possibility for detaching from the complacency that thwarts and stifles our ability to work hard to reach our aspirations.

As Oscar Wilde declared, "Skepticism is the beginning of faith."[6] For without a skeptical attitude toward truisms, we can never gain the mature conviction and wisdom that are born of hard intellectual and spiritual labor. Or as Chögyam Trungpa Rinpoche says (with his typical flair for the controversial), a worthy recipient of spiritual teaching must first be a total cynic:

> *At this point, we are talking purely about the beginner's level and the preparations that might be needed in order for spiritual transmission to occur in the very early stages. It is necessary for us to sharpen our cynicism, to sharpen our whole critical attitude towards what we are doing. That cynicism provides a basis for our study and work.*[7]

While faith, then, is the antidote to one kind of doubt, another kind of doubt is thus the necessary correlate to faith itself. Freedom from suffering and the attainment of true happiness cannot come from passive acceptance of the status quo. It is doubt that impels us to start questioning what we have hitherto blindly accepted, and it is that questioning and rational inquiry that leads to conviction—a reasoned faith that frees us from ignorance and complacency.

And there is also a danger that our spirituality will ossify into a fundamentalism that retards our progress rather than impels it. Doubt here must be reintroduced in order to keep one's spiritual life dangerous and powerful—like a tiger, not a broken-down nag. Complacency is the enemy of progress, and a skeptical, questioning attitude is its antidote.

"Good doubt" (as opposed to the "lazy doubt" described above) is, therefore, not at odds with faith but rather is its requirement and also its complement. Without faith or conviction, reason is stunted, marooned in indeterminacy and shallow pessimism. And without doubt, faith can preclude the hard work of thinking that keeps one moving along instead of stuck in some fundamentalist rut.

We live in a cynical age, and that's not exactly all bad. It's important to be critical and rational as part of our spiritual path and in life as a whole—to embrace healthy doubt and even cynicism, to never accept things blindly. A mature spiritual discipline does indeed call upon us to be skeptics and rationalists. But we can begin by targeting the very doubt that precludes faith and keeps us in our suffering state; we can be cynical about the value of the "hip cynicism" that so pervades certain segments of modern life.

If we are to be proactive in creating a desirable future, we must not be complacent about "lazy doubt" nor taken in by "hip cynicism," the "cool" kind of modern doubt which is really no more than indolence, confusion, and resignation posing as worldliness, wit, and intelligence. We must avoid the despair that comes from a sense of impotence. Rather, it is faith—springing from "good doubt" and healthy skepticism, and grounded in reasoned conviction—that can set us free.

Discovering the Real Secret

The wish to gain control over the future is, of course, wholly understandable. We human beings abhor uncertainty and powerlessness. In our search for mastery over what will come, we have put our hopes in the kinds of things and enterprises—The Big

Five—we discussed in the last chapter, and, relying upon a false version of causality, we spend our whole lives pursuing them. We work long hours in the hopes of making more money, not realizing that hard work actually isn't the true cause of money. We spend hours at the gym or yoga center, not understanding that exercise cannot guarantee health and long life. Remember, the definition of a cause is something that brings about its effect *every time and for all people*. Conversely, if something really is a cause, then without it the effect cannot come about.

In addition to adopting this seemingly commonsensical but nevertheless erroneous version of causality, some of us have turned to another and supposedly more direct method of realizing our desires for the future. It is a variety of what is usually labeled "magic," an alternative form of causality based on what science regards as spurious principles or laws. Examples include the law of similarity ("like affects like," e.g., rain is produced by pouring water on the ground, or your enemy's body is racked with pain because you've stuck pins into a doll); the law of contagion or contiguity (a part can influence the whole, e.g., manipulating a lock of hair influences the person from whom the hair was taken); and the law of antipathy or opposition ("opposite drives out opposite," e.g., the grease of a hairy bear serves as the remedy for baldness or holy water drives out evil spirits).[8]

Magical thinking about causality has recently been resurrected in the form of yet another "law," the so-called law of attraction, the operative principle of which turns on the idea that we attract desirable things to us by . . . well, by really desiring them. Don't have enough money? Just fervently wish for more money and send that desire out there into The Universe. The money you want will be attracted to you by your very desire for it.

There is certainly a place in the spiritual life for desire, as we shall see in chapter 9. And intention plays an important role also in how karma works. So far, so good. But the deficiencies of thinking that we get what we want merely by the wanting are rather obvious. "Why don't I have enough money?" *Because you haven't wanted it enough.* "No, but I have!" you might protest. "I really do want money!" The response? *Ah, but you haven't **really, really,** wanted money enough to attract it to you.*

According to this theory of how we "attract" things to us, if we don't have what we want, it's because we haven't empowered our desire to a high enough degree to make the desire work. The solution to any failure to achieve the coveted result is simply to amplify the craving until the desired result is realized.

Even when adorned in the garb of a causal "law," thinking that we could and should get things just because we want them is not much of a secret. We've all been practicing this methodology in some form or another our entire lives. And we're all quite conservative; we stick to the old methods even when they have demonstrably and repeatedly failed us. It's not for lack of trying that selfishly wanting things hasn't worked out for us in the past. If *really, really* wanting what we think will make us happy actually produced happiness, don't you think it would have done so by now?

As it says in Master Shantideva's *Guide to the Bodhisattva's Way of Life*:

If all beings got whatever they wished for,
Then there would be no one at all who would be suffering,
For there is no one at all who wishes for suffering.[9]

It is pretty obvious that we don't get things simply by longing for them. And as we intimated above, this version of magical causality is not just ineffectual; it is actually *antithetical* to how things really happen and thus serves as a formidable barrier to taking up the correct method and way of life.

According the system of karma, we do not get things simply by wanting them for ourselves—or even by *really, really* wanting them for ourselves. *We get the things we want only by wanting them for others.* In this regard, the "law of attraction" is really diametrically at odds with an elementary principle of karma. While the former asserts that we get what we want *because* of our selfish desires for those things, the latter posits that *it's only by giving up our selfish desires that we actually get what we want.*

To be the master rather than the victim of karma will require a much more radical shift in our *modus operandi.* We will need to think of ourselves more as fountains than as drains; we'll want to concentrate on what we can do for others rather than what others (or "The Universe") should do for us.

It is due to our ignorance that we have repeatedly failed at producing our own happiness. We've disregarded a fundamental principle of karma—that our happiness depends upon our *first dedicating ourselves to the happiness of others.* Because of our selfishness and willful spurning of what religious traditions, worldwide, have always taught—and what, deep down, we know to be right and true—we replicate over and over the causes for our suffering.

This cycle of disappointment *is* what is meant by the Sanskrit term samsara—repeatedly creating the causes for the very things we wish to avoid. We are on a gerbil wheel of suffering, and although we're not wholly unaware that there's an escape door, we haven't availed ourselves of it. We want to be happy, but we don't do what at some level we know we should do to live the good life.

Our unhappiness is not because we haven't thought enough about ourselves. It's not that we have failed to really, really desire what we think will make us happy, and it's not that we haven't really, really wanted to make our pain go away. Our future happiness will never come from our continuing to blithely ignore morality and the effect our actions have on others. Living the good life (i.e., the happy life) depends on living the good life (i.e., the ethical, selfless, compassionate life).

Our happiness will come when we stop worrying about our own happiness and start worrying about the happiness of others. The real secret for creating a pleasant future, the foundation underlying the system based on karma, is embodied in Master Shantideva's famous verse:

All the suffering in the world has come
From wanting happiness for yourself.
And all the happiness in the world has come
From wanting to make others happy.[10]

How Things Really Work: The Laws of Karma

Once we overcome our resistance to adopting the real techniques for creating a better future, we'll be able to put our (reasoned) faith into a method that actually does succeed. But in order to work the system to our advantage, we must explore the details of how it functions.

The "laws of karma" aren't really that complicated or mysterious. We can find very simple summaries in the world's religious scriptures:

- "There is a connection of cause and effect. Meritorious deeds bring pleasant effects; bad deeds bring unpleasant ones." (Yoga Sutra 2.14)
- "No action in this world goes for nought or brings about a contrary result." (Bhagavad Gita 2.40)
- "Do not be deceived: God is not mocked, for you reap whatever you sow." (Galatians 6:7)[†]

Or, as the folk wisdom found in modern popular discourse would put it,

- You get what you give; what goes around comes around.

This is the crux of karmic cause and effect. As opposed to the fake causality we talked about, karma provides answers to not only the "hows" of things but also the "whys." This true causality, karma, furnishes the only truly satisfactory answers to what we have called the "Why, Daddy?" question. With some belief in and knowledge of karma, we can easily provide explanations of both the present (it's the result of past causes) and the future (it'll be the result of present causes).

This principle of cosmic reciprocity and justice we might dub "the boomerang effect": what goes out comes back, and this is both the essence of real causality and the core of any moral system. This is the first "law of karma": karma is unwavering and definite. *Meritorious deeds bring pleasant effects and bad deeds bring unpleasant ones; you shall reap what you sow.*

Not *sometimes* or *hopefully*, but as an invariable law. Without such an unfailing rule, all bets are off when it comes to any real compelling reason for leading an ethical life. There is no moral *system* if doing selfless, kind, and compassionate deeds only *sometimes* brings you a good result and *sometimes doesn't.* If this first principle is not definite, then we are in danger of regressing into the idea that the effects of actions are wholly unpredictable. And such a viewpoint spells the end of both the rationale for living a moral life and any hope for gaining control over one's future.

Also entwined in this fundamental assumption of karma are two very practical ramifications: (1) *If we produce the real cause for the effect, the effect* ***must*** *occur.* If we are kind to others, others will in turn be kind to us. If we lie and cheat in our relations with other people, we will experience the same from them. Conversely, (2) *if we don't generate the true cause, the effect* ***cannot*** *occur.* If we haven't been honest with others, it should be no surprise that we regularly encounter deceitful people. And, on the other hand, if we haven't been envious of others' successes, we won't have people resenting our own achievements.

We've spoken in this chapter of obstacles like laziness and holding to false forms of causality. But if we are to accept karma as the real reason that things happen the way they do, we still have to wrestle with the apparent inconsistencies. There are times when doing good doesn't immediately produce a pleasant result, and when doing bad isn't instantaneously followed by an unpleasant result. We have to think about causality and remember that *there is always a gap between cause and effect.* There is no "instant karma"; we have to "mind the gap" and maintain our confidence that, as the Bhagavad Gita puts it, "No action in this world goes for nought" (i.e., there's never *not* an effect following a cause) "or brings about a contrary result" (meaning that something good can *never* come from a bad cause, and vice versa).

The ancient texts sometimes state another karmic law: *karma grows*. Even a small cause, good or bad, can result in a large effect, just like an acorn can grow into an oak tree. This principle suggests, on the one hand, that we should be very careful to avoid even little acts of unkindness to others, for they can grow into major problems for us in the future. On the other hand, it also suggests that we should not eschew even seemingly insignificant attempts to make life more pleasant for others. It is the accumulation of small acts of goodness that can flower into a future beyond our wildest dreams!

So, to summarize, here is one way to state the main principles of karma:

1. *Actions are definite—they are certain to produce similar consequences.* If the cause is an act motivated by selflessness and kindness, then the consequence it produces will definitely be positive, and never negative; and if the cause is an act inspired by a harmful or selfish intention, then the consequence it produces can only be negative, and never positive.
2. *There can be no effect without a cause.* If you don't create the cause, you will never experience the consequence.
3. *There can be no cause without an effect.* If you do create the cause, the consequence must occur.
4. *Karma grows.* The effect, either desirable or undesirable, will be greater than the cause.

THE THREE LAWS FOR CONTROLLING THE FUTURE

Karma does not require a Cosmic Judge sitting in front of a bank of supercomputers on Alpha Centauri, determining whether your actions are virtuous or not and then entering them into some database. There's no external Santa Claus figure who "knows if you've been bad or good."

You act as your own judge and jury. Your own consciousness records your actions, positive and negative, like a videotape. And the "karma cam" is always on; you can't run away or hide from yourself. Time passes and then the tape is played back: you yourself experience some version of what you've done, said, or even thought vis-à-vis others.

These experiences are either pleasant or unpleasant (leaving aside "neutral" experiences, which are also produced by karmic causes). What makes a karma "good" or "bad" in terms of its outcome is simply a matter of whether you find the resulting experience agreeable or disagreeable. While the specifics of what individuals regard as pleasant or unpleasant are obviously variable and a matter of taste, it is universal that no one wants to suffer; everyone seeks pleasure and happiness. No one wants to be harmed: physically hurt, lied to, betrayed, insulted, or cheated. Everyone wants to live a life free from such unpleasantries and replete with the enjoyable things that make up the good life.

Our confusion and ignorance do not really center around karmic results. We know that we desire pleasant things and do not want the unpleasant. Rather, it's karmic causes that we seem fuzzy about, even though, as suggested above, it's not because we haven't heard about them before.

Later on in this chapter we'll review the "karmic correlations"—if you want *X*, do *Y*; if you don't want *A*, don't do *B*. Conforming our actions to these straightforward rules of life will instill confidence that everything will work out fine in the future.

But for now, we can summarize all the specific correlations into three basic (although, given the level of our ignorance and resistance, seemingly counterintuitive) propositions:

If you want something, make sure someone else gets it first.

"Hey, wait a minute! You got it all turned around! If I want something, shouldn't I try to get it *before* someone else does?"

See, there's our ignorance talking again, masquerading as "common sense." But this proposition is the hallmark of karmic causality: If you want something—enough money, good relationships, fun leisure-time activities, a healthy body, or whatever it is—the real cause for it will be to see yourself trying to help others obtain it.

This is hardcore karma. And as contradictory as it might seem to us—especially here in the age of the apotheosis of the self and its demands for instant gratification—it is a universally taught guideline for living the good life that most of us are familiar with in the form of the Golden Rule: Do unto others as you would have them do unto you. Try to make other people happy and you will be happy; provide for others and everything will come back to you. What goes around comes around . . .

And please note: The code here requires us to *first* "do unto others" if we want to obtain the desired result ourselves. The maxim is not "What comes around goes around." Most of us are pretty good at reciprocation. When something pleasant "comes around," when someone does something nice for us, it is just good manners to return the favor and "pay it forward."

This karmic principle is more radical and less practiced than mere reciprocity. But this is how things really work. If we want something, we must first make efforts to see to it that others get it. Remember: there can be no effect without the cause.

If you don't want something done to you, never do it to others.

The second principle is just the reverse of the first, a negative version of the Golden Rule (sometimes called the Silver Rule): *Do* **not** *do to others what you would* **not** *have them do to you.*

In addition to wanting the pleasant things in life, we all wish to avoid unpleasant events. If you don't want people lying to you, don't lie to them. If you don't want your partner cheating on you, don't cheat on them, even mentally.

Simple to say, harder to do. We ignore this major ground rule when it is inconvenient ("It's just a little white lie") or when we are overcome by our negative emotions and refuse to "turn the other cheek" ("Sorry, but she really had it coming!"). In neither case is karma somehow suspended. *There are no karma-free zones.* Our actions do not just dissipate into the vapor; they cling to us like our shadow.

If you don't want unhappiness, don't do the things that make other people unhappy—no matter what kind of self-serving justification you might have for acting otherwise.

If you want to keep something, give it away (or at least share it).

If the first two principles seemed a bit oxymoronic, well, what about this one? Come on! If I want to keep something, how can I possibly do that if I give it away?

This is ignorance piping up again. Master Shantideva puts it even more strongly. This miserly way of thinking is actually evil or "demonic":

> *"If I give this, what will I have left to consume?" This is the selfish thinking of demons.*
> *"If I consume this, what will I have left to give?" This is the selfless thinking of the gods.*[11]

It's not only "nice" or "godlike" to give away what we have; it's actually the *only* way to keep what we value in our lives. In a world of constant change, we cannot retain things by grasping to them. Rather, we have to work the system; *we can only keep things by keeping them in circulation.*

We can't lose it if we realize we never had it and stop clinging to it. Want money? Be generous. Want a nice relationship? Set the partner free. You never owned them anyway!

This really goes against our inclinations, which are reinforced by certain parts of our culture. We are encouraged to be parsimonious and thrifty if we want to keep our money (or at least we used to be before the mandate to spend and consume became preeminent). And the whole Hallmark Valentine's Day mentality (with its many subsidiary arms, reaching into our soap operas, novels, popular songs, and so on) inculcates a different message when it comes to our romantic relationships. To love somebody, we are told, is to take possession of him or her: *I love you, you're mine, I love you! Don't talk to him! I love you! You're mine!*

But we don't even own our things, let alone people. And the proof of that is very simple, so simple it constantly eludes us. The proof that we don't own things or persons (husbands, wives, boyfriends, girlfriends) is that *we can involuntarily lose them at any time.* Money, people, relationships, consumer goods—these are all changing things. We can't keep them by being stingy and grasping, by hoarding them or locking them down or keeping close tabs on them.

What goes around, comes around. But, again, it has to go around first. We can only be sure that we will continue to have desirable things and beings in our lives by letting them go. And then, boomerang-like, they must come back.

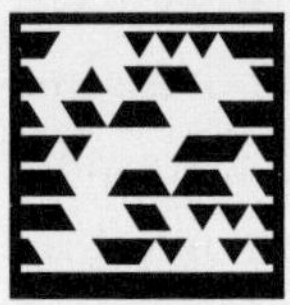

The Three Laws of Karma
http://bit.ly/renegade8

Karmic Correlations: Ten Ways to Create a Good Future

Having outlined the general principles, we can now go into a little more detail about how, precisely, we can create the causes for a future we can look forward to not just with hope but with confidence and assurance.

I'm not sure why so many different traditions came up with the same number, but it does seem like a kind of consensus has formed around the number ten.

There are, of course, the Ten Commandments in the Bible: (1) love, fear, and honor God and do not commit idolatry; (2) do not take the Lord's name in vain; (3) remember the

Sabbath and keep it holy; (4) honor your father and mother; (5) do not kill; (6) do not commit adultery; (7) do not steal; (8) do not commit false witness against your neighbor; (9) do not covet your neighbor's home/house; (10) do not covet your neighbor's wife, your neighbor's donkey, or any other of his possessions.[12]

And there are also ten "restraints" (*yamas*) and "observances" (*niyama*) in the yoga tradition: The five restraints are not to harm (*ahimsa*), to tell the truth (*satya*), to not steal (*asteya*), to not engage in sexual misconduct (*brahmacarya*), and to not be greedy (*aparigraha*). The five observances or commitments are to maintain purity (*shauca*), to stay contented (*santosha*), to practice austerities (*tapas*), to engage in daily spiritual study (*svadhyaya*), and to serve your guru or spiritual teacher (*ishvara pranidhana*).

And then there are the ten "misdeeds" one should avoid (and their positive opposites one should adopt) in Buddhism that we will enumerate below.

But it's not just the count that's comparable; many of the particular moral strictures found in these lists are similar or even identical. Advice like don't kill, don't steal, don't commit adultery, don't lie and cheat others, don't covet what others have and be envious—these and other such familiar ethical instructions comprise a kind of universal code of behavior.

Some of us, however, resent the "thou shalts" and "thou shalt nots." Nobody really likes being told what to do and what not to do, and there's a sort of natural, knee-jerk, reactionary tendency to "Just say 'no!'" when we hear that we should or should not do something. But giving in to our petulant inner three-year-old will not change the karmic system. The laws will still stand, whether we like it or not.

It helps a lot to know *why* we "should" or "must" do something, and the Western traditions have been a bit weak on providing any persuasive rationale for morality. For many of us spiritual renegades, it's not going to be enough to say, "Just do what you're told." But if we come to see that it is *intelligent* to do or not to do something, if the rule makes sense to us, then we are much more likely to conform our actions to it. And if it further appears to serve our desire to live a happy life, then we're even more inclined to actually use these instructions to guide our behavior.

This is why the "karmic correlations" we find in texts from the Buddhist and yogic traditions are so very valuable to us. These lists delineate the particular effects one can expect from specific actions. The correlations provide not only the reasoning for why one should avoid creating negative karmic causes of body, speech, and mind (because we don't want the negative results that will inevitably follow); they also present us with a potential blueprint for consciously constructing a future we truly desire.

The following are the "Top Ten" correlations for the main actions that we should avoid (since none of us wishes for the negative consequences that these actions bring) and that we should cultivate (since we all seek the future results that these positive actions will bring). While the list comes from the Buddhist tradition, the specific correlations are derived from a number of different texts (Hindu, Buddhist, and yogic).[13] Although there are some small variations, it's remarkable how much agreement there is across various religions and lineages as to what effect follows from what cause.

This is a handbook of life; these are the rules of the game. With these guidelines we can avoid all the major undesirable things we worry will come in the future and, instead, create the causes for the kind of life we all really want.

Don't kill / Protect and honor life

Number one, with a bullet, on the Top Ten hit parade, and in so many different religious traditions and ethical systems: Practice nonviolence; don't kill or physically harm others—*ahimsa* in Sanskrit, a concept Mahatma Gandhi made famous. As individuals, we've heard this dictate our whole lives, and as cultures it has been propounded in one form or another for millennia—but still we ignore it, literally at our own peril.

It is especially important with this, the first of the rules for living the good life, to understand the reason for it. Why shouldn't I try to kill or hurt my enemies, especially if they have hurt me and I am just retaliating? Why shouldn't I kill other living beings once I've deemed them a "pest" rather than "pets" (just one letter transposed makes such a difference!)? What if I desire their meat?

The rationale here is very simple, once again so simple that it eludes us (especially those of us who choose not to think, or are led around by our mental afflictions). No one wants a premature death, or sickness, or physical pain of any sort. No one. Not your enemy, not animals or even insects and bugs, and certainly not you. Why would one want to inflict on others what one abhors oneself, unless, of course, one has lost sight of the fundamentals: *do unto others ... don't do unto others ... what goes around, comes around.*

According to the karmic correlations found in many texts, killing or causing bodily harm is the cause for all types of physical health issues (sickness, injury, physical weakness, handicaps, and short lifespan, to name a few). "Killing" covers all forms of taking the life of a sentient being (plants are usually not regarded as having sentience), including the slaughter of animals of all sorts (great and small), murder, abortion, and suicide. Just supporting the killing that others perpetuate (e.g., sanctioning war, especially if your tax dollars are underwriting it) also sows this kind of negative karmic seed.

Conversely, all forms of health and longevity come from respecting and caring for the lives of others. So, if you want to prolong your own life and insure a future of minimum physical illness and other bodily problems, then you must refrain from harming others and do what you can to protect and promote their physical well-being.

In the Yoga Sutra, an even more radical claim is made regarding the karma of *ahimsa*. In that text, it is said that the karma of never harming other living beings is that "in your presence all conflict comes to an end,"[14] which implies that the strict practice of nonviolence also reduces your perception of violence in the world around you. If everything is caused, and the real underlying causality is karma, then even large-scale events in the world ultimately must be coming from our own actions. War itself is the result of causes created by those who experience or perceive it.

In close relationship with physically hurting or killing others is anger, which is, if we're honest, really nothing more than the wish for harm to come to the object of our anger. Anger can have the same sort of karmic effect as the injurious actions that it often motivates. And the opposite of anger, patience, is sometimes stated to be another cause for health and long life.

Interestingly, the karma of anger is said to bring about a particular physical problem—ugliness. As you may have noticed, people in the throes of rage are really not very attractive. It's like your mom said: if you scrunch up your face like that over and over, it will freeze into an unappealing mask. And so it is really patience—not cosmetic surgery or buying a new outfit or working out at the gym—that is the true cause for physical beauty.

Don't steal / Treat other people's things with respect and practice generosity

Stealing means taking what doesn't belong to you. It includes the obvious (shoplifting, burglary, armed robbery), but just because you haven't knocked off any liquor stores lately doesn't mean you're wholly innocent of this one. Stealing also includes things like cheating on your taxes, shady business dealings, pilfering office supplies or making personal calls while at work, not repaying your debts, and other more commonplace acts of taking what is not yours. At a more macro level, one could argue that using up way more than our fair share of the world's resources and depleting them to the point that those in the future will be without is a particularly poignant form of stealing.

Stealing is the karmic cause for all real and perceived material shortages—not having enough money or food, adequate shelter, consumer goods, and so on, or living in a place where there is famine. Ensuring that you will have a sufficient supply of money and other material things, or that your business ventures in the future will succeed, requires lifting the obstacles that stealing imposes and also planting the seeds that produce prosperity. The positive correlative to stealing is generosity and respecting others' property. *Give, and you shall receive.*

Don't hurt others with your sexual activity / Respect and foster others' relationships

This stricture is best known to most of us in its biblical enunciation: "Thou shalt not commit adultery." Having sexual relations with someone other than your partner (assuming you have mutually agreed not to), or, if single, with someone who is married or otherwise seriously and exclusively committed to another—this is what's meant by adultery. Sometimes we call it "infidelity," which points to the main problem with this sort of sexual misconduct: you hurt another person by betraying their trust. It's actually like a composite of the previous two rules—harming another with your bodily actions, and stealing or "cheating on" them—and the next one in the lineup, lying.

All the problems we encounter with unfaithful spouses derives from this very karmic cause. And yet another ripening is the experience of others constantly hitting on our partners. Some texts say that in general the people around you—your friends, office mates, family members—will seem untrustworthy if you have this karma. One source declares that with such karma you can expect to have lots of enemies, which makes sense: one certainly does make some real enemies with this kind of behavior!

Our karma is responsible not just for the social environment we find ourselves in, but also for the particulars of the physical world we as individuals experience around us. Another consequence of sexual misconduct is said to be, interestingly enough, the perception of one's habitat as being polluted. One person's pollution is another's purity. Some people don't seem to notice what others are completely obsessed with. Right? Why? Karma.

If we perceive air or water pollution problems in our locale, it is because of our own "dirty" sexual behavior.

If we want a trustworthy sexual partner, as well as friends and associates we can count on (and a clean environment!), we need to refrain from negative actions that would preclude such an outcome, and remember to be proactive in instigating the positive causes. Respect and support others' relationships. Do what you can to foster harmonious feelings in couples, and what you send out you'll get back, with interest!

Don't lie / Tell the truth

Lying means giving someone an impression different from the one that you have. It's interesting to note here that what is *actually* the case is irrelevant when it comes to lying. The definition of lying turns on your *thinking* the reality is one way and then intentionally representing the situation differently to someone else. When you know you have tried to give another person what *you* regard as a false impression, that makes a negative imprint on your own consciousness. That's the karma that is set into motion by lying.

Sometimes people feel that it is better to lie than to hurt someone with the truth. And yes, it's never a karmically good idea to upset others. If someone asks you how you like their new polyester dress, the one with huge purple polka dots that they got at Kmart for ten dollars, it's obviously not a compassionate act to say, "No! It's butt ugly. It totally sucks!" But first off, does it really *totally* suck? Isn't there *anything* nice you can say about the damned dress? "It fits you well!" or "I really like the shade of purple of those polka dots!" or even "You got a great deal on that particular item!"

And then there are cases people bring up that will occur, oh, say once every four or five lifetimes. "What if there's a refugee being chased by jackbooted, Gestapo-like policemen who if they catch that person will torture and kill them, and this poor person comes to me for asylum and I shelter them in my house, and then the jackbooted, Gestapo-like policemen come knocking on my door demanding to know if the refugee is inside. . . . Can I lie then?"

I would say yes. By all means, lie. Tell the jackbooted, Gestapo-like cops, "Nope, no refugees in here." *And be completely willing to take onto yourself the karmic consequences of lying.* Because it's still giving another an impression different from your own, isn't it? It's still lying, regardless of the good intention. (It's important to note that the motivation or intention of a karmic act *does* count, and we'll come back to this in the next section.)

The karmic consequences of your lying will obviously include the experience of being lied to by others. All incidents of people trying to deceive you verbally can be traced back to lying. Furthermore, you'll find that people don't believe you even when you aren't lying—the "Boy Who Cried Wolf" syndrome.

Telling the truth is sometimes difficult to do, especially in situations where it doesn't appear that there is an immediate advantage in doing so. In fact, in certain circumstances, it may well seem beneficial in the short-run to fib to another person, particularly when telling the truth might be embarrassing or incriminating. But karma is "definite," and having faith in its workings will help us to do the right thing even in tough situations.

The practice of telling the truth will result in people not lying to us and in their trusting what we say. And according to the Yoga Sutra, another consequence of practicing *satya*—

a word that means not only "truth," but "reality"—is that the things you say "bear fruit" or come to pass.[15] Your words have power. Because in the past you have matched your words to reality, what you say really happens!

Don't use your words to drive a wedge between people / Speak in ways that bring people together

Avoid what is known as "divisive speech"—using your speech to divide or estrange people from each other. This means speaking to person *X* about person *Y* with the intention of creating a rift between the two.

The karmic correlation here is that you lose friends easily. And the karma can also come back at you in the form of people who slander or defame you. You may find yourself in situations where people are constantly bickering with one another, unable to get along.

Or you may perceive your environment as one where travel is difficult—e.g., you find yourself living in a place where the traffic seems to be an issue. Again, whether the traffic is "bad" or not is not an objective fact, but merely a perception forced upon a person by his or her karma. I, having lived in L.A., do not think there is any problem at all with the traffic in Tucson, but when in Tucson, I heard many Tucsonians complain about the traffic snarls. Such is the karma of divisive speech. Tearing people apart through your words comes back to you as the feeling that you are having a hard time joining yourself to your destination!

The positive version of this karma is to use your speech to bring people together rather than divide them. Say nice things about other people, especially when they're not around. This will generate loyal friends and more harmonious relationships for you in the future.

Plus it will help clear the traffic jams!

Don't hurt people with your words / Use words that are kind and pleasing to others

Harsh speech includes anything said that hurts another person. You can do this at the top of your lungs and with a lot of four-letter words, or sarcastically and ironically, or even softly and gently, with honey dripping off your lips. The particular modality doesn't matter. What does matter is if the intention is to cause pain to another person with your verbal utterances.

Orally abusing others is the reason why others insult you or, in general, say things you don't want to hear. Some people seem to always be being challenged by others. They go into a bar and people try to pick fights with them. That comes from this karma.

Hurting people with your words is also the real cause of noise pollution in your life. I used to live on a street in New York City where motorcycles without mufflers would drag race all night long. While everyone living in New York seems to have some form of harsh speech karma—it's surely the world's noisiest city!—my version of this was unmistakably striking.

To avoid all sorts of unwanted sounds, ranging from people's insults or criticism to the sound of leaf blowers or chain saws outside your window, make pleasing instead of disagreeable sounds. Kind, pleasant speech will plant the seeds for a more euphonious future.

Don't engage in useless speech / Make your words meaningful and sincere

Useless or "idle" speech comes in a number of forms. It can take the appearance of gossiping about other people (usually about their problems). In the Buddhist texts, another form of idle speech is said to be just blah-blah-blahing your mantras or prayers without thinking about what you're saying. Useless speech can also include engaging in meaningless debate with others about stuff you really don't know that much about and with the outcome of the debate serving no real purpose.

A particularly virulent form of useless speech is saying you will do something and then not doing it. While we may think it doesn't really matter when we don't follow through on our promises—when we casually say "Let's do lunch sometime" when what we really mean is "I don't ever plan to see you again"—what we say does have an effect. Our words don't just evaporate into the ether. When we make promises we don't intend to fulfill, Mr. Karma (who is none other than our own consciousness and conscience) takes note and will make sure there are repercussions.

The karmic consequence of this misdeed is that no one pays any attention to what you say. If in the past your words have been meaningless, the karma comes back at you as having people regard your speech as, well, meaningless. No one thinks your speech has any value because you yourself haven't valued your words in the past.

But even worse, because you haven't respected your own speech, you come to believe that you have no value or worth in general. Lack of confidence, depression, and low self-esteem spring from idle speech. It makes sense: you hear yourself "talking trash" and you come to think of yourself *as* trash.[16]

The positive trait to cultivate here is matching our words with our actions and doing what we say we will. This is one very important way to make your words meaningful: *Write no checks with your mouth that your body can't cash.* By doing so, we'll feel better about ourselves and others will respect us more.

Don't be envious of other people's lives / Rejoice in the little things that bring pleasure to others

This guideline is sometimes known as "coveting" and it makes an appearance under that name in the Ten Commandments. It is, simply put, being bummed out when we don't have what someone else has. Or, to put it even more pointedly, it means being unhappy and resentful about the fact that someone else has obtained some crappy little thing here in this suffering world that brings them a modicum of happiness for a little while—until they lose it.

As usual, such self-centered thinking is wholly irrational. Your neighbor didn't somehow get his new car at your expense, and your competitor at work didn't get her promotion because you didn't. Other people obtain desirable things because of their own good karma, not because of your bad karma. Their acquisitions and success actually have nothing to do with you. When it comes to real causality, it's never a zero-sum game: another's gain does not come at your loss. If you didn't get the new car or the promotion, it's because you didn't have the karma for it: *there can be no effect without a cause.*

This kind of envy of others is basically a form of greedy discontent, and its karmic fruit is a personality dominated by insatiability. All forms of addictive personality and compulsive behavior spring from this cause—alcoholism or addiction to drugs, food, gambling, sex, shopping, video games, or whatever. Because you have thought you didn't have enough, you later feel that you can never get enough.

As a result of craving and coveting, your desire is unquenchable and you live in an environment of shortages and decline. The particular karmic consequence will also depend upon what, exactly, you're envious of. If you wish you had the good looks someone else has, the result might be feeling ugly. If you covet another's wealth, the karma could be a sense that you never have enough money.

The opposite of envy is to practice contentment ("*Om, I have enough, ah hum*") and rejoice about that which brings happiness to others. This not only creates the karma for a future in which you will feel satisfied with what you have, but also it's just plain sensible in all kinds of ways. It makes no sense to be upset about other people's successes, so why not just "pile on"? Join in and be happy for others' happiness and you'll be . . . happier!

Don't be happy about other people's pain or problems / Be compassionate and empathetic

This is the opposite of the previous instruction and is also called "ill will" or "malice." It means taking perverse pleasure in the suffering of others and/or wishing that others have difficulties. It includes things like being pleased when your enemy has problems or your rival fails, and also encompasses rubbernecking at an accident on the freeway and indulging in much of what passes as modern info- or entertainment (which, as we noted in the last chapter, basically entails watching, listening to, or reading about other people's suffering for our own amusement).

Not getting the help we need and a personality dominated by anger, sadistic tendencies, or, interestingly enough, paranoia (and also an environment that promotes paranoia, where others really are plotting against us) are listed in the texts as effects stemming from this cause. Because we've had the mindset of wanting suffering to come to others, we later experience the sense that others are out to get us.

The remedy and antidote for ill will is compassion. Really, it is just to be fully human—to be a real *mensch*—and feel empathy for, not perverted pleasure in, the suffering of others. The karma of cultivating this positive virtue is a future in which we can trust and rely upon others, a feeling of camaraderie with, rather than suspicion and mistrust of, our fellow human beings.

Don't adhere to erroneous views / Adopt viewpoints that are correct

The last one in the Top Ten list is in some ways the worst since it tends to make possible and enhance the others. By "erroneous views," what is meant is some form of nihilism, the belief that life is meaningless and nothing we do really matters—the conviction that there are no laws of karma or morality, that what goes around *doesn't* come around. "Nothing harmful, immoral, or illegal that I do or say will have any detrimental consequences to me—as long as I don't get caught."

Unfortunately, such a corrosive belief system is fairly prevalent these days. The stronger one stubbornly holds to wrong views, the more serious the negative karma created. In this case, it's much better to be only casually or unthinkingly nihilistic than to be professing it with certainty and conviction.

In general, karma replicates itself. If we repeatedly do something—positive or negative—we find ourselves later with a predisposition to do it again. So in this case, one of the karmic consequences of holding erroneous beliefs is the tendency to gravitate again to such viewpoints in the future. Worldview begets worldview. Another karmic ramification is that we find ourselves living amongst others who agree with us—who think wrong is right and what's harmful is somehow OK.

By becoming entrapped in such a large-scale error, one finds oneself later unable to think clearly about pretty much anything. So it is that stupidity, low IQ, is karmically caused by holding to wrong views.[17] With a proclivity to continue to clutch to a nihilistic worldview and the inability to think straight about what's what, one easily creates a whole host of problems for oneself. Some texts identify the karmic consequence of this misdeed as self-destructive tendencies. Embracing erroneous worldviews leads to a downward cycle of ignorance and delusion and the suffering that derives from them.

If you want to be smart and clever in general (get high marks in school, know how to balance a checkbook, and solve sudoku puzzles), as well as be wise (be able to figure out what to give up and what to take up for your own and others' happiness), adopting the correct worldview is the karmic cause.

And the correct worldview, in case you were somehow still wondering, is karmic causality. Having overcome our obstacles and put our faith in the true understanding of how things really work; having contemplated the general principles of karma that have been taught in both Eastern and Western traditions;

and having been presented with a set of specific correlations that link our present actions to subsequent results, the tools for creating a desirable future are now truly in our own hands.

The Three Steps of Karmic Management

Theory is one thing; action is another. Future suffering can be avoided; it is possible to rest easy in the present with confidence and trust that a happy future is ensured. To attain those desiderata, however, there are three things we must do: (1) stop creating new bad karma; (2) start creating new good karma; and (3) purify our old bad karma and strengthen our new good karma.

The first of these requires retraining what we think of as our instincts. In fact, there really are no "instincts" to retrain. We are not hardwired, one way or the other. It's really just the force of habit that impels us to return violence with violence, anger with anger, criticism with criticism. Bad habits can be broken, but it takes effort, discipline, and vigilance.

Let's say you have a problem with anger. Interrupting the tendency to lose one's temper involves, first of all, really wanting to do something about the problem. You begin by reviewing over and over the karmic principles and relevant rules. You think repeatedly about the disadvantages of anger and the advantages of no longer being the slave to this particular bad habit. And then you systematically monitor your behavior all day long. By maintaining alert self-awareness, you will be able to catch yourself as you start becoming angry. And then it's showtime! You bring to mind what you have practiced thinking about: "All actions have consequences. If I get angry, there will definitely be consequences. And I know that those consequences will be undesirable. Not getting angry will preempt such negative future results." And you try to restrain your inclinations by deploying your wisdom and your sense of enlightened self-interest.

Need it be said, you will lose many of these inner battles before finally winning the war. But if you don't start fighting those nasty, self-destructive tendencies, they will continue to bring you exactly the kind of future repercussions you worry about and want to avoid. A little wisdom goes a long way; just knowing what to give up and why (because it hurts you and those around you) helps you to actually do it.

And then there's what to take up. As you are training yourself to avoid re-creating the causes for undesirable future outcomes, you will also want to be cultivating positive actions that will have desirable, pleasant results. This too requires practice, self-discipline, and attentiveness. Every day try to do things for others—small acts of kindness, especially anonymous ones where the element of self-interest is minimized. Which, paradoxically, are the best kinds of things you can do for yourself!

His Holiness the Dalai Lama sometimes says, "If you can't help others, at least don't hurt them." But it's even better to not hurt *and* to help others—daily and systematically. At the end of this chapter, you'll find an Action Plan that can help you develop this kind of karmic self-discipline. Keeping a spiritual diary where you're tracking your actions all day long is one of the most effective ways to take control of your future.

Which brings us to the third thing we must do to really solidify a future we can look forward to. We must defuse old bad karma so it doesn't ripen into unpleasant results, and supercharge the positive acts we do so they will bring us maximum benefit.

Can we really purify our negative deeds of the past? What about that karmic rule: *There can be no cause without an effect*? Fortunately, there is something of an escape clause here. You can't, of course, actually *undo* what you have done, but it is certainly possible to *get it off your conscience.* And since Mr. Karma does not exist apart from or outside of your own mind, if you clean your conscience of the negativity you thereby disable its power to flower in the future.

Here's how it's done: First, *admit it.* Take responsibility for the bad deed, and don't make excuses or otherwise try to somehow legitimize it. Second, *regret it.* Which doesn't mean "feel guilty." Regret and guilt are two different things. Guilt, a therapist friend of mine once pointed out, is what we feel so we don't have to feel regret. We think that if we just beat ourselves up enough it might be sufficient penance. Regret, on the other hand, entails the intention to change. It is how you would feel if someone told you that the water you drank five minutes ago was laced with arsenic. You wouldn't feel guilty about it—*Oh, I'm such a bad person for drinking that water!*—but you surely would regret it. And if you understand karma you will feel this way about bad deeds you've done that you know are just ticking like a time bomb, waiting to bring you unwanted consequences.

Third, having admitted and generated some regret for your mistake, make a promise to yourself to not do it again. For some serious bad actions, you might want to swear never to repeat the action for as long as you live. But usually it's best to set a time limit that you can keep: "I promise to not steal supplies from the office for the next month"; "I vow to not lie to my girlfriend for a week." Or even, "I swear to restrain myself from feeling envious for an hour." And then having made the vow, keep it.

Finally, in addition to restraining yourself from repeating the act you're cleaning from your conscience, you can also actively take up the opposite and positive action. If you are purifying some act of stealing, be proactive in giving to others. If it is lying you're working on, be attentive to telling the truth. If envy is the problem, practice being happy about what other people have.

These four steps—admit it, regret it, refrain from it, and do some kind of act of restitution—have to be repeated until *you* feel it's been sufficient, until *you* can say honestly that it is off your conscience. You are, remember, your own judge and jury, and you are also the only one who can grant you absolution. But when you have done a practice like this sincerely, at a certain point (and when that is, exactly, only you will know) the negative karma you've been working on will be cleaned.

Together with purifying the old bad karma that we've already done, we can also strengthen the acts of good karma that we have newly created. There are several factors that can energize karmic seeds. To get the biggest bang for the buck when it comes to creating good karma for the future it's wise to take advantage of these techniques.

Probably the most important factor of all is motivation or intention. We touched on this earlier in our discussion of the once-in-every-five-lifetimes lie to save the refugee from the Gestapo-like police. The negative karma of lying in that scenario would be severely mitigated by the goodness of the intention. Similarly, our motivation for doing karmically beneficial acts also makes a big difference. I think we all know that it is quite possible to do good acts with a bad motivation, like, for example, making an ostentatious display of an act of generosity solely to impress others. Conversely, a truly selfless, loving, and compassionate motivation makes even small acts of goodness more powerful.

A strong intention creates a more powerful karma than an act that's done spontaneously or with little forethought and feeling. Just thinking about doing good things for others engenders good karma. And every time you think about helping others, another little karmic seed is added to the pile. So another way to increase the power of a good deed is to plan it carefully and in advance, with *premeditation,* to amp up the purity and goodness of your motivation.

Thinking about doing nice things is good; thinking about them over and over again is better; but then actually doing what you've been thinking about is best. Implementing a good deed, especially one you've repeatedly and carefully plotted in advance, makes for a stronger karma than something you've done spontaneously or just in your imagination. And repeatedly doing something good, just like repeatedly thinking about it, digs a deeper groove and produces a more potent result.

Certain kinds of beneficial acts are intrinsically better than others. It's good to give someone something to eat, but it's even better to teach that person how to grow their own food. And it's best to help others by sharing with them the real methods—the ones we've been discussing in this book—for reaching their highest goal: true and abiding happiness.

Yet another factor for supercharging karma centers on the object. Good acts done for certain kinds of people in our life are more powerful than good acts done for others. Such special people include our parents, teachers, and others who have helped us greatly. People who depend entirely upon us to assist them are more powerful objects of karma than folks who might have others who are available to help them. Supporting people who are helping lots of other people—doctors who treat many patients, aid workers who provide relief to many in need, or spiritual teachers who teach these principles to numerous students—is an especially good way to multiply the karmic energy of your act.

Finally, it's important to really "own" your good deeds, to take justifiable pride in the little things you do for others and to revisit those acts in your mind. This too makes a deeper imprint and creates a more powerful effect. We're not just hopeless losers; we are, in fact, constantly doing small acts of kindness for others all day long. Pay attention to what you're doing right and really rejoice in your own goodness! As my teacher used to say, we need not only a "confessional" in order to purify our old bad karma; it's equally crucial to have a "rejoice-ional" where we can fortify our good seeds.

"Me First" or "The Last Shall Be First"?

Unhappiness in the present derives in part from projecting ourselves into an uncertain and scary future. But apprehension and stress are not inescapable conditions of life. *Future suffering can be avoided,* and so too can present nervousness about what lies ahead. We can indeed move from worry and anxiety to trust and control.

But not without wisdom and effort. *The future is in our hands*—always. Whether we are aware of it or not, at every moment we are putting the causes in place for future results. Taking control of that process requires, first and foremost, the recognition that it is only our own inertia, doubt, and delusion that have made us feel like helpless victims, that have either immobilized us or misguided us, or both.

We all have a deep-seated tendency to think and act in ways that are counter to our own happiness. Our habitual responses to the events of our lives are mostly 180 degrees wrong. Being stingy when we feel we don't have enough, yelling back at someone who yells at us, and generally cutting corners in our moral lives because we think it doesn't matter—living life like this, we should indeed worry about what tomorrow will bring.

In order to create a happy future, we must fight our own inclinations and resist the siren song of a culture that encourages and exacerbates our own worst tendencies. Living in the thrall of consumer capitalism, with its ceaseless promotion of greed and its deification of the ego, we find it hard to do anything but continually obsess about our selfish desires. A constant barrage of advertizing spurs on this myopic concern with ourselves and our never-ending "needs." An inner syllogism of twisted logic unfolds like this:

I can imagine it, therefore I want it.
I want it, therefore I should have it.
Because I should have it, I need it.
Because I need it, I deserve it.
Because I deserve it, I will do anything necessary to get it.

Notice the prevalent use of the first-person pronoun in this formula. We have been seduced by a force that depends upon our perpetual dissatisfaction, our continual craving, and our compulsive acquisitiveness. We've thrown out the tried-and-true moral principles of our authentic spiritual traditions in favor of a secular ideology that ratifies our selfish inclinations.

The basic assumptions of consumerism are rearticulated in certain sectors of the modern self-help movement. Ego-oriented therapeutic methodologies with their emphasis on self-fulfillment and the narcissistic wish-fulfillment of the more simplistic forms of positive thinking function as the pseudo-spiritual arm of consumer capitalism. In the end, it's really just good old-fashioned self-centeredness that's once again being sold, notwithstanding the glitzy packaging. Vanquishing our deeply rooted mistaken thinking and defeating the negative habits that follow from it will require a more radical change than that entailed by self-affirmation or magical thinking. It will demand a more thorough-going inversion of our selfish orientation, both inborn and learned, and the assumptions that follow from it.

"Me first"—in all the many forms it takes—cannot and will not ensure future happiness.[18] *Au contraire!* It's like Jesus said in what constitutes a nice summary of how karma really works: "Many who are first will be last, and the last will be first."[19]

At the heart of the karmic system lies an apparent paradox: *We will get what we want only when we let go of our selfish wanting.* Our happiness comes not by indulging or increasing our own egotistical cravings. It comes when we replace selfish desire with the desire that *others* be happy. It is our own stubborn ignorance that inverts the true secret of happiness. The way to achieve our own happiness isn't to worry about ourselves all the time; it's to be concerned about somebody else's happiness.

This is the "enlightened" part of "enlightened self-interest." One's real self-interest is furthered only by working to help further the interests of others. As Emerson said, "It is one of the most beautiful compensations of life that no man can sincerely try to help another without helping himself."[20]

If your actions are guided by this compass, there's absolutely no need at all to worry about the future. Furthermore, virtue, they say, is its own reward. You will become who you are now. You'll be happier in the present not only because you know you're doing the intelligent things, the things that are conducive to your future security, but also because you'll be living the kind of life you know you should be living.

Couch Potato Contemplation: How to Get What You Think You Need

Think about what it is that you don't have that you think might make your life better, what you do have that you'd like to be rid of, and the elements and possessions of your present life that you value and enjoy.

Then review the three possible coherent and comprehensive explanations of how the world is working: (1) things are just random, (2) God is micromanaging everything, or (3) everything lies within the nexus of causality.

Now apply the principles of karmic management to your own situation. Work the system! What would be the causes for getting what you don't have but want, for getting rid of what you do have and don't want, and for keeping the desirable aspects of what you already have, by creating the seeds for more desirable things in the future?

Action Plan: Charting Karmic Connections

Keep a spiritual diary and monitor your morality six times every day. Using the "Top Ten" list of karmic correlations we discussed in this chapter, every two or three hours stop what you're doing and check in on yourself. Be especially vigilant about the positive and negative actions related to a goal you're working for. For example, if you are interested in better health, be especially observant about monitoring actions that avoid harming the bodies of others and instead actively foster their physical health.

Part IV

Relaxing into the Present

8

Honking in Gridlock and Pop-Ups in Horrorland: *Staying Happy—All Day, Every Day*

> Let us learn from the past to profit by the present,
> and from the present to live better in the future.
> —William Wordsworth

Being Here and Now Happily, No Matter What

We've seen that living a happy life requires generating a healthy, accepting attitude about the past and a positive outlook on the future. Making such adjustments will automatically result in a happier present. When we heal those parts of ourselves that are preoccupied with bitterness about the past and anxiety about the future, we purge a great deal of what has been contaminating the present.

But life doesn't stand still. Completing the spiritual renegade's project of inciting happiness and achieving our goal of revolutionary contentment and radical peace of mind demands also that we learn how to live wisely in the ongoing present. We'll need to develop survival skills for dealing with whatever challenges we may confront, such that we stay happy all day long—no matter what!

Putting our anger and resentment about past events to rest and learning how to think optimistically about the future will allow us to spend more time in the only time that really exists. When we stop worrying about what might be and rehearsing what has already been, we can finally stop ignoring what is actually happening—right here, right now.

The importance of living in the present—of "being here now," as Ram Dass famously put it back in the 1960s—is a spiritual truism.[1] And like most truisms, there's more to it than at first meets the eye.

Staying attentive to what's going on in the moment is without question a crucial component to living a good life and to psychic health. Reality is literally invisible to you if your mind is stuck in the past or future. Abraham Maslow, one of the towering figures of modern psychology, declared, "The ability to be in the present moment is a major component of mental wellness."[2]

Too much attention on the past and future can detract from life as it's unfolding. If we have one eye on yesterday and the other eye on tomorrow, we're going to be cockeyed today. Focusing on life as it is happening in the only time that actually exists is a key to contentment and happiness.

Peace and contentment come in various flavors. One variety is to be satisfied with what we have instead of always craving more (*"Om, I have enough, ah hum!"*). But another version of contentment entails being OK with what's happening in the present instead of casting one's mind forward or backward or to some place other than where you are right now. To be content with the "here and now" instead of always bailing into the "there and then" is a crucial step for inciting real happiness in our lives.

But even if we manage to wrench our minds out of the imaginary past and future and finally focus on the present, we need to have the wherewithal to deal with what's happening with intelligence and grace. There are right and wrong ways to relate to the here and now. A sophisticated spiritual practitioner has to learn to "be here now" wisely.

Living in the present is necessary, but it is not sufficient. We need to know *how* to "be here now." Being in the moment *unhappily* is really not so different from being miserable due to resentments regarding a time gone by or fearful and anxious imagining a time yet to come.

Living life consciously and in the present does not in and of itself automatically produce contentment. One of the reasons we try to avoid what's actually going on by escaping into the past or future is that we're not happy with what's actually unfolding. We suffer not just because we're not "here and now," but also because we aren't prepared to cope with whatever occurs in the present. If we are unhappy with what's actually happening, whatever it may be, being presentist can just turn out to be another modality of suffering.

We will succeed in staying in the moment *only if we really want to be there*—and this requires that we learn to willingly accept whatever life throws our way without turning our backs on reality and wishing things were different. We will be much, much more likely to be living in the present if the present seems to us to be a good place to be.

How can we make this happen? It's relatively easy to embody the present moment when things are going well. We're attracted to the pleasant and therefore attentive to the present when it's enjoyable. But what about when things are difficult? When events are apparently not going right? When unwanted things occur? Can we be fully "here and now" even in these disagreeable circumstances?

Staying Happy All the Time

There's a verse in the Yoga Sutra that reads *sthira sukham asanam*, usually translated to mean something like "The physical poses (*asanam*) bring you long-lasting (*sthira*) happiness (*sukham*)."[3] Which is, of course, the point of doing yoga or any other spiritual discipline—to obtain true and enduring happiness. But that important verse can also be read differently, in a way that is equally descriptive of what yoga is really all about: "Stay fixed or steady (*sthira*) in the perspective (*asanam*) of happiness (*sukham*)."

Or, more loosely, "Stay happy all the time."

This is, as we've repeatedly reiterated, the purpose of life itself, to learn how to be happy and stay that way always. Doing so begins with truly taking to heart a simple fact of life that we've touched upon before: *There's never a time when it makes sense to be anything other than happy*. And that includes the present moment, no matter what's happening.

It's worth reminding ourselves here that, by "happiness," we don't mean some kind of shallow, chuckle-headed attitude where you just ignore the realities of pain, suffering, and the difficulties of life. Nor is happiness some kind of unremitting flow of sensual pleasure. Rather, true happiness is a deep, ongoing, imperturbable mental state where one remains calm and unflustered by the twists and turns of outer events. It's a state that arises not through gaining control of the external world but through gaining control of ourselves.

Whenever we feel unhappy, it is not because of outside events or confrontations with dislikable people—although it might indeed seem like outer circumstances are clearly to blame. Our emotional distress is really due solely to our own self-destructive responses to these situations. It's not the things that happen to us that disturb us. It's being disturbed that disturbs us.

We are unhappy because of one or another of the mental afflictions—anger, jealousy, pride, greed, and so on. These negative emotions grab us by the neck and fling us about like puppets. We lose control and no longer think straight. We forget that *being upset is never an effective strategy for dealing with any situation.*

The point is not so much to change our reactions as it is to change our reactions to our reactions. Instead of automatically embracing and affirming our negative responses to things, we can stop and notice that our knee-jerk responses are neither logical nor conducive to our own enlightened self-interest.

If we can sustain a rational perspective on life, we will always choose to be happy. Because getting upset never helps the situation; in fact, it just makes it worse.

No matter what unwanted thing happens to me
I will not let my joy be disturbed.
Being upset does not help me get what I want,
But rather just causes me to lose my well-being.[4]

This is the beginning of learning how to live happily in the present: recognizing that responding to *any* situation with anything other than a calm, chillaxed, and peaceful state of mind simply makes no sense. It's just not an intelligent, sane way to live, let alone a strategy for living a happy life.

Appreciating and remembering this is the first step to knowing why it's always your smartest play to "*sthira sukham asanam*," "stay happy all the time."

Knowing What You Can Change and What You Can't

Realizing that it's never sensible to be anything other than happy is buttressed by another bit of wisdom for living rationally and happily: knowing the difference between things we can change and things we can't, and taking the corresponding and appropriate measures.

The *Guide to the Bodhisattva's Way of Life* puts it simply and succinctly:

> *If there is something you can do about it*
> *Why be unhappy?*
> *And if there is nothing you can do about it*
> *Why be unhappy?*[5]

If there's something we can do about a lamentable situation that may arise in our lives, then what's the point of being upset? Just do what needs to be done and get on with it already! Being upset about what's fixable only diverts us from taking the necessary measures to bring about the change we desire. And if there's nothing we can do, well then, what's the point of being upset? It is useless to get angry or depressed or anxious about what is completely out of our hands.

Such ancient wisdom has been restated more recently in Reinhold Niebuhr's famous "Serenity Prayer":

God, give us the grace to accept with serenity the things that cannot be changed,
Courage to change the things that can be changed,
And the wisdom to distinguish the one from the other.[6]

So the question that immediately arises is *which is which*? What is it we can't change, and what actually is within our power to alter?

The answer is not what we might expect.

Generally, people believe that what we can't change is the past ("What's done is done") and the future ("Que sera, sera; whatever will be, will be"). But as we've seen in previous chapters, it's actually the past and the future that we *can* change. We transform the past by substituting forgiveness and gratitude for anger and resentment, thereby endowing ourselves with new and more wholesome memories. And we steer the trajectory of the future by paying close attention to our actions in the present, with full knowledge that we are sowing what we later will reap.

Surprisingly, what we actually *can't* change is the *present.*

And herein lies an extremely important aid for maintaining a calm, cool demeanor all day long, no matter what may transpire. Realizing that *we cannot change the present in the present* will help us relax and accept what is, for now, unalterable.

Building on the insights about karma that we gained in the last chapter, let's turn our attention again to the nature of causality. *The present is a result of previous causes.* We were *once* in control of our present, but that was in the past. And we are, *in the present, in control of the future.* But *we are not in control of the present in the present.*

This is the way things are; this is how causality works. Resistance is futile . . . and detrimental to our happiness.

Since this revolutionary idea seems so antithetical to what we've assumed our whole lives, it is important to rehearse the logic from various angles. Once we think about it, it will become more and more obvious that we have no control over the present in the present.

Let's do a thought experiment, remembering what we learned earlier about what a "cause" really is—something that brings about its effect all the time for everybody. Let's say there's an irritating person in your life. Later we'll talk about the real (and only) way to get rid of such a person by working the system of cause and effect. But that takes time, and usually we want the irritating person to go away or to stop being irritating right now!

If we could change the present in the present, there would be a way to make this happen, a foolproof method that would work every time for everybody.

Let's review the two main options in our hypothetical case. Which of the following will change the present in the present and make the irritating person go away or stop being irritating: (a) being irritating back to them, or (b) being tolerant and kind instead?

Being irritating back is a method most of us have definitely tried in the past. And what was the result? Did your indignant response seem to cause the irritating person to stop being irritating? Well, perhaps it seemed to . . . some of the time. When we respond to provocation with anger, the provocateur sometimes shrinks back in the face of our formidable ire.

But then sometimes just the reverse occurs, right? The irritating person gets even more irritating because of our hostility.

So being irritating back to an irritating person can't actually be the cause that ends such unpleasant encounters. Why? Because it doesn't work all the time for everybody.

So let's try the opposite tack. You've been reading this book and have decided you will try to be a better, kinder person. So when you run into the irritating person, you're soft-spoken, apologetic, and friendly in your response. Does that work to change the present in the present?

Again, sometimes it does seem to have the desired effect. When you don't "rise to the bait," sometimes the offender stands down. But sometimes the annoying person just gets angrier by your "goody two shoes" appearance of moral superiority—and becomes even more irritating!

So being kind to an irritating person isn't the cause for changing this sort of behavior in the present either. Such a strategy doesn't always succeed, and therefore cannot be the true cause for stopping the unpleasant experience.

Neither one—being irritating back or just chilling out and staying calm—works to change the present in the present! And the reason is that *neither strategy works all the time.*

It's really hard to accept this plain and simple fact. We've lived our whole lives trying to change the present in the present. But if we were actually able to do it, wouldn't you expect we'd be better at it after all these years of practice? Don't you think that by now we'd have hit upon the surefire method for instantly revamping what we don't like? If this were possible, why would we ever again willingly opt to have a bad day or encounter an unpleasant person or have any unwanted experiences at all? Instead, when such events occurred, we'd just transform them in the twinkle of the eye into something more desirable, wouldn't we?

But we can't. Which explains why we fail so often when we try. Any success we seem to have in changing the present in the present actually *isn't because of present actions.* The modification is coming from—yep, you guessed it—past karma. If the karma is there for there to be the *appearance* of changing the present in the present, there will be change. And if the karma is not there, there won't be such an appearance of change in the present—no matter what you do—until the karma for the unwelcome event wears out.

Later in this chapter we'll talk about something that we *can* change in the present: our *understanding* or *interpretation* of what's happening. While the externals of life are not within our immediate control, if we are fortunate enough to have been exposed to some wisdom, we thereafter will always have a choice. That's what a bit of the truth offers us—a choice. We can choose to indulge habitual responses, or we can try something different. When confronted with difficult situations, we can always *think* about them in a more healthy-minded way.

But what's happening externally in the present can't be changed in the present. It's happening—the toast is burning, the car isn't starting, the boss is yelling, the cancer's getting worse—and *not* wanting it to happen won't suddenly make it just disappear. Closing our eyes and holding our breath didn't work when we were children. And some grown-up version of this tactic won't make the unwanted person or event instantly evaporate either.

It's a little like gardening. Actions of body, speech, and mind plant seeds. Time elapses and those seeds sprout, bringing us present events. And once the consequences of past actions have flowered there's nothing we can do in the moment to ward them off or change them. It's like trying to push the plant back into the ground because we didn't want what grew out of the seed we ourselves had planted.

Or to use another simile: Actions are like wet cement that we have poured out and shaped in a certain form and image. Time passes and the concrete hardens. Our present is the dried and now quite solid stuff of our past karmic artistry. And if you don't like the way the concrete has congealed, banging your head on that wall is not going to do anything other than give you a headache.

Or here's yet another image I like. Being unhappy about what your own past karma has brought to you is like *honking your horn in gridlock.* Maybe you've seen people do this (or maybe you've done it yourself!). You're in gridlock, which (for those of you living in rural areas . . . or Tucson!) means *the traffic is not moving.* You're at a standstill, with stopped cars behind and in front of you.

And then someone (is it you?) starts blowing their car horn. Sure, it's frustrating to be in a traffic jam, but what is honking supposed to accomplish? Does the stymied driver think that the sound of the horn will somehow magically part the traffic, like Moses and the Red Sea? Or does he or she expect that the people in the cars in front will hear the horn, look back, and say, "Oh, sorry! We didn't know *you* were back there! We'll get out of your way immediately so you can get going again!"

Honking your horn in gridlock will not unlock the grid, and just makes you and the people around you (similarly stuck and unable to do anything about it) feel worse about a situation that *can't be changed in the present.* There's nothing to do about gridlock except to wait it out. You can relax and accept that, or you can vent your frustration meaninglessly and ineffectually by getting upset and blasting your horn.

Which of these two choices makes sense? Which option is rational? Which one is conducive to a happy and sane life, and which one perpetuates your misery?

And, you see, every situation that arises in life is exactly like being stuck in a traffic jam. There's nothing you can do about a seed that has sprouted, or about concrete that has hardened, or about traffic congestion once you're caught in it. Attempts to make disagreeable events or people instantly disappear or transform by becoming distressed and acting out are totally futile.

Getting upset about what you cannot change—honking your horn in gridlock—*never helps* and *never makes any sense at all.*

It's like the text we've quoted above says: If there's nothing you can do about it, why get upset? Relax and stay happy. What's the point of any other response? Contentment in this case means choosing to accept the choices that have already been made—past causes have now become present effects. And, as the quotation also says, if there is something you *can* do about it, why get upset? Get busy instead of getting angry! Take control of what is within your control—the past and the future—and chill out already about the present.

And that's really the only reasonable way to live, isn't it? Such a radical shift in thinking and behaving is not some kind of airy-fairy departure from hard-headed rationality. On the contrary, it is our reflexive and habitual responses—honking in gridlock; beating our heads against the dried concrete—that have deviated from good old common sense.

It's just smart to stay calm and collected, no matter what's happening, and dumb to take the self-destructive option of losing one's cool—also no matter what.

Breaking the Chain of Pain

In the last chapter, we pinpointed where undesirable events and experiences come from, the "karmic correlations" that link effects to their causes. While there's nothing we can do about the present in the present, what we can control is our *response* to the ongoing flow of events. We can choose to do the smart thing in the present to create a better future rather than just mindlessly replicating the causes that are guaranteed to bring us more future suffering.

There's no sense at all in getting our "bowels in an uproar," as my mother used to say, about what we cannot change, but we can avoid re-creating the causes that brought the undesirable result in the first place. Although we aren't in control of present events in the present, we do have the option to do what we know is the right thing and restrain ourselves from doing what will just perpetuate our suffering.

But it's often hard in the moment to do what we *know* we should and refrain from what we unthinkingly *feel* like doing. We regularly find ourselves honking our horns in gridlock, which not only spoils our present happiness, but also creates the seeds for more gridlock in the future. Instead of doing what we can to solve our problems—relax about what we can't change and work hard and wisely for a different future—we do exactly the wrong thing: We respond to stressful situations with stress, to anger with anger, insult with insult, violence with violence.

We know we should "turn the other cheek" when we are provoked, not necessarily because it's "nice," but because it's *smart.* But instead, we do the wrong thing . . . just because we *feel* like it!

The ancient texts of India and Tibet delineate the structure of the cyclical reproduction of the causes of our unhappiness. We can call it the "*chain of pain.*" It begins, as we've intimated in the last chapter, with ignorance about what's what. Ignorance here doesn't mean *not* knowing something. *Ignorance is ignoring what is.* It is disregarding what's true—because we are too lazy to discover it, too cool to adopt it, or too overcome with our own wants and needs to acknowledge it—and instead adhering to an erroneous view about how things work.

Rather than using our heads, we follow our untrained instincts. And how's that worked out so far?

In our ignorance, we believe that the desirable or undesirable qualities we see in things are inherent in those things. It is the syndrome we investigated in the last chapter: "If only I had more money and things, a better job, a nicer and more attractive partner, more channels on the cable, and a better looking body . . . then I would be happy."

So out of our ignorance comes what some texts call by the interesting Sanskrit term *asmita*, literally meaning "I-amness"—the belief that things like The Big Five we discussed in the last chapter have *intrinsically* or *essentially* happiness-making qualities, whereas traffic jams and unpleasant people have the *inherent* power to *make us unhappy.*

And then, because of this mistaken conviction that people and things have such essential natures, we ignorantly like and dislike them. There's nothing wrong with liking or disliking, but the "ignorantly" part relates to our misguided belief in the *innate* likeability and dislikeabilty of things, experiences, and people, as if they existed "out there," objectively, apart from our own karmic actions of the past.

Based upon such erroneous assumptions, we proceed to do what we think will procure for us what we regard as desirable and keep what we find to be undesirable at bay. If we want a better salary and promotion, we ruthlessly jockey for a better position; if we don't like an annoying person, we yell insults at him. If we don't like terrorists, we hunt them down and assassinate them.

All such uninformed, emotionally driven actions are like honking the horn in gridlock. The only result we will get by acting like this is more unwanted events in the future.

Egocentric, hurtful, and ill-conceived actions simply replant again and again the seeds for continued unhappiness. We, as individuals and groups, make the same mistakes over and over again. Whether it's terrorists who fly planes into buildings or someone who insults, cheats, or harms us personally—either circumstance invokes the same vengeful and vindictive response. Consumed by primitive, unchecked emotions, we ignore the truth and respond by doing precisely that which brought the unwelcome event to us in the first place. We twist up the Golden Rule and do back to others as we would not have them do to us.

We've heard it said before, many times and in many ways: If we want to attain happiness and avoid repeated suffering, we have to stop the cycle of retaliation and break the chain of pain. It's all over the Christian scriptures:

- "Love your enemies, do good to those who hate you, bless those who curse you, and pray for those who abuse you." (Luke 6:27–28)[†]

- "Do not repay evil for evil or abuse for abuse; but, on the contrary, repay with a blessing. It is for this that you were called—that you might inherit a blessing." (1Peter 3:9)†
- "Do not be overcome by evil, but overcome evil with good." (Romans 12:21)†

And it is echoed also in Buddhism:

- "One should conquer anger with love, evil with goodness, stinginess with generosity, and lies with the truth." (Dhammapada 223)*

It is by training ourselves to actually do the right thing instead of just giving lip service to it that we will break the chain of pain in our lives. Living happily in the present will entail not just relaxing about what we can't do anything about; it will also involve constantly recalling that future suffering can be avoided—but only if we do what we know we should and act wisely in the here and now.

Three Stages for Disappearing an Irritating Person

Sometimes I think of life as one of those scary rides at the amusement park where they buckle you into a little train car and then it goes creaking down the track until it pushes through a pair of doors . . . and suddenly you're in the pitch blackness of Horrorland. And then as you slowly proceed through darkness, one by one all these pop-ups suddenly arise: "Oooh, a ghost! A skeleton! A vampire!"

An untrained, nonspiritual life in which one is just the perpetual victim rather than the master of karma is indeed a kind of "Horrorland" with one pop-up after another making an appearance: "Oooh, a traffic jam! Money problems! Boss yelling at me!"

Let's suppose that in your own personal version of Horrorland, one of the pop-ups is an irritating person. You're going through your day, minding your own business, and then, wham! A pop-up appears, seemingly out of nowhere. Suddenly you're confronted with a truly exasperating individual.

Let's acknowledge right off the bat that annoying, irritating people are not conducive to one's happiness. If it's our purpose in life to learn how to be truly happy (so we can be helpers instead of helpees), having irritating people pop up is not helpful to our mission. The amusement park ride of life will be a Horrorland as long as there are such pop-ups.

So it's OK to want to disappear such people from our lives. We need not feel guilty about wanting fewer (and eventually no) obnoxious people in our lives.

The question is how to do it. How do we put to rest the scary pop-ups in our life? How do we "go postal" on the irritating person?

First, let's remember the strategy that won't work—the one we've tried most often in our lives: When the irritating person pops up, we get upset and are irritating back. An irrational and dysfunctional response. Won't help. But it will guarantee the return of the irritating person. They'll pop right back up, sooner or later. They might have a different face or gender, but they'll be the same annoying person making your life miserable.

And also, don't forget, being tolerant and turning the other cheek also won't always make the pop-up instantly pop down either. Can't change the present in the present, no matter what you do.

But we can change the future by learning from the past. In order to break the cycle and put an end to the pop-up, we need to bring to mind the truth: There are no irritating persons in our lives that haven't come from us previously being irritating to others.

We take responsibility for what we used to be in control of, but what we can't control now. Annoying people are our own karmic creations, the results of past causes. We realize that the present pop-up has come from our own past actions and we can't just make jack get back into his box because we don't like the looks of him.

In the moment, we have only two choices—neither of which will change the present in the present. We can *freak out* or we can *chill out*. We can be unhappy about what's happening in the here and now and have our day ruined, or we can say to ourselves, "Wish I hadn't created the karma for this unpleasant event, but I must have and there's nothing I can do about it now that the result has come."

And that's what we need to do about what we can't change. But this is not an argument for mere fatalism. We have to take another step; we have to realize what we can change. Having taken responsibility, we then take control. When the pop-up appears, we remain aware that the future is in our hands; we decide to shift the course of the future trajectory of things by taking a different tack in our present response to people we find annoying and difficult.

We can, in the present, stop re-creating the causes for more scary pop-ups in the future and instead plant the seeds for a more pleasant amusement-park ride. We can get rid of unwanted people and events. But in order to do so, we have to use a method that will actually work—every time, for everybody.

There are, I think, three phases to the process of changing an unwanted pop-up, of disappearing an irritating person.

The first is to run away!

To be sure, this is just an initial step and by no means the final solution. Running away from your problems does not solve them. But getting yourself out of a situation before you do the wrong thing (again) is a start. Reacting wrongly won't make it right. Rather than re-create the causes that brought you the aggravating person in the first place, you extract yourself from the confrontation before you have a chance to act on your self-destructive impulses.

"Run away" is the strategy to adopt when the irritating person pops up in your life and you take stock of your own psychic strength and come to the conclusion that you're not yet tough enough to do the right thing, the intelligent thing, the thing that will break the chain of pain. There are lots of ways to "run away": apologize and hang up the phone, make yourself scarce, spill your coffee, excuse yourself and go to the bathroom, take a sick day at work, move to Barbados—but one way or the other, get out of a situation you can't, at present, handle.

And then go back to the spiritual gym and start working out. If you can't do the right thing in a challenging situation, it means that you need to get stronger, wiser, and more resolute in your quest to live a good, happy life. Review the facts over and over: "This is not an essentially irritating person; everything is karmically caused; it makes no sense at all to be anything other that happy in any situation; you can't change the present in the present so there's no point in getting upset about what you can't alter." Then think: "I can change the future by present actions, but it will require breaking old, mindless habits and doing what I know is right."

The second stage of the process of disappearing the irritating person: When you encounter this pop-up in Horrorland and they start doing their irritating thing (it might be something they do or say, or perhaps just their very appearance and presence antagonizes you), *you just shut up and take it*!

This is a lot harder than running away. But you've been preparing yourself and you're feeling stronger and more self-confident. And so when the pop-up occurs, you just stay there and endure it. No matter what they do or say, you do not say or do anything to retaliate.

A whole cacophony of name-calling and four-letter words might be going through your head, but nothing comes out of your mouth. You become like a "bump on a log," as one Indian text on patience puts it. You grit your teeth and bear it until it's over.

And when, you may be asking yourself through gritted teeth, will that be? When the karmic energy that brought you the irritating person runs out. Your ordeal will be over when the force of the cause that brought you the irritating person in the first place wears out—and not until then, no matter what you do. So in stage two, you just wait it out without re-energizing the karma by yelling back.

This phase of disappearing the irritating person obviously presupposes a lot of self-discipline. Since yoga is so popular these days, I have personally invented a yogic pose you can take when you need to get through such challenges. It's called *mukha bandha asana*. When the irritating person begins to irritate you, you can say, "Excuse me, but I need to do some yoga."

And then take the pose.

Mukha means "mouth." *Bandha* means you keep it shut. *Asana* means the pose you've assumed.

Mukha bandha asana—way harder than a backbend or twist. But it's the only way to begin the process of breaking the chain of pain, of putting jack back in his box, of disappearing the irritating person.

After probably months of training (and in some hard cases it could take years), eventually you'll be ready for stage three of the process. When you meet the person formally known as "irritating" and he or she starts doing what used to irritate you, instead of feeling irritated you think something like the following:

"This is an unhappy person. I remember what it was like to be so angry and mean that you would want to say or do hurtful things like this. I felt terrible and was lashing out, and this person is in the same position. What a shame! I feel so sorry for someone who is so unhappy! I wonder what I could do here to help make this person happier?"

When you reach stage three, you will have finally succeeded in disappearing this irritating person through the only method that actually works.

And you will have finally and fully realized a fundamental truth: *There is no irritating person unless you are irritated.* Don't like having irritating people pop up in your life? Then don't get irritated! How else did you think it would work?

If instead of irritation you feel compassion and sympathy for a person who is obviously not happy themselves (happy people are not interested in irritating others), you have put that pop-up to rest. That karmic cycle is finished. One down.

And then you can start on the next pop-up. And each time that you succeed in doing the right thing instead of perpetuating your own pain, it gets easier. Keep it up and eventually you'll have no more unpleasant pop-ups at all! Whatever occurs, you'll find yourself managing it with wisdom and compassion.

Through practice, the time spent in stages one and two diminishes and you become more and more accustomed to the mind-set that characterizes stage three. You've learned what you can and can't change and you're on your way to reinventing life, transforming the Horrorland ride into something a lot more agreeable.

The Irritating Person
http://bit.ly/renegade9

Presto Chango: How to Instantly Transform Problems

Staying happy all day, every day, centers on recognizing what is and what is not within our control in every one of our life experiences. With such discernment, we'll then be able to take the appropriate action to maintain an easygoing state of mind. This is how to live sensibly and happily in the here and now: We chill about what we can't change, we work hard to change what we can, and in either case we remain happy all the time.

We've repeatedly asserted that we *can't change the present in the present,* but we've also pointed out that there are better and worse options available to us as we go through life's vicissitudes. We can, in the present, be creating the causes for a different future. But in addition we always have available another way to transform present difficulties.

We can *reinterpret* them.

There are no such things as problems that exist as such, out there, on their own. What we call a "problem" or "difficulty" is an interpretation, not a fact. A "problem" is just a *label*, not an intrinsic defining quality of the thing, person, or event being labeled. Something or someone exists as a problem *only because we are seeing it that way*—and it is always possible to look at things differently and in a more useful light.

Most people go through their whole lives without realizing that problems are not intractable and need not be simply endured. But you are now no longer one of those disempowered people. You have read something that gives you a choice that others aren't even aware of. You're a spiritual renegade, armed and dangerous when it comes to your own unhappiness.

So here is something we can actually do in the present about the present: we can adjust our *understanding* of what's happening in the here and now.

Just as we can change the past by reinterpreting it, we can change the present by seeing it as a constant flow of unfolding life lessons. And *when problems become teachings, they are no longer problems.*

The techniques for doing this we've already touched upon in chapter 5, where we spoke about ways to stay grateful by reflecting on the advantages of difficulties. The advice given there we can briefly review here in the context of transforming problems into opportunities:

See the "problem" as an opportunity to eliminate egoistic pride.

When things are going too right for us, we not only have the tendency to get lazy and complacent—we can also develop a sense of entitlement: "This is the way my life *should* be. Other people have problems—that's too bad for them—but that's not me!" And this, we might think, is somehow the natural and eternal order of things.

Such arrogance is seen not only among individuals but within entire cultures and societies. We tend to believe that it is hard-wired into the nature of things that other people's children should labor in sweatshops for pennies so that our children can wear relatively inexpensive, trendy clothing. But there's nothing set in stone about such international economic arrangements, and things can turn around very quickly and dramatically.

Economic downturns, health problems, career reversals, and a myriad of other problems can instill in us some needed humility. They can remind us that we are not somehow supernaturally privileged or protected, that it is not our God-given right to be immune from suffering while others must endure it. When we encounter difficulties in our own lives, we are made to notice that all of us are in the same boat; none of us has an exceptional birthright that automatically provides shelter from life's troubles.

If a problem can reveal to us our own arrogant and prideful assumptions and knock us down a notch from our regal perch, then that "problem" has actually made us a better and more humble person—and it can't really be called a "problem" anymore.

Use the "problem" to cultivate compassion for others.

This is perhaps the most important of all the methods for transforming a problem into something positive and spiritually helpful. Every misfortune that befalls us can be an opportunity to reflect upon the fact that *others have always been suffering like this.*

So now it's you. Now you really know what it's like to lose your job, or a loved one; to not be able to pay your bills; or to have a cherished dream shatter. "Oh, so *this* is what it feels like."

Now you really know how others in the same situation must feel—how they've *always* felt, even though up until now you weren't fully aware. Now you can really generate some true compassion for the suffering of other people. Until and unless we experience the pain, we really don't know what it feels like.

Without suffering ourselves, we could never really empathize with the suffering of others. When troubles come to us, we can most effectively *jujitsu* them by making them serve to increase our compassion for others and their difficulties. When a problem turns out to afford us a unique opportunity to finally break out of the confines of selfishness and callousness about the suffering of others, how can we say it is a "problem"?

See the "problem" as a lesson about karma.

We've touched on this strategy several times now. When an undesired event occurs in our lives, we can always use it as a teaching about karma. Instead of ranting and railing about how unfair it is that this undesirable occurrence has arisen, we can stop and think: What must have been the cause that would have brought me this result?

We can, in other words, review the "karmic correlations" we outlined in the last chapter in order to carry out a "search and destroy" mission. If, for example, we encounter a difficulty with another person—say a handyman we've hired cheats us—we can stop and conduct a little life review: *Have I ever cheated anyone in the past?* Chances are pretty good that if you're honest you'll be able to pinpoint at least one incident in your past that could have served as the cause for this unpleasant present event.

Just doing this much reinforces our conviction that *things don't happen for no reason.* We can use difficulties in our lives to review the options as to why we are now experiencing a problem (no reason, just random; or is God micromanaging everything in my life?), and, as a result of the review, strengthen our belief in the only explanation that actually empowers us and gives us the tools to change our lives: karma.

Once we have identified the cause of our "problem," we can go on to do the second part of the "search and destroy" mission. We can begin the work of purifying the karma. We can clean our past mistakes from our conscience by employing the method we discussed in the last chapter: We admit our misdeed, truly regret it, restrain ourselves from repeating it, and do something to make up for it.

Sometimes it happens that we are unable to remember anything that might be the karmic cause for what we're experiencing now. But even if we can't recall doing, saying, or even thinking something that we can establish as a possible karmic cause, *there nevertheless must have been one!*

There are lots of things that have happened in our lives that we can no longer consciously remember. If the karmic worldview is correct, there is always a cause for any effect. We can just assume that if someone hurts us or lies to us, or if we have money problems, we *must* have created the cause for it in the past—even if that cause has now been forgotten.

Mr. Karma is constantly screening the home video of your life. If you don't like what's on, think about how it was produced and how you could make a different show to watch in the future.

See the "problem" as pointing to something we need to fix.

Problems often occur because we are grasping onto something we want to keep or to keep from changing. And then when the changing, impermanent thing shows us its true nature—when the car doesn't start, when the relationship ends, when we lose our health or our youth—we become unhappy and bemoan our fate.

If you trace back the pain, you'll usually find an attachment or a delusion—for example, a belief that changing things won't change and that the way to keep something is to hold on to it as tightly as possible. And so a problem of this sort is just pointing toward our own possessiveness and clinging.

Or the problem may be that we're irritated with an irritating person, angry about something that someone said or did, or envious about something that someone else has. In some way or another, *our buttons have been pushed.*

But this need not be a "problem" at all! *If we didn't have buttons, how could anyone push them?* The button-pushers in our lives are not "problems," they're teachers:

> *Thank you for being so annoying! I thought I was a tolerant person, but you've shown me that I need to work on my patience. Thank you!*

No one can push your buttons if you don't have any. If you've learned something about yourself and what you need to work on to become a happier and more secure person, then the lesson—painful though it may be—isn't just a "problem."

In addition to these methods for transforming problems (or problematic people) into opportunities to learn and grow, we can also always use this one as well:

See the "problem" as a teaching about the true nature of life.

While no one wants problems, life is after all often problematic. This is the reality. And this is what the Buddha meant by the first "Noble Truth": Life is suffering. He wasn't kidding and he wasn't just having a bad day. Things go wrong all the time—disasters (large and small) befall us. Sh*t happens.

So when the samsara hits the fan in your particular corner of the universe, you can take it as a friendly reminder. "What did you think? Did you think you would never have any difficulties in life? That you, uniquely, would be spared disappointment, loss, thwarted hopes, and unexpected tragedies? That your life was somehow special and immune?"

And, of course, the answer will probably be "Yes, somehow I did think that nothing bad would ever happen to me, and now I'm unhappy because what I naively expected didn't come to pass."

Life has to repeatedly slap us around to keep us alert and paying attention. It's sometimes said that samsara is kind because we never have to wait too long before it reminds us of its true nature. But unless we have made revolutionary changes in our thinking and actions, we will repeatedly be taken by surprise when we fail to get what we want, when we get what we don't want, and when we lose what we want to keep.

When life is going well for us, the danger is that we can become complacent and fail to continue to proactively reproduce the karmic causes that brought about the good life. Problems can be life's wake-up call, instigating us into action. Instead of being bewildered that some displeasing thing has happened, we can be grateful for the reminder that, unless we are actively working to create the causes for a good life, we will continue to bounce from one unmanageable difficulty to another.

"Problems" help us to get serious about life and what we need to do to negotiate it successfully. And if they perform this function—if they inspire us to think more realistically and to make important adjustments in our lives—then they have become motivators, not "problems."

The external events of our ever-evolving present may not be within our immediate control, but our mental and emotional take on them always is. Staying happy requires relaxing about the gridlock, fixing the pop-ups in Horrorland, and taking the most positive view on everything that happens.

Things do not always go as expected, but the spiritual renegade sees that they have gone "just right." When you are tempted to become *upset* consider it a *setup*—an opportunity, not a problem.

With such an attitude we can indeed practice being "here and now," because we know that, no matter what happens in the present, we will be able to deal with it skillfully, in a way that is maximally beneficial for preserving and furthering our happiness.

We can stop beating our heads against what can't be changed—no more honking in gridlock!—and instead maintain a calm acceptance of the intractable. But we can also be enterprising in exploiting the opportunities afforded by any event that may arise. We can get busy gardening for the future, taking advantage of the fact that any "problem" we think we have is reinterpretable. For someone who is truly interested in squeezing the juice out of life and staying happy always, there's nothing that isn't just grist for the mill.

We need never be victims—not of what has happened, what is happening, or what will happen. The past is changeable, and so is the future. And both are here in the present moment, the only time that really exists. "The present contains all that there is," writes the philosopher Alfred North Whitehead. "It is holy ground; for it is the past, and it is the future."[7]

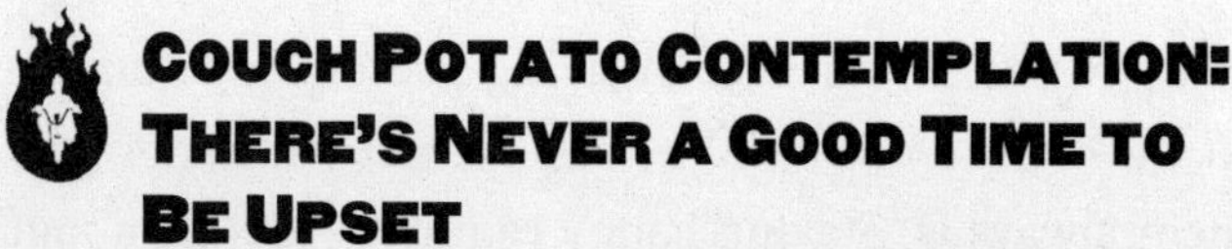

Couch Potato Contemplation: There's Never a Good Time to Be Upset

Review the sections of this chapter which argue that there is never a good time to be anything other than relaxed and happy. Think about whether this is indeed the case. Does it ever improve a situation to get stressed out, angry or upset? Does it make you and those around you feel better or worse when you are perturbed, anxious, or depressed? Resolve to maintain your equilibrium no matter what happens in your daily life, knowing that remaining calm, cool, and collected is always your most intelligent strategy.

Action Plan: The Complaining Fast

For the next week, declare a moratorium on whining. Just try to go through the next seven days without complaining about anything.

Whatever happens, try to accept it without complaint, realizing that cause and effect is at work! If there's nothing you can do about it, why get upset? It is the result of a previous karma—the cement has hardened. What's the point of honking in gridlock? If you don't like what is happening, instead of uselessly grumbling about it, think about the karma that brought the unwanted event to you and how you could avoid a repetition in the future by planting different karmic seeds in the present. Finally, see if there is any way you can reinterpret what's happening in order to see it as something other than a "problem." Can you learn anything from this experience?

Check in with yourself at the end of each day and see how you did. Did you complain today about anything? If so, why? What good did it do? How could you respond better—with wisdom about what you can change and what you can't—the next time you find yourself in such a situation?

9

Good Enough to Be Perfect: *Overcoming Liberphobia and Working Hard to Relax*

At the end of our exploring we'll arrive where we started,
and know the place for the first time.

—T. S. Eliot

You wander from room to room hunting for the diamond necklace
that is already around your neck!

—Rumi

Relaxing and Working Hard / Working Hard to Relax

Throughout this book, I've stressed how happiness does not come to us serendipitously—it is not something that we may or may not just stumble upon—nor will it occur only when external events finally "go right" or when, at long last, other people decide to *make us happy* (and to stop *making us unhappy*).

Our happiness is our own responsibility. And it is also our most fundamental human right.

If we are to succeed in achieving the true purpose of our lives, we must recognize that genuine and long-lasting satisfaction—as opposed to fleeting sensory pleasure—is neither a trivial nor superficial thing. Happiness is our deepest desire and our sole motivator—whether we admit it or not. It's what we're pursuing, consciously and unconsciously, in every action we take.

Nor is it merely self-serving to want to be happy. Our own happiness is also the condition of possibility for living a life of service to others. Happy people are in a position to be helpful people, whereas unhappy people make life difficult not only for themselves but for those around them as well.

When we get clear about the real mission here—to achieve true happiness so we can assist others in getting there too—we're then ready to think seriously about how we're going to accomplish this mission. While we all have been chasing happiness and trying to avoid suffering every minute of our lives, we have done so unthinkingly and wrongheadedly, failing to scrutinize what works and what doesn't.

At bottom, our biggest mistake is thinking that our own happiness comes from selfishly pursuing it at the expense of others—a mistake that's reinforced at every turn by a secularized consumerism that venerates the self and its endless, insatiable desires. Despite its claims to the contrary, consumer capitalism is aligned squarely against our search for contentment, creating, stoking, and reinventing the discontentment that impels voracious consumption.

We'll never be happy if we succumb to the advertisers and their claim that happiness is just around the corner in the next purchasable commodity. To really go for it will require a revolutionary inversion in our usual patterns of thought, patterns that have been instilled in us and intensified at every turn by our culture and media.

Nor can we achieve our end by embracing the current pervasive worldview that promotes randomness and meaninglessness. Here too we must "fight the power" if our quest for happiness is to succeed. If we uncritically subscribe to our culture's official vision of a universe grounded in a causeless first cause and randomly mutating ever since, we will be left with only fatalistic resignation and nihilistic hedonism as our personal philosophy.

If we are ever going to *incite* happiness in our lives, we not only must stop blaming other people, outer circumstances, or our lack of the latest consumer gadget for our perpetual discontent. We'll also need to have the guts to ask the "Why, Daddy?" question of ourselves and of our cultural mavens.

Our present scientific establishment is good at explaining *how* things work, but it's failed miserably at giving an answer to the question of *why*. When it comes to learning how to live the good life, answers to why things happen such as "no reason" or "luck" are as unsatisfactory as "God's inscrutable will."

Radical, desperate, and intelligent spiritual renegades and happiness-seekers require a worldview that sees that effects invariably come from causes, and that the true causes for things are based upon one's own moral actions. The karmic worldview puts the means of production of our happiness into our own hands. If we don't have a belief in karma, we don't believe we're in control of our own destinies and we'll remain, to a greater or lesser extent, powerless victims.

But if we adopt such a worldview, it's then entirely up to us! Inciting happiness requires a willingness to change our old habits and assumptions—a willingness born out of both desperation (nothing else has worked, nor could it) and conviction (we believe a new approach might work because we've reasoned our way to it). And so we're ready to do the hard work it will take to live differently, happily.

Realizing that it's within our power to reshape the past, we decide to cease masochistically clinging to painful memories. To that end, we resolve to no longer resurrect the Frankenstein monster of past resentments. We understand that *not* forgiving is hurting no one but ourselves, and we buckle down to do what we have resisted doing for so long: We forgive those who have hurt us—unilaterally and preemptively—knowing that we will never be happy until we do.

We then finish the task of rehabilitating the past by moving from forgiveness to gratitude, recognizing the kindnesses so many people have shown us in the past and paying attention to what others continue to do for us. Even those who have hurt, betrayed, or otherwise disappointed us in the past can teach us something we can be grateful for. Remember, it's not happiness that makes us grateful but gratitude that makes us happy.

Having overhauled the past, we then turn to the future, realizing that Nietzsche was right: "The future influences the present just as much as the past." Our present happiness depends not just on gifting ourselves with a better backstory but also on learning how to think both realistically and optimistically about the future.

A more realistic view about the future is obtained when we stop looking for happiness in things that can't deliver it—what we called The Big Five of money and possessions, the job, relationships, entertainment, and the physical body. We learned that happiness requires *renunciation*, and that what renunciation really means is that we give up thinking that external things and other people have the ability to impart happiness. When we finally relinquish the notion that our future happiness is pinned to these things and get more sensible about what *doesn't* work, we can then turn to what actually will bring us the future we desire.

We gain optimism about the future, and thus more peace of mind in the present, when we take control of life's operative mechanism—karma. Having overcome the paralysis of lazy or cynical doubt, as well as the seductive, if puerile, notion that we get what we want simply by wanting it, we finally embrace the real secret: It is only by giving up our selfish desires and turning our attention to what's good for others that our future happiness can be guaranteed.

Once we take appropriate actions to change what we can—the past and the future—because all the parts of time are interrelated, our present will also radically improve. Having cultivated acceptance and gratitude when it comes to the past, and confidence and trust about the future, our present state of mind will be dramatically happier.

We're now ready to face the ongoing challenges of life in the constantly unfolding present with wisdom and discernment. Calmly accepting what is unalterable without "honking in gridlock," we remain vigilant about gardening for the future, planting seeds for a happier tomorrow. We stay on the lookout for ways to *jujitsu* any "problem," turning it into an opportunity. And we stay happy always, knowing it's the only rational way to live.

To repeat: once we understand (a) how happiness is really obtained (through thinking about others and how we can help promote their happiness) and (b) what the point of it is (so we can become better helpers, having ceased ourselves to be helpees), happiness can no longer be regarded as a selfish goal. We can't be of real use to others until we have learned how to fix ourselves.

And as we've also emphasized throughout this book, the attainment of radical happiness will require a major mobilization of effort. When it comes to inciting happiness in your life, if you're looking for a helping hand you'll have to rely chiefly on the one at the end of your arm.

Relax and work hard—it boils down to that. Relax about what you can't change, and work hard to change what you can. That's really the essence of the method we've covered so far.

The Most Revolutionary Idea of All

In this final chapter, we recall again that our goal in life is to reach a state of perfect contentment—what we've called "entry-level happiness." There is no form of happiness—joy, bliss, ecstasy, euphoria—that doesn't presuppose plain old contentment. In fact, if we achieved contentment, by definition we wouldn't want anything more. Contentment would be *good enough to be perfect.*

It is important to work hard, wisely, and effectively, for a happy life. If we're haunted by painful memories, we need to confront them and do what's necessary to transform them. If we are anxious about the future, we'll want to take the appropriate actions that will convince us that everything will be OK. And if there are things that one believes need fixing about one's present situation—financial shortages, relationship problems, unsatisfactory job, health difficulties—then we need to address these concerns. Study the real principles of cause and effect and then work the karma to make the necessary adjustments.

If there's something you can do about, why get upset? Just do it!

But as we're working hard to improve our lives, some part of us also needs to be aware that this assumes that our lives *need improvement,* that the way things are is faulty or deficient. And this attitude is by definition *not one of contentment.*

To attain real contentment we need to believe that life is good enough as it is; that things do not need to be different before we can be happy. If we are actually going to realize the goal, we at some point must notice that continuously striving to change our lives and ourselves is the very opposite of the contentment we are striving for.

There has to come a time when the antecedent mandate to "relax and work hard" is at least complemented—if not wholly superseded—by the injunction to "work hard to relax."

The practice of working *toward* contentment then becomes the practice *of* contentment—right here, right now. *Aspiring* converts into *accepting*. The distinction between the end and the means to the end collapses: the path to the goal becomes using the goal as the path.

And really, how else did we think it would happen? How else will we ever achieve contentment other than . . . just being content? At some point, the spiritual renegade's hard work of improvement in order to incite more happiness in his or her life must give way to the most revolutionary idea of all: that one's present life, *as it is,* is *good enough to be perfect.*

Freedom and Liberphobia

Way back in chapter 1, we discussed our resistance to happiness as a kind of devil. We were encouraged to identify which parts of ourselves *didn't want to be happy* and then exorcise those demons. We'll never motivate ourselves to work for happiness if we think we shouldn't or that somehow we don't deserve it. Refusing to make happiness the supreme goal of life is the first of our self-imposed obstacles.

But silencing that particular devil isn't something we can do easily once and for all. Fighting our perverse reluctance to be happy is an ongoing process—and it's as relevant at the end as it was in the beginning.

The disinclination to even try to obtain true happiness gets repositioned later as the *fear of finishing.* We get addicted to *working toward* happiness instead of . . . being happy!

Having been in the academic world for most of my life, I can tell you that a similar phenomenon is well known there. A fear of finishing the dissertation that would complete their requirements for the desired PhD degree can surface among advanced graduate students. They have become so comfortable with the role of "student"—a status they've inhabited their whole lives—that they seize up and are unable to complete the final requirement for graduation. Instead of earning their PhD, the "Doctorate in Philosophy," such students are jokingly said to have only attained the ABD: "All But Dissertation."

When, after perhaps years or decades of hard spiritual work, we start to get nearer to our goal of happiness, a similar condition can arise. We have to again fight our enslavement to suffering which now takes the form of a disinclination to let go of our old identity and graduate into the as yet unknown status of a *happy person.*

We discover that we all have a fear of freedom—what we might call *liberphobia.*

"Realize that happiness is freedom," wrote the Greek historian Thucydides.[1] The Buddha, along with many other religious leaders, would agree: Nirvana, defined as freedom from suffering and its causes, "is the highest happiness."[2] In the Hindu traditions, it's called *mukti* or *moksha*—"liberation" or "freedom." It's a freedom *from* unhappiness and suffering, and the freedom *to* really be of use to others. "Because he is free, he obtains happiness; because he is free, he achieves the highest. Because he is free, he is in nirvana; because he is free, he goes to the highest state."[3]

It is freedom that we strive for, but it is also freedom that we perversely dread.

Liberphobia. It's actually been apparent all along. Because of this fear it can be hard to even start one's spiritual journey. We are all deeply traditionalist; we all resist change. We have made peace with our captivity and with the status quo, and we're afraid of the great unknown that is contentment.

We have, in some dark recesses of our subconscious, realized that as long as we're not free we're also not responsible. The following observation is attributed to no less an observer of the mind than Sigmund Freud: "Most people do not really want freedom, because freedom involves responsibility, and most people are frightened of responsibility."[4] We gravitate toward worldviews that suggest we are impotent in the face of blind luck or inscrutable divine whimsy because of the fear we have of being our own masters.

As long as we can avoid freedom and duck responsibility, we can go on blaming others for our difficulties. We can continue to point the finger at something or somebody outside of ourselves. Some part of us prefers to be an imprisoned victim rather than a free agent, and we are forever repositioning who or what to blame for the bondage we ourselves have embraced.

When we begin our spiritual journey we work to liberate ourselves from the crudest of our own untrained instincts: the mental afflictions—anger, jealousy, pride, greed—that have always governed our actions. We realize that we have never been—nor will we ever be—free until we gain a modicum of self-control.

And so we train to liberate ourselves from the fetters of our ignorant and self-destructive impulses, and through practice we gain more and more self-mastery. We learn to respond both to events and to other people intelligently rather than impetuously. We gain a bit of composure and with it the freedom to choose how we are going to respond to challenges and provocations.

And even with this much freedom we gain a great degree of happiness. But there are still more subtle forms of bondage to be cast off. At the later stages of our practice, we find that we're still clinging to our suffering, still reluctant to be happy.

As we get closer to real freedom and real happiness—as we approach the place where our lives are *good enough to be perfect*—we discover an inner resistance. Just as at the beginning we had to combat the demon that tried to stop us from pursuing a course that would lead to happiness, as we approach the end of our path a similar demon appears who suggests that *we aren't ready to finish*—and never will be!

That's why a serious spiritual practitioner, at all stages of the journey, needs to be something of a daredevil, willing to risk the unknown. In the beginning we're desperate enough to want to cast off our habitual patterns of self-inflicted pain and take a different direction. Bravely embarking into the uncharted waters of new responses and behaviors, we rebel against the status quo of perpetual dissatisfaction and the indulging of ignorant instinctual responses. We engage in a serious, take-no-prisoners practice that isn't just a hobby or a part-time job, but rather a full-on crusade. Out of desperation, we become spiritual renegades.

But we carry the liberphobia that aids and abets our imprisonment into even a mature practice. We get used to working *toward* happiness instead of actually arriving there. Settling into our new and improved way of life, we become complacent and perhaps a bit proud of our progress so far. We forget that the point of *practice* is to *make perfect*.

Once we get used to being a "practitioner" it's a safe position to remain in; we settle for the ABD instead of going for the PhD. Identifying with the role of perpetual seeker, we're always keeping the goal at arm's length.

We need that daredevil, renegade spirit to push us further, to go beyond the familiar and the comfortable, to realize that *seekers eventually must become finders!*

Bad Desire, Good Desire, No Desire

We will remain unhappy—to one degree or another—as long as we remain discontent, as long as we are *seeking* and have not yet *found*. That is why in the Eastern traditions the root cause of our suffering is often identified as "thirst" (*tanha*), "craving" (*tirshna*), or "desire" (*kama* or *raga*).

As long we think we'll be happy only if we have something we don't have, or didn't have something we do have (desire in the form of aversion), contentment will elude us.

Identifying the source of unhappiness as desire can be a bit confusing, however. Firstly, as we shall see later in this chapter, the opposite of desiring is not some kind of self-satisfied smugness that renders us insensate to the needs of others. Contentment does not mean that we become disinterested and dormant. And secondly, if the ultimate goal is a state of desirelessness (or to put it positively, perfect contentment), we need to utilize a certain kind of desire to get us there.

We must distinguish between "bad" or problematic desire and "good" or helpful desire, the latter of which is the force that will actually bring us to our final objective.

"Bad" desire we've already talked about in several different contexts. Desiring things that won't bring the happiness we think they will—The Big Five—is bad desire. It's "bad" because it leads nowhere. It just perpetuates itself, and it doesn't result in satisfaction. A second dimension of what makes desire "bad" is that it is permeated with ignorance—the ignorance that believes that the desirability of an object is an inherent quality of that object; and the ignorance that thinks that the way to get the desirable object is to do anything other than *try to help others get objects they regard as desirable.*

But there's also "good" desire, and it is a crucial component of the spiritual quest. What is it that motivates us to want to relinquish our suffering and unhappiness and work toward contentment if not some form of desire? You can call it "will" or "motivation" or "drive" or whatever, but we actually *must* have the desire to eradicate our mental afflictions, to be kinder, more compassionate, wiser, if we are to develop these qualities.

Underlying all desires—"bad" and "good" alike—is *the* desire: the desire to be happy, to be content; the desire to *no longer be plagued by endless desires.* The fundamental impulse behind every action, every decision in our lives, is the desire to be happy and content (i.e., the state of desirelessness).

So the tension we observed above between the imperative to *relax and work hard* and the instruction to *work hard to relax* can here be rephrased:

We cultivate desire in order to get motivated to work hard for what we want, which will bring us enough of what we desire to get us to the point where we realize that what we really desire is the end of desire.

Whew. But there it is, the complete summary of our spiritual trajectory. We start by strongly desiring a change—we decide we've wasted enough of this precious and limited life being unhappy, and we look for an alternative. This "good" desire motivates us to do the hard work that's involved in reorganizing our priorities, retraining ourselves, and developing the gumption to do difficult things like forgiving, paying close attention to our morality, and controlling our foolish and self-destructive responses to life's challenges.

Things improve. We start waking up happier, looking forward to rather than dreading the day. Our relationships with others get easier; the circumstances of our lives seem more positive; our sense of well-being rises. Life gets *pretty good.*

But at some point we must come to the conclusion that what we regard as "pretty good" might be "good enough." When we're more or less satisfied with the life we've created through our spiritual labor, it's time to take the final leap and cultivate the last desire . . . the desire for total contentment.

And then one more twist. The only way to fulfill this last desire is to give it up; we must, in the end, let go even of the desire to be content. How else could it happen? We can't be content if we still want something we think we don't have. We achieve contentment only when we stop *not* being content.

It's the great paradox of life, a paradox that also lies at the heart of the karmic system: we get what we want only when we stop wanting it.

And that's what we've wanted all along.

It's the end of wanting that we've always really wanted.

Dropping What "Should Be" for "What Is"

Discontentment is articulated in conditional sentences, statements that begin with *if only* or *it should be* (and the negative version, *it shouldn't be*). *If only* I had this, or didn't have that . . . *then* I'd be happy. My life *should* be (fill in the blank: more of this, less of that), and *until then* I won't be satisfied.

Dissatisfaction, like desire, can play an important role in the spiritual life. We *should be* (to use the conditional!) dissatisfied with our unhappiness and suffering. We should be dissatisfied enough to do something about our dissatisfaction! This kind of discontentment is the twin of what we've identified as "good" desire. Both "good" desire and "good" dissatisfaction motivate us to work for improvement.

But dissatisfaction, if not controlled and restricted, can easily become an interminable condition. We can get so habituated to the conditional—*if only*—that we perpetually postpone the contentment we're *working toward* but never *arrive at.* Ultimately, the only way to achieve contentment is by putting an end to discontentment.

Here's another angle on the same problem: It's important to have *ideals* that we aspire toward—visions of what *should be.* We set up goals for ourselves and we then try to reach them; indeed, without goals, how would we know what to work for?

But to the extent that our ideals are unrealistic or kept just beyond our grasp, we find ourselves coming up short. And if that happens too often we get discouraged or maybe give up altogether trying to improve our lives. This would be bad enough; instead of training ourselves to succeed we'd be conditioning ourselves to fail. But even worse: not only would we never realize our ideals, we would likely feel guilty about such failures. Setting up goals and then repeatedly not reaching them is obviously a recipe for frustration and depression—and not for the happiness that such goals were supposed to help us attain.

This phenomenon seems fairly common among spiritual practitioners. We posit what I would call *surreal* goals, wholly different from our commonplace reality, and then we deploy the conditional: *Unless and until I become* (and here fill in the blank according to your tradition: an omniscient Buddha, a perfected saint, an angel of light, or whatever) *and the world I live becomes* (again, pick your idealized version of a perfect environment—a heaven or "Pure Land"), *I won't be satisfied with myself and with my life.*

If we're honest we can't really say that such surreal visions are totally impossible. Who really knows? Such seemingly fantastical goals might be realizable some day. But what most of us can say with certainty is that ideals like these are *radically different* from the reality we are experiencing in the here and now. In comparison to such idyllic future scenarios our present lives might very well look rather shabby and ordinary.

Focusing too much on remote and extraordinary attainments could easily function to increase, rather than decrease, our discontentment with our present lives. Perhaps it would be better to learn how to disabuse ourselves of *all* of the fantasies that undermine our contentment with reality as it is. Perhaps it would be more conducive to our happiness not to obsess about surreal goals, but rather to fully embrace life in a way we might describe as *hyperreal.*

Religious traditions have not only endorsed pie-in-the-sky ideals; they have also promoted attainments that are much closer at hand. When Jesus was asked where the "kingdom of heaven" was located, he didn't offer a Star Wars answer: "In a galaxy far, far away." "The kingdom of heaven," Jesus said, "is within you."[5]

Similarly, in the Ashtavakra Gita, a text from the Hindu tradition, we find a description of the *jivanmukta*—a person who has achieved "liberation in this very lifetime." Such a perfected being is not depicted as looking or acting dramatically different from others—no wings, no body of light, no golden halo, and no flying in the sky or walking on water. The transformation has occurred within: "The wise man, even though he may be living like an ordinary person, is completely different."[6] Perfection is not represented as some kind of transcendent, other-worldly status but as a hyperreal contentment with ordinary life: "One whose mind is completely at peace stays happy in his everyday life. He sleeps happily, he comes and goes happily, he speaks happily, and he eats happily."[7]

In Buddhism too the goal is portrayed in terms that make it a lot less surreal and a lot more realistic—and therefore realizable. The title of "Buddha" comes from a Sanskrit verbal root that simply means "to wake up." A Buddha is someone who has *awoken to reality*. Nirvana—the "blowing out" or extinction of everything that obstructs perfect happiness—is described not as a destination that one needs leave samsara in order to arrive at. Nor is it a state or condition that one needs to "attain." Nirvana is a potentiality of life here and now; it is a perspective—not a place.

The aim of one's spiritual life is to arrive at the realization that there has never been anything at all that we need to "acquire" or "obtain"—to see that reality as it is is "good enough to be perfect." We don't "reach" nirvana, contentment or happiness; we *recognize* and *realize* that it has always been a possibility right here, right now. To quote the great Arya Nagarjuna:

There is nothing whatsoever
That distinguishes samsara from nirvana
Or nirvana from samsara. . . .[8]

Samsara and nirvana are just two different takes on our present reality. Our idealization of the perfected state as some sort of never-never land, some heavenly realm completely and utterly *different* from where we are now, keeps it always in abeyance and at arm's length. Anam Thubten, in his *No Self, No Problem*, writes:

Nirvana is not some kind of beautiful, celestial garden filled with peaches and mangos, a place where everybody is walking around with beautiful halos. It is not a place where everyone is in a constant state of bliss. . . . It's not even a transcendent state of mind that we are going to achieve. It is not a beautiful, ecstatic, trancelike state of mind that we can cherish. That's not really nirvana. Rather, nirvana is a great cessation of the separation between us and the truth. It is the mere acknowledgment of what has been the case all along. It is like waking up from a nightmare. It's a great relief to discover that nothing has to be done.[9]

We're deferring our own happiness by demanding the appearance of "mangos, peaches, and halos" in the outer world.

Nirvana and samsara are merely different viewpoints on our present reality. There is no nirvana to *achieve* through hard work and practice (although without hard work and practice nothing will happen). We will, eventually, simply *notice* enlightenment, not *procure* it.

In this sense it is true that, as Voltaire said, "Man is free at the moment he wishes to be,"[10] a sentiment restated in the Ashtavakra Gita:

The one who regards himself as free is free.
The one who thinks himself bound is bound.
It has often and truly been said:
As one thinks, so one becomes.[11]

The nirvanic way of thinking is characterized by perfect contentment and peace of mind, with nothing that needs changing or correction. And the samsaric point of view is the opposite. It is *defined* by discontentment, striving, effort, thirst and craving for something more, something different, something new and transformed from what is.

The samsaric viewpoint is conditional—*if only*. The nirvanic perspective is an unconditional acceptance and embrace of the indicative—of *what is*. And until the conditional gives way to the indicative—until we drop what we think *should be* and fully affirm *what is*—we will continue to be discontented and unhappy.

Nirvana, Here and Now
http://bit.ly/renegade10

Contentment Is Not Complacency: The Way of Desireless Action

What the Indian texts call "samsara" can be defined as the ignorant, self-centered, and mentally afflicted perspective, a frame of mind that causes us to experience our lives as at best problematic and fraught with difficulties, and at worst tragic and disastrous. The samsaric mind-set also leads us to re-create the causes for more of the same. Our untrained habitual responses to the "pop-ups in Horrorland"—returning hatred with hatred, anger with anger, violence with violence—re-create the very causes that brought such unpleasantness to us in the first place.

It is crucial for our happiness to replace this kind of samsaric perspective with one that is infused with wisdom, and with the enlightened self-interest that will help us restrain our worst impulses and act in ways that will bring about a happier life. We work hard to replace the samsaric viewpoint with a more intelligent and rational one that will then guide us to act in ways that are conducive to, rather than destructive of, the happiness we seek.

But from another angle, the samsaric mentality can be defined a bit differently. "Samsara," declares the Ashtavakra Gita, "is nothing other than having something that needs to be done."[12] As we've said above, the samsaric perspective is conditional—if I do *x*, then *y* will occur . . . and *then* things will be better.

The *compulsion to act* is the opposite of freedom. The feeling that we must always stay busy fixing, replacing, improving, or correcting things—this is characteristic of the discontented view of life. And it is also the very antithesis of the peace of mind we are seeking through such activity:

> *How can there be happiness for one whose heart is scorched by the heat of the sun—the pain of having things that need to be done—without the refreshing shower of the nectar of tranquility?*[13]

The liberated person—someone who has reached the goal of true happiness in this very lifetime—is described in the texts as being free from the compulsion to act. Such a person has nothing they feel they *need* to do, a feature of the state of mind of true contentment. Or, to put it differently, the two forms of discontentment—wanting something one doesn't have and not wanting something one does have—have been put to rest: "There is no feeling that one needs anything or needs to get rid of anything in the wise man who delights in himself and whose nature is cool and clear."[14]

Now if you're like me you're probably having an attack of liberphobia at about this point. We resist freedom, and this very much includes the freedom of having *nothing that needs doing.* This aspect of liberation might appear to us as irresponsible indolence. "What about helping others? What about a social conscience? Don't we *need* to do something about the pain and suffering in the world?"

Such objections miss the mark. The liberated individual is neither self-absorbed nor inert. The free person of course feels responsible to do what he or she can to alleviate the suffering of others. But having thoroughly trained themselves in the wisdom that accords with living the good life, the actions of such a being are *automatically* kind and compassionate. A truly liberated person is liberated from indecision about what the right thing to do is and from the unwillingness to actually do it.

Contentment is not complacency. It is possible to be *both* satisfied with reality as it is *and* always working for the betterment of oneself and others. There need not be a contradiction here: complete acceptance includes happily embracing the opportunities we have to help make the world a better place. We stay content with what comes our way; we make the best of whatever hand we're dealt and play our cards to the maximum benefit.

When the rewiring of our inclinations and proclivities is complete, we will be able to trust ourselves to *spontaneously* do the right thing in any given situation. We will be happy and content with whatever arises and *do what there is to be done.* Our actions will no longer be motivated by ignorance, nor will they require correction through discipline. In fact, our actions won't be "motivated" at all. Spontaneous and free, the liberated person is childlike—not in the sense of being naïve and untrained but rather being uncontrived, unaffected, and genuine.

The positive qualities associated with children are taken up again in the person who has given birth to a new and happy self and who sees the world with nirvanic, and not samsaric, eyes. "Truly I tell you," Jesus proclaimed, "unless you change and become like children, you will never enter the kingdom of heaven."[15] This hard-won kind of simplicity, this willed second childhood, is the result of training and wisdom. As it says in the Ashtavakra Gita: "Knowing that everything is only a projection"—that things aren't coming *at* us but rather are coming *from* us—" the self is free and eternal. So it is that the wise man behaves like a child."[16]

The liberated person goes through life like a kid at play—energetic and skilled, yet without any ulterior motive or feeling that something *needs to be done.* Just as a child has *no purpose* in playing other than that it is *fun* to do so, so too the free man or woman no longer acts with an eye on the fruits of action.

This kind of contented, desireless way of living is what the Taoists call *wu-wei* ("actionless action") or what the Bhagavad Gita terms "karma yoga": "One does what needs to be done while remaining unattached to the results of this action."[17]

Enlightened action is action done for its own sake. It's like dancing or singing. There's no real *reason* or *purpose* or *motive* for acting when one has become perfectly content, any more than there's a reason for dancing or singing a song. "Desireless, free, spontaneous, liberated from all bondage, he moves like a dried leaf blown by the wind of karmic imprints."[18]

The truly free person is no longer *trying* to become free. The seeker has become the finder; the hard work has paid off, and has come to an end. There's nothing more to achieve. Work is replaced by play, as dissatisfaction and struggle give way to contentment and affirmation. One says yes instead of no to life and all it has to offer.

The modern Indian spiritual teacher known as Bhagwan Shree Rajneesh (and later as Osho) described this state of perfect contentment, where one squeezes the juice out of every moment of life, without desire or expectation:

> *You accept, you become loose and natural. You simply start floating with existence, not going anywhere, because there is no goal; not moving to any target, because there is no target. Then you start enjoying every moment, whatsoever it brings—whatsoever, remember. And you can enjoy it, because now you have no desires and no expectations. And you don't ask for anything, so whatsoever is given you feel grateful. Just sitting and breathing is*

so beautiful, just being here is so wonderful that every moment of life becomes a magical thing, a miracle in itself.[19]

Living Your Life Like It's Golden

Buddhist scholar Robert Thurman has observed that a spiritual practitioner must have a high tolerance for cognitive dissonance. Spiritual renegades hell-bent on inciting happiness in their lives are going to have to get used to driving with both the brake fully engaged and the accelerator floored.

The road to true happiness is rarely straightforward—although we might wish it were. Spiritual truths generally do not conform to our desire for black-and-white divisions. Instead, they often appear to us as paradoxical or even contradictory.

The word "paradox" comes from the Greek "*para*" ("beyond") and "*doxa*" ("belief"); *paradoxos* means "beyond belief" or "conflicting with expectation." And the truth does indeed often "conflict with expectation!" When we hear that the best thing to do when someone hurts us is to forgive them and love them back, this does not accord with our impulsive and habitual urges. When we read that "the first shall be last and the last shall be first" we wonder if there hasn't been some mix-up at the printer. When we are told to relax and work hard, and then to work hard to relax, and then to not work at all but just play or dance our way through life—well, we might feel that the giver of such advice should get their story straight.

The spiritual desperado, however, must get comfortable with the risky ambivalence of contradiction, incongruity, and conundrum. We must try to be a bit more like the Queen of

Hearts in *Alice in Wonderland*, who upon hearing Alice's claim that she can't believe "impossible things" replies, "I dare say you haven't had much practice ... When I was your age, I always did it for half an hour a day. Why, sometimes I've believed as many as six impossible things before breakfast."[20]

The deeper reaches of the spiritual quest are neither for those who grasp to the safety of received opinion nor for people who insist on what Emerson memorably called a "foolish consistency is the hobgoblin of little minds."[21] On the path to true and lasting happiness we employ methods that take us closer to our goal. But when they have fulfilled their function we abandon them for practices that will take us further.

Clinging to what is no longer useful is a form of liberphobia. The Buddha is said to have told his disciples that his teachings were like a raft. They could be used to get to the other side of the river of suffering but upon arrival the conveyance can be cast aside. Once it has served its purpose, the raft can be discarded.

There is a time to be thoroughly dissatisfied with our unhappiness and suffering in order to get motivated to start living differently. We should strongly desire a life that isn't driven by the endless bait-and-switch game of consumer capitalism or our own deluded notions that happiness could be found in anything outside of ourselves. It is crucial to discipline ourselves in order to curtail free rein of our worst inclinations and to aspire to live up to our own ideals. And when it accords with our own best interests, it can be useful to feel the compulsion to act when to do so helps to combat the habitual urges of our mental afflictions.

But as many Type A personality spiritual practitioners quickly find out, it is possible to bring all the stress we associate with our secular life into our spiritual life as well. We can worry, get tense, feel anxious and insecure, and in general get all worked up about the very thing that's supposed to bring us relief from such agitation. If your spiritual practice has become a source of anxiety and stress, it ain't a spiritual practice anymore.

It's important to work hard on the path to improve and perfect ourselves. But it is equally important to cultivate a relaxed and stress-free attitude about the path. The way can get in the way if it becomes the source of anything other than happiness and joy.

So relax while you're working hard. We've been rehearsing here time-tested techniques for inciting true happiness in our lives: forgiveness and gratitude when it comes to the past; paying attention to karma and your ethics so we can trust in the future; and accepting whatever comes in the present as a teaching on how to live the good life. And if we follow these guidelines, there will come a time when it will be possible (and necessary) to loosen up on the hard work and discipline, to make the final push to overcome the liberphobia—to take the goal as the path and the end as the means.

There will come a time when our highest practice will be, as the Jill Scott song would have it, to "live your life like it was golden."

The only way we'll ever truly realize contentment and perfect happiness is by trying to inhabit these states of mind—in other words, by pretending to be content and happy. We impersonate a happy person; we fake it until we make it, which actually turns out to be a powerfully effective technique.

Nearly two decades ago, Dr. Madan Kataria started the first of the so-called laughing clubs in India. These clubs, which have now spread around the world, practice what is called "laughter yoga." Now there are now over 6,000 such groups in 60 countries.[22] The technique is rather simple: "Laughter is simulated as a body exercise in a group; with eye contact and childlike playfulness, it soon turns into real and contagious laughter. The concept of Laughter Yoga is based on a scientific fact that the body cannot differentiate between fake and real laughter. One gets the same physiological and psychological benefits."

Fake laugher becomes real laughter—and this is also the principle underlying some of the most advanced techniques of the esoteric traditions of India and Tibet. The seasoned practitioner is instructed to pretend that life is perfect, to imagine oneself as an enlightened being living in a faultless world. This "make-believe yoga" plants the seeds for actually seeing oneself and the world as indeed perfect. One foreshadows the attainment of true happiness by practicing the feeling of true happiness.

Truth be told, however, we won't get very far simply making believe things are perfect when we really don't think they are. We mustn't fall into the trap of what Lama Surya Das has cleverly called "premature emaculation." We need to work hard to fix what we think needs fixing before we can convincingly imagine that there's nothing left to do.

But even as we endeavor to improve ourselves we should also realize that there is theoretically no end to this tinkering with what is; that, in fact, such dissatisfaction with reality is the opposite of the contented state of mind.

It's totally possible to be happy—not in some otherworldly heaven or Pure Land, but in the here and now. And no one has a better chance to realize this than people like us.

You can do it! But you have to work hard to get to the point where you have persuaded yourself that the life you are leading is good enough to be satisfied with—that it's good enough to be perfect.

You can't fool yourself about this. No one but you can determine whether your life is truly golden or needs more polishing. But contentment and happiness won't come until discontentment ends and you cease to wish things were otherwise.

Is it good enough yet?

Is it good enough for you to finally be content?

Is it good enough to be perfect?

Couch Potato Contemplation: Everything's OK, Here and Now

Relax into a comfortable physical position while remaining mentally alert. Try to prevent your thoughts from migrating to the past or future. Be here now—and keep up with the ever-changing present. Just notice what is happening in the here and now: the smells, the temperature of the room, the sounds you hear, the inhalation and exhalation of your breath.

Notice that when you actually occupy the present everything is OK, here and now. It's when the mind wanders and begins to worry about the future or re-lives the past that our contentment is destroyed. But here and now, everything's usually fine.

Relax into that contented state of mind here in the present, with nothing that needs to be different, nothing that needs to be done. Try to feel that everything is perfect, just as it is, here and now.

Action Plan: The Perfection Mantra

Spend at least ten to fifteen minutes a day consciously practicing contentment with your life as it is. Review all the events of the day, inclusive of those planned and unplanned, desired and unwanted. Then repeat (with conviction!) the mantra of acceptance and affirmation: "Yes! It's good enough to be perfect!"

Epilogue:
Inciting Happiness 24/7—The Components of a Sane Life

It's one thing to finish a book like this and think, "Yeah, that all sounds well and good . . . now what should I read next? Where's that Deepak Chopra paperback I bought a while ago?"

It's quite another thing to stop all the reading, put the books down, and actually start living differently. Resolve to do what Master Shantideva advises, "I will put these teachings into actual practice, for what's the point of just reciting words? How will those who are sick benefit by just studying medical books?"[1]

The medicine has been prescribed, but it's up to the patient to take it. The horse has been led to water, but is Trigger ready to drink?

Living the life of a spiritual desperado isn't about shaving one's head, ringing bells, wearing funny clothes, or speaking in foreign tongues. Each one of us can live much happier within the contours and structure of our ordinary daily routine. It just takes a few minor adjustments to make a big difference.

And, of course, it takes the willingness to really go for it. The life of a true spiritual renegade will be different from the norm—and proudly, defiantly so! The norm is boring (not to say ruinous), and blessed are the bored and the desperate for they're the ones really ready for a change.

I leave you with nine essential components for living a sane life in these insane times. If you do all of these regularly and consistently, your life will definitely change for the better.

You can do it. No excuses. Just a few small changes and your life can be so much happier.

Stop reading books about doing it and just do it! You'll be glad you did it once you've done it.

Every night, get a good night's sleep.

Sounding good already, right? Most of us are cheating ourselves of proper rest on a regular basis, and that isn't good for us or the people around us. Caring for your body and mind is a crucial part of one's spiritual practice. Watching what you eat and drink and especially avoiding intoxicants are specifically mentioned in many religious texts. But you are also doing yourself and those around you a disservice by skimping on sleep and going through your day cranky and crabby. Every night get enough sleep so that you are properly restoring your mind and body and are in a calmer, more controlled state of mind less likely to be perturbed by the little irritations of daily life.

epilogue

Every morning, before getting out of bed, loll about in bed for a while (and throw away the alarm clock!).

Many of us feel our lives to be so busy and stressful that at the first moment of consciousness in the morning we jump out of bed and maniacally begin to run around getting ready for our day.

And whose idea of a sane life was it that our first moments of consciousness should be listening to the most irritating sounds science has invented? Go to sleep early enough so you wake up on your own, without the bleating of the alarm, refreshed and happy.

Then spend some time each morning in bed setting a more peaceful tone for the rest of your day. Luxuriate in that delicious semiconscious state between waking and sleep and begin your day thinking about what a total miracle your life is, how many things are going right, how many advantages you have. But also realize that this kind of life will not last forever. We all will die, and we don't know when. Recalling our mortality helps us get our priorities in life straight. So start every day appreciative of your life. Determine not to take this precious opportunity for granted and instead get out of bed resolved to make the very most of it.

Every morning, meditate.

A daily meditation practice of at least twenty or thirty minutes is an important component of any spiritual practice. Make it an essential part of your day. You can use one or another of the Couch Potato Contemplations at the end of each chapter of this book as your meditation topic. Stick with one for at least three or four weeks, meditating on it every day, in order to get the real benefit. Then, when the topic begins to get routinized and dry, switch to another one and do it for the next month or so. But do it every day. A little every day is better than a lot once in a while.

Keep track of your moral life, all day long.

A real spiritual practice will also involve checking one's morality periodically during the course of the day, preferably by keeping a journal or diary and consulting it every two or three hours. For detailed advice on how to "keep your book," download "The Book: How to Make Your Dreams Come True," online at http://www.acidharma.org/aci/online/thebook.pdf.

Do something for someone else.

Learning to live a selfless, other-directed life and diminishing our tendency to think only about ourselves is another crucial part of any renegade's spiritual practice. Every day do at least one little act of kindness for someone else. And keep track of it and be happy that you are doing things like this in your life. This reinforces the tendency to do more altruistic acts in the future, thereby creating the real causes for your own happiness and well-being.

Every day do some form of physical exercise.

It could be yoga, tai chi, dance, a morning run—but it's crucial to get some movement every day in order to have the inner energies flow better. And be sure to do it with the right attitude and intention! Moving with thoughts of helping others in mind rather than narcissistic or competitive motivations transforms your daily exercise regimen into an important component of your spiritual life.

At the end of the day, do the Couch Potato Contemplation on the goal.

At the end of your workday, instead of vegetating in front of the television or reading a magazine, curl up in your favorite chair or sofa, shut your eyes, relax, and think about what it would be like to achieve the goal of your practice—complete and total happiness. What would it be like to have no problems, physical or mental? What would it feel like to have a heart that's completely open and loving toward all beings? What would it be like to have no doubts about anything, no fears, no anxieties or worries?

This is actually a crucial component of a spiritual practice. If you can't conceptualize the goal, how do you expect to reach it? So every day, spend some time visualizing your own future perfection, thereby creating some of the causes and conditions for realizing that perfection.

Every evening, spend some time studying a spiritual text.

Instead of watching television or reading a trashy novel, finish your day with the study of a text that is designed to make you a happier person. Any text that teaches you to be less selfish and more compassionate and loving toward others is a "sacred" text, because it will help you be happier and live a better life. It's nice to end the day like this so as to have these kinds of thought swimming in one's unconscious as one sleeps.

Once a week, take a day off.

Taking a holiday or "observing the sabbath" once a week is a time-honored spiritual practice. Having worked hard for six days, set aside a day for complete relaxation, restoration, and fun. Cultivation of your spiritual life should be regarded like running a marathon, not a sprint. Protect your practice by keeping it fresh and avoiding burnout. Take your weekly holy day of rest, and then return the next day to your life as a spiritual renegade, refreshed and happy!

Notes

Religious Texts

* Dhammapada translations by author.

† *The New Standard Version*, Copyright © 2007 by HarperOne.

‡ *The Middle Length Discourses of the Buddha: A New Translation of the Majjhima Nikaya*, Copyright © 1995 by Bhikku Nyanamoli and Hikku Bodi, Wisdom Publications.

§ *The Qur'an with Annotated Interpretation in Modern English*, Copyright © 2007 Ali Unal, The Light, Inc.

|| *The Mahabharata, Book 3 of 18*, Copyright © 2008 Kisari Mohan Ganguli, Forgotten Books.

Introduction

1. **"Human beings by nature want happiness"**
   His Holiness the Dalai Lama, *Kindness, Clarity, and Insight* (Ithaca, NY: Snow Lion Publications, 1984), 180.

2. **happiness is "the human good"**
Aristotle, *Nicomachean Ethics* I.7, cited in Nicholas White, *A Brief History of Happiness* (Oxford: Blackwell Publishing Ltd., 2006), 2.

3. **"the desire for happiness is essential"**
Saint Augustine, "Saint Augustine Quotes," *The-Philosophy*: http://www.the-philosophy.com/saint-augustine-quotes.

4. **"how to gain, how to keep, how to recover happiness"**
William James, *The Varieties of Religious Experience*, cited in Darrin M. McMahon, *Happiness: A History* (New York: Grove Press, 2006), xii.

5. **what do they [i.e., human beings] demand of life**
Sigmund Freud, cited in White, *A Brief History of Happiness*, 2.

6. **claiming we are "very happy" or "happy"**
Richard Layard, *Happiness: Lessons from a New Science* (London: Penguin Books, 2006), chapter 3.

7. **"ordinary unhappiness"**
"This is Freud's famous avowal that the goal of what he would first term 'psychoanalysis' . . . was in fact relatively humble. It aimed to cure gratuitous or self-imposed suffering—neurosis—in order to restore 'common' or 'ordinary' unhappiness (*gemeines Unglück*)." McMahon, *Happiness: A History*, 442.

8. **it takes only about $10,000 for us to say, "I'm pretty happy"**
According to Ruut Veenhoven, Professor of Happiness Studies at Erasmus University in Rotterdam, Holland, those who have an income of less than about $10,000 a year are generally unhappy, but in countries where the average annual income is more than $10,000, money and happiness stop having much of a relationship; those with $100,000 a year are only marginally happier than those with $11,000. Cited in Merryn Somerset Webb, *Love Is Not Enough: A Smart Woman's Guide to Money* (HarperCollins E-books, 2007), chapter 11, "A Facilitator of Happiness, Not a Source of It."

9. **an increase of a mere 20 percent would be enough to make them happy**
Richard A. Easterlin, "The Economics of Happiness": http://www-rcf.usc.edu/~easterl/papers/Happiness.pdf. Other studies seem to indicate that happiness for most people is a relative term. We are "happy" when we think we're better off than we were in the past, or are better off than significant others with whom we compare ourselves. As H. L. Mencken observed,

a happy man is one whose income is slightly higher than his brother-in-law's. See His Holiness the Dalai Lama, *The Art of Happiness* (New York: Riverhead Books, 1998), 22–23 and Layard, *Happiness,* chapter 4.

10. ***by* happiness *I mean here a deep sense of flourishing***
    Matthieu Ricard, *Happiness: A Guide to Developing Life's Most Important Skill,* trans. Jesse Browner (New York: Little, Brown and Company, 2006), 19.

11. **"what about me, what about me?"**
    Check out the video and rap by Mipham Rinpoche called "What about Me?" posted on YouTube at http://www.youtube.com/watch?v=FDSAAl rqAHM.

Chapter 1

1. **O Lord! Shout for Joy!**
   "Shout for Joy," negrospirituals.com: http://www.negrospirituals.com/news -song/shout_for_joy.htm.

2. **"first-world problems"**
   For a musical, satirical, and lucid take on this issue, watch the "The First World Problems" rap on YouTube: http://www.youtube.com/watch?v= D2p5svFJ9cQ.

Chapter 2

1. **"there are only two ways to live your life"**
   Albert Einstein, "Einstein Quotes," The Albert Einstein Site: http://www .alberteinsteinsite.com/quotes/einsteinquotes.html.

2. **"God is dead"**
   Friedrich Nietzsche, *The Gay Science,* trans. Walter Kaufmann (New York: Vintage Books, 1972), 181.

3. **recent polls show that most of us are in deep revolt**
   A Harris Poll conducted in November of 2007 found large percentages of us believing in angels (74%), heaven (75%), hell (62%), the devil (62%), and ghosts (41%). A whopping 82% reported that they still believe in God (well over a century after Nietzsche officially declared Him dead!), and an equally startling 79% say that miracles occur. "The Religious and Other Beliefs of Americans," Harris Interactive (11/29/07): http://www.harrisinteractive.com/ vault/Harris-Interactive-Poll-Research-Religious-Beliefs-2007-11.pdf.

Another poll also done in 2007 by the Pew Forum on Religion and Public Life confirms these percentages: 92% of Americans believe in God or in a universal spirit (including, curiously enough, one in five of those who call themselves atheists!) and 74% believe in heaven (but only 59% in hell). Sixty-eight percent believe in the existence of angels and demons who are active in the world. One third say God answers our prayers and that they have experienced or witnessed a divine healing of an illness or injury. And, again, despite the establishment's official view against it, 79% of us contend that miracles do, in fact, occur. "Summary of Key Findings," Pew Forum on Religion and Public Life: http://religions.pewforum.org/pdf/report2 religious-landscape-study-key-findings.pdf.

4. ***there is nothing more deluded***
   Shantideva, *Guide to the Bodhisattva's Way of Life*, 4.23. All translations from this text are my own.

5. ***you must make use of this boat***
   Ibid., 7.14.

6. **pining for some solitariness and peace**
   Ibid. See verses 85–88 of chapter 8.

7. **everything's amazing**
   Louis C.K. interview on *Late Night with Conan O'Brien*, 2001. "Everything's Amazing and Nobody's Happy," YouTube: http://www.youtube.com/watch?v=8r1CZTLk-Gk.

8. **and my teacher was right**
   "Yoga Journal Releases 2008 'Yoga in America' Market Study," *Yoga Journal* (2/26/08): http://www.yogajournal.com/advertise/press_releases/10 (*accessed 10/16/10*).

Chapter 3

1. ***a cause of something is that thing***
   Paraphrased from Shantideva, *Guide to the Bodhisattva's Way of Life*, 6.104.

2. **the fact that statistics now suggest**
   The 25 percent figure is cited, and disputed, in an online article entitled "Yoga 'Injuries' Don't Add Up," by Susan Eggins, online at Australian Yoga Life: http://www.ayl.com.au/pdf_docs/A4L_issue_10_INJURIES_22.pdf. But see also "Yoga Injuries on the Rise," Impact Lab (1/9/07): http://www.impactlab.com/2007/01/09/yoga-related-injuries-on-the-rise/.

Also check out the recent article, "How Yoga Can Wreck Your Body," published in the *New York Times* (January 5, 2012), online at http://www.nytimes.com/2012/01/08/magazine/how-yoga-can-wreck-your-body.html?pagewanted=all.

3. **"no action in this world goes for naught"**
   Bhagavad Gita, 2.40. All translations from this text are my own.

Chapter 4

1. ***people who want to be rid of suffering***
   Shantideva, *Guide to the Bodhisattva's Way of Life*, 1.28.

2. ***children want no suffering***
   Ibid., 6.45.

3. **"it is a simple but sometimes forgotten truth"**
   Robert G. Menzies, cited in Tom Crisp, *The Book of Bob: Choice Words, Memorable Men*, 2nd ed. (Riverside, NJ: Andrews McMeel Publishing, 2007), 171.

4. **"the past is not dead"**
   William Faulkner, *Requiem for a Nun*, in Faulkner: *Novels 1942–1954* (New York: Literary Classics of the United States, Inc., 1994), 535.

5. **"I'm an old man"**
   Mark Twain, cited in *The Yale Book of Quotations*, ed. Fred R. Shapiro (Chicago: R. R. Donnelley and Sons, 2006), 782.

6. **"we seem to be going through a period of nostalgia"**
   Art Buchwald, "Art Buchwald Quotes," ThinkExist: http://thinkexist.com/quotation/we_seem_to_be_going_through_a_period_of_nostalgia/339028.html.

7. ***when one has the thorn of anger***
   Shantideva, *Guide to the Bodhisattva's Way of Life*, 6.3.

8. **85 percent also said**
   This Gallup poll finding is cited in R. L. Gorsuch and J. Y. Hao, "Forgiveness: An Exploratory Factor Analysis and Its Relationship to Religious Variables," *Review of Religious Research* 34, 4: 351–363.

9. **"for I do not do what I want"**
   Book of Romans 7:15.

10. **studies have shown that people who forgive are happier**
See, for example, Fred Luskin, *Forgive for Good: A Proven Prescription for Health and Happiness* (New York: HarperOne, 2003).

11. **International Forgiveness Institute**
Their website is located at http://www.forgiveness-institute.org.

12. **"an eye for an eye makes the whole world blind"**
Louis Fischer, *The Life of Mahatma Gandhi* (New York: Harper, 1950), chapter 11.

13. **"it is the foregoing of resentment or revenge"**
"About Forgiveness," International Forgiveness Institute: http://www.forgiveness-institute.org/html/about_forgiveness.htm.

14. **"there is only one defect in forgiving persons"**
Udyoga Parva, Section XXXIII.

15. **"the weak can never forgive"**
Mohandas Gandhi, *My Religion* (Ahmedabad, India: Navajivan Publishing House, 2007), 59.

16. **"holding a grudge takes mental, emotional, and physical energy"**
Cited in "How to Let Go of a Grudge," *The Argus-Press* (Owosso, MI), July 18, 1997: 4.

17. **"I shall allow no man to belittle my soul"**
Booker T. Washington, *Up from Slavery: An Autobiography* (New York: Doubleday, Page & Co., 1907), 165.

18. **"forgiveness is not an occasional act"**
Martin Luther King, Jr., *The Papers of Martin Luther King, Jr., Volume VI: Advocate of the Social Gospel, September 1948–March 1963*, ed. Clayborne Carson (Berkeley and Los Angeles: University of California Press, 2007), 488.

19. **there is nothing that remains difficult**
Shantideva, *Guide to the Bodhisattva's Way of Life*, 6.14.

Chapter 5

1. **"nothing more detestable does the earth produce"**
Cited in *Many Thoughts of Many Minds: A Treasury of Quotations from the Literature of Every Land and Every Age*, ed. Louis Klopsch (New York: The Christian Herald, 1896), 145.

2. ***throughout history***
   Richard Carlson, *Shortcut through Therapy: Ten Principles of Growth-Oriented, Contented Living* (New York: Plume, 1995), 150–51.

3. **"gratitude is not only the greatest of virtues"**
   Marcus Tullius Cicero, from his *Pro Plancio*. The Quotations Page: http://www.quotationspage.com/quote/2035.html.

4. **Research Project on Gratitude and Thanksgiving**
   For more information, see http://psychology.ucdavis.edu/labs/emmons/PWT/index.cfm.

5. ***let us rise up and be thankful***
   See Beliefnet: http://www.beliefnet.com/Quotes/Buddhist/General/T/The-Buddha/Let-Us-Rise-Up-And-Be-Thankfulfor-If-We-Didnt.aspx.

6. **"to educate yourself for the feeling of gratitude"**
   Cited in Lenore Skomal, *LifeLessons: Gratitude* (Kennebunkport, ME: Cider Mill Press, 2006), 80.

7. **"I have learned silence from the talkative"**
   Kahlil Gibran, *Sand & Foam: A Book of Aphorisms* (London: William Heinemann, 1927), 42.

8. **"good things about suffering"**
   We return to this topic below in chapter 8 in the context of how to transform what would otherwise be problems into positive opportunities for furthering our progress toward a totally happy life.

9. ***and besides, there are good things about suffering***
   Shantideva, *Guide to the Bodhisattva's Way of Life*, 6.21.

10. **"we come nearest to the great"**
    Rabindranath Tagore, *Stray Birds* (London: Macmillan and Co., 1921), 15.

11. ***obtaining honor is a bond***
    Shantideva, *Guide to the Bodhisattva's Way of Life*, 6.100–101.

12. **"if the only prayer you ever say"**
    Cited in Gordon S. Wakefield, *The Westminster Dictionary of Christian Spirituality* (Philadelphia: The Westminster Press, 1983), 124.

Chapter 6

1. **"the distinction between the past, present and future"**
   Cited in *Albert Einstein: Historical and Cultural Perspectives*, eds. Gerald Holton and Yehuda Elkana (Princeton, NJ: Princeton University Press, 1982), 149.

2. **"I have realized"**
   Alan Watts, *In My Own Way: An Autobiography, 1915–1965* (Novato, CA: New World Library, 1972), 3.

3. **"all that is happening in the present"**
   Andrew Solomon, *The Noonday Demon: An Atlas of Depression* (New York: Touchstone, 2001), 29.

4. **"if you don't steer clear of the fire"**
   Shantideva, *Guide to the Bodhisattva's Way of Life*, 8.135.

5. ***birth is suffering***
   From the Dharmacakra Pravartana Sutra, cited in Geshe Tashi Tsering, *The Four Noble Truths: The Foundation of Buddhist Thought*, Volume I (Boston: Wisdom Publications, 2005), 3.

6. **recent studies seem to show**
   In a survey of 450,000 Americans, researchers found that the further people's annual income fell below a benchmark of $75,000 per year, the more unhappy they said they were: "Researchers found that lower income did not cause sadness itself but made people feel more ground down by the problems they already had. The study found, for example, that among divorced people, about 51% who made less than $1,000 a month reported feeling sad or stressed the previous day, while only 24% of those earning more than $3,000 a month reported similar feelings. Among people with asthma, 41% of low earners reported feeling unhappy, compared with about 22% of the wealthier group. *Having money clearly takes the sting out of adversities*." (emphasis added) Belinda Luscombe, "Do We Need $75,000 a Year to Be Happy?" *Time* (9/6/10): http://www.time.com/time/magazine/article/0,9171,2019628,00.html.

7. **"a large income"**
   Jane Austen, *Mansfield Park*, ed. Eleanor Donlon (San Francisco: Ignatius Press, 2010), 218.

8. **study after study has repeatedly demonstrated**
   See, for example, a 2001 survey of the scholarly literature where Ed Diener and Robert Biswas-Diener note that "subjective well-being" (SWB) is corre-

lated to income only up to the point where basic needs are fulfilled, and that "Economic growth the last decade in most economically developed societies has been accompanied by little rise in SWB . . ." Ed Diener and Robert Biswas-Diener, "Will Money Increase Subjective Well-Being?: A Literature Review and Guide to Needed Research," *Social Indicators Research* 57, 2 (Feb. 2002): 119–169.

Also found at http://siteresources.worldbank.org/INTEMPOWERMENT/Resources/486312-1095970750368/529763-1095970803335/dienerpdf.

For most people living in affluent, Western countries, happiness has not increased since 1950, and the richer among these countries are no happier than the poorer. In countries with an average per capita income above $20,000, additional income does not produce more happiness. See Richard Layard's *Happiness: Lessons from a New Science* (New York: Penguin Books, 2005), especially chapter 3 ("Are We Getting Happier?"). Cf. Eric Quiñones, "Link between Income and Happiness Is Mainly an Illusion," Princeton University (6/29/06): http://www.princeton.edu/main/news/archive/S15/15/09S18/index.xml?section=topstories.

9. **"anybody who thinks money will make you happy"**
Cited in *The Rich Are Different: A Priceless Treasury of Quotations and Anecdotes about the Affluent, the Posh, and the Just Plain Loaded*, ed. Jon Winokur (New York: Pantheon Books, 1996), 10.

10. **"what's the use of happiness?"**
Henny Youngman, *Take My Wife, Please!: Henny Youngman's Giant Book of Jokes* (Secaucus, NJ: Citadel Press,1998).

11. **the median household income in America**
The Evolution of the U.S. Household (1950s to Today)," Kaleazy Creative (4/13/11): http://kaleazy.com/infographic-the-evolution-of-the-u-s-household-1950s-to-today/.

12. **"the only way not to think about money"**
Edith Wharton, *The House of Mirth* (New York: Charles Scribner's Sons, 1905), 110.

13. ***the more one possesses the more one will suffer***
Nagarjuna's Letter to a Friend, with commentary by Kyabje Kangyur Rinpoche, trans. Padmakara Translation Group (Ithaca, NY: Snow Lion Publications, 2005), verse 35, 102.

14. **"it's easier for a camel"**
Mark 10:25.

15. ***of all types of wealth***
Nagarjuna's *Letter to a Friend*, verse 34, 102.

16. **"by 1985 people could be working"**
Quoted in Kerby Anderson, "Time and Busyness," Leadership U: http://www.leaderu.com/orgs/probe/docs/time.html.

17. **leisure time enjoyed by the average American**
The Harris Poll results are cited in "Leisure Time Plummets 20% in 2008—Hits New Low," Business Wire (12/4/08): http://www.businesswire.com/news/home/20081204005072/en/Leisure-Time-Plummets-20-2008---Hits.

18. **a 2006 study discovered**
Sage Software Survey (2/07), cited in "Time Management Statistics," Key Organization Systems: http://www.keyorganization.com/time-management-statistics.php.

19. **one survey found**
Anderson, "Time and Busyness."

20. **Fifty-four hours per week**
Sage Software Survey (2/07), cited in "Time Management Statistics."

21. **and more than half cite "self-imposed pressure"**
Society for Human Resource Management (2009), cited in ibid.

22. **we're not only working more**
NationMaster: http://www.nationmaster.com/graph/lab_vac_min_vac_tim_aro_the_wor_leg_req-time-around-world-legally-required.

23. **give back some 465,000,000 vacation days a year**
Expedia.com (2010), cited in "Time Management Statistics."

24. **30 percent of all employed adults**
A Harris Interactive poll, findings published in *Yoga Journal* (11/05), and cited in ibid.

25. **an estimated 71 percent**
Accenture Survey (2009), cited in ibid. The same source reports that 49 percent of generation Xers and 38 percent of the members of generation Y said they worked while (supposedly) on vacation.

26. **we are, to some degree, working for a higher income**
According to the Federal Reserve, the consumer debt (not including mortgages) in the United States had reached $1.9 trillion dollars by 2003, which comes to an average of $18,654 per household, up 41 percent from 1998.

According to this same source, 43 percent of American households spend more than they make each year and carry some $8,000 of credit card debt. http://federatedfinancial.com/debtcompare.html.

27. **"as the pace of our lives has increased"**
Anderson, "Time and Busyness."

28. **"the worst loneliness"**
Cited in Steve Deger, *The Nightly Book of Positive Quotations* (Minneapolis: Fairview Press, 2009), 196.

29. **Amusing Ourselves to Death**
Neil Postman, *Amusing Ourselves to Death: Public Discourse in the Age of Show Business* (New York: Penguin Books, 1985).

30. **let's run the numbers**
Michael Malone, "TVB Study: Adults Spend Twice as Much Time on TV Than Web," Broadcasting and Cable (5/25/10): http://www.broadcastingcable.com/article/453033-TVB_Study_Adults_Spend_Twice_as_Much_Time_on_TV_Than_Web.php.

31. **television watching is now at an all-time high**
Jill Sergeant, "U.S. TV viewing at all time high in 2008–09," Reuters (11/10/09): http://www.reuters.com/article/2009/11/10/us-viewing-idUSTRE 5A94QY20091110.

32. **of the internet worldwide increased 200 percent**
"Healthcare and Emerging Rich Web Technologies," Scicasts (5/21/08): http://scicasts.com/specialreports/86-healthcare-it/1828-healthcare-and-emerging-rich-web-technologies-the-web-20semantic-web-challenge-and-opportunity/.

33. **amount of time that we are spending online**
Robin Wauters, "The Rumors are True: We Spend More and More Time Online," TechCrunch (12/23/09): http://techcrunch.com/2009/12/23/harris-interactive-poll/.

34. **294 billion emails are now sent every day**
Heinz Tschabitscher, "How Many Emails Are Sent Every Day?" About.com: http://email.about.com/od/emailtrivia/f/emails_per_day.htm.

35. **43 percent of us check our emails first thing**
AOL, Opinion Research Corp study (7/26/07), cited in "Time Management Statistics."

36. **according to a Nielsen poll**
Nielsen Co. (2009), cited in "Time Management Statistics."

37. **more than 200 messages a day**
http://pewresearch.org/pubs/1716/adults-cell-phones-text-messages; cf. http://pewinternet.org/Reports/2010/Teens-and-Mobile-Phones.aspx.

38. **so-called social networks**
"Time spent social networking up 82%," Digital Media (1/25/10): http://www.digital-media.net.au/article/time-spent-social-networking-up-82/509915.aspx.

39. **over 10 million such procedures**
"2010 News Release: Demand for Plastic Surgery Rebounds by Almost 9%," Plastic Surgery Research.info (4/4/11): http://www.cosmeticplasticsurgerystatistics.com/statistics.html.

Chapter 7

1. **"future suffering can be avoided"**
Yoga Sutra 2.16.

2. **faith**
C. S. Lewis, *Mere Christianity* (New York: HarperCollins, 1952), 140.

3. **"as the wise test gold"**
Cited in The Dalai Lama, *Dzogchen: The Heart Essence of the Great Perfection*, trans. Geshe Thupten Jinpa and Richard Barron (Chökyi Nyima) (Ithaca, NY: Snow Lion Publications, 2004), 35.

4. **if we were to put our minds**
This quote appeared on Rinpoche's "Glimpse of the Day" (10/06): http://www.rigpaus.org/Glimpse/Glimpse.php.

5. **"because of the faith one has in it"**
Nagarjuna, *Precious Garland* 1.5. The translation is mine.

6. **"skepticism is the beginning of faith"**
Oscar Wilde, *The Picture of Dorian Gray*. (New York: Barnes & Noble Classics, 2003), 200.

7. ***at this point, we are talking purely***
Chögyam Trungpa Rinpoche, *Journey without Goal*, in *The Collected Works of Chögyam Trungpa*, Vol. IV, ed. Carolyn Rose Gimian (Boston: Shambhala Publications, 2003), 53.

8. **examples include**
The classic study of magic in pre-modern societies is Marcel Mauss's *A General Theory of Magic,* trans. Robert Brain (New York: Routledge, 1972).

9. ***if all beings got whatever they wished for***
Shantideva, *Guide to the Bodhisattva's Way of Life,* 6.34.

10. ***all the suffering in the world has come***
Ibid., 8.129.

11. **"if I give this, what will I have"**
Ibid., 8.125.

12. **Ten Commandments**
I'm grateful to Reverend Anne Deneen for the phrasing of the Ten Commandments.

13. **A number of different texts.**
The textual sources I've consulted for the karmic correlations are the *Lam Rim Chenmo,* by Je Tsongkapa; *Wheel of Knives,* by Dharma Rakshita; Yoga Sutra, by Patanjali; the Buddha's *Sutra of the Cause and Effects of Actions*; *Guide to the Bodhisattva's Way of Life,* by Shantideva; *Tenrim Chenmo,* by Geshe Drolungpa; *Liberation in the Palm of Our Hands,* by Pabongka Rinpoche; *Precious Garland (Ratnavali),* by Nagarjuna; and the *Manusmriti,* an ancient Hindu law book.

14. **"in your presence"**
Yoga Sutra 2.35.

15. **the things you say "bear fruit"**
Yoga Sutra 2.36.

16. **lack of confidence, depression, and low self-esteem**
Since depression is such a pervasive affliction, it's important to add here that pride and arrogance are also given as karmic causes for low self-esteem. Pride is said not only to bring a life devoid of joy and happiness, but also a low social status. Because you've felt superior to others, you later experience what it's like to have others look down on you.

17. **stupidity, low IQ, is karmically caused**
Another karmic cause for intellectual dullness is ingesting intoxicants—a rare case where in addition to creating a future effect the action more or less instantly brings about its result! Pride (presumably in one's own intelligence) and encouraging immoral behavior in others are also listed as causes for stupidity. One text says that a person becomes "thick" or "blockheaded"

(*maurkya*) if he or she feels they have nothing to learn from a spiritual teacher.

18. **"me first"**
For an entertaining music video that makes this same point, check out Sakyong Miphram Rinpoche's rap posted on YouTube at http://www.youtube.com/watch?v=RUA-x6fBPqw&feature=related.

19. **"many who are first will be last"**
Matthew 19:30.

20. **"it is one of the most beautiful compensations"**
Ralph Waldo Emerson, "Ralph Waldo Emerson Quotes," ThinkExist: http://thinkexist.com/quotation/it_is_one_of_the_most_beautiful_compensations_of/181419.html.

Chapter 8

1. **"being here now"**
Ram Dass, *Be Here Now* (Santa Fe, NM: Hanuman Foundation, 1971).

2. **"the ability to be in the present"**
Cited in *The Book of Positive Quotations*, 2nd ed., compiled and arranged by John Cook (Minneapolis: Fairview Press, 1993), 107.

3. **"the physical poses"**
Yoga Sutra 2.46.

4. **no matter what unwanted thing befalls me**
Shantideva, *Guide to the Bodhisattva's Way of Life*, 6.9.

5. ***if there is something you can do about it***
Ibid., 6.10.

6. ***God, give us the grace***
Reinhold Niebuhr, *The Essential Reinhold Niebuhr: Selected Essays* (New Haven, CT: Yale University Press,1986), 251.

7. **"the present contains all that there is"**
Alfred North Whitehead, *The Aims of Education and Other Essays* (New York: The Free Press, 1967), 3.

Chapter 9

1. **"realize that happiness"**
   Thucydides, *The Peloponnesian War*, trans. Martin Hammond (New York: Oxford University Press, 2009), 44.

2. **nirvana**
   Dhammapada 204: *nibbanam paramam sukham.*

3. **"because he is free, he obtains happiness"**
   Ashtavakra Gita 18.50. All translations from this text are my own.

4. **"most people do not really want freedom"**
   Cited in Alex Lowy, *No Problem* (Bloomington, IN: AuthorHouse, 2007), 64.

5. **"the kingdom of heaven"**
   Luke 17:21.

6. **"the wise man"**
   Ashtavakra Gita 18.18.

7. **"one whose mind is completely at peace"**
   Ibid., 18.59.

8. ***there is nothing whatsoever***
   Root Verses on the Middle Way 25.19. The translation is my own.

9. **nirvana *is not some kind of beautiful, celestial garden***
   Anam Thubten, *No Self, No Problem* (Ithaca, NY: Snow Lion Publications, 2009), 31.

10. **"man is free at the moment he wishes"**
    E. R. Dumont, ed., *The Dramatic Works of Voltaire. Vol. VII* (New York: The St. Hubert Guild, 1901), 256.

11. ***the one who regards himself as free is free***
    Ashtavakra Gita 1.11.

12. **samsara**
    Ibid., 18.57.

13. ***how can there be happiness***
    Ibid., 18.3.

14. **"there is no feeling"**
    Ibid., 18.23.

15. **"truly I tell you"**
Matthew 18:3.

16. **"knowing that everything is only a projection"**
Ashtavakra Gita 18.7.

17. **"one does what needs to be done"**
Bhagavad Gita 6.1.

18. **"desireless, free, spontaneous, liberated"**
Ashtavakra Gita 18.21.

19. ***you accept, you become loose and natural***
Bhagwan Shree Rajneesh, *Tantra: The Supreme Understanding* (Poona, India: Rajneesh Foundation, 1975), 46.

20. **"I dare say you haven't had much practice"**
Lewis Carroll, *Alice's Adventures in Wonderland, in Collected Works of Lewis Carroll* (Charleston, SC: BiblioBazaar, 2007), 132.

21. **"foolish consistency is the hobgoblin of little minds"**
Ralph Waldo Emerson, "Self-Reliance," *Essays: First Series*, 1844.

22. **6,000 such groups in 60 countries**
For more details on laughter clubs, see Laughter Yoga International: http://www.laughteryoga.org.

Epilogue

1. **"I will put these teachings into actual practice"**
Shantideva, *Guide to the Bodhisattva's Way of Life*, 5.109.